SIXTH 1985 EDITION

COINS OF CANADA

by J.A. Haxby and R.C. Willey

W9-BMD-636

Editor
Don Wainwright

Editorial & Pricing Committee
Brian Cornwall
Andrew Kossman
Charles Moore
Ed Solski

THE UNITRADE PRESS
TORONTO

Printed and Bound in Canada
The Unitrade Press • P.O. Box 172, Station A • Toronto, Ontario M5W 1B2
Tel: (416) 787-5658

ISBN 0-919801-18-8
Telex: 06-969719

Copyright © 1984, 1983 Unitrade Associates
Copyright © 1982, 1977, 1972, 1971 Western Publishing Co.

ISBN 0-919801-18-8
Printed and Bound in Canada
Typesetting by Mastertype of Canada Ltd., Toronto
Photo credit: New coins illustrated in this edition were provided by
Ed Solski of The Coin Shop, Toronto.

IMPORTANT NOTICE

The sixth edition of COINS OF CANADA has been completely reset in a new and larger format. Many new illustrations have been added with expanded listings and data to provide the collector with even more information than ever before. Completely new sections include Specimen Sets from 1858 to 1976, Bullion Guides for common silver and gold coins and a Glossary. More additions have been planned for next year!

The editors have attempted to provide the most accurate, up-to-date retail prices for all Canadian coins, tokens and paper money. Our pricing committee consists of established experts who submit current prices from across Canada. These submissions are averaged with current auction results. However, collectors should note that the prices quoted in any catalogue should be considered as a guide only as many factors must come into consideration when purchasing a coin.

While every care has been taken to ensure accuracy in putting together this catalogue, the publisher cannot accept responsibility for typographical errors.

ACKNOWLEDGMENTS

The authors wish to express their sincere thanks and appreciation to the following individuals for assistance and contributions, both direct and indirect, to this and past volumes.

Walter D. Allan	R. H. M. Dolley	Andrew Kossman	Dick Robinson
Larry Becker	Stephen Dushnick	Glen Lacey	K. S. Sargent
R.C. Bell	Graham Dyer	Wilf Latta	Neil Shafer
G.H. Bishop	Harry Eisenhauer	Michael Levy	Thomas Shingles
R.F. Blandford	J. Douglas Ferguson	C.F. Martin	Thomas S. Shipman
George Blenker	R.P. Findley	Ruth McQuade	Ed Solski
Fred Bowman	Guy Gibbons	Michele Menard	F. Stewart Taylor
Bill Boynton	Robert J. Graham	Charles Moore	Richard Thompsen
K.E. Bressett	E.C. Grandmaison	Eric P. Newman	Pierre Van Wissen
Patrick Brindley	Friederich D. Grosse	Walter Ott	Don Wainwright
Major Sheldon S. Carroll	Leslie C. Hill	Gary Patterson	Holland Wallace
Freeman Clowery	Klaas Hirsch	Alfred E.H. Petrie	Randy Weir
Myron Cook	Dr. Douglas D. Hunter	Major Fred Pridmore	Harold Whiteneck
Brian Cornwall	Dr. J.P.C. Kent	R.K. Robertson	Warren X.
Michael Curry	James D. King	Douglas Robins	G. Gordon Yorke
Earl Davis			

TABLE OF CONTENTS

Royal Canadian Mint
1983 Report

In 1908 when the first Canadian coins struck in Canada reached the hands of coin collectors, few if any could have foreseen the scope and popularity of Canada's numismatic program in the 1980s.

Each year since 1976, the Royal Canadian Mint has struck a limited mintage of $100 gold coins featuring a design by a Canadian artist interpreting a theme of national importance, a practice that began with the Olympic Games held that year in Montreal.

In 1983, the $100 gold coin celebrated the 400th anniversary of the landing of Sir Humphrey Gilbert in Newfoundland on August 5, 1583 and his formal acquistion of the land in the name of Queen Elizabeth I. The design depicts the Cabot Tower on Signal Hill in St. John's to the right of a central anchor which symbolizes the seas from which Newfoundland draws its sustenance, with a ship similar to Sir Humphrey Gilbert's to the left. The obverse bears the effigy of Queen Elizabeth II as it has every year since the series began, thus providing a line of continuity for the entire series.

A first in Canadian coinage was introduced with this $100 gold coin which carries the word "Canada" marked on its edge, a feature which is bound to heighten collectors' interest. Originally known as security lettering, nowadays it is strictly an aesthetic enhancement.

In 1983, two other items of great interest to collectors worldwide were struck, a commemorative silver medal on the occasion of the visit to Canada of Their Royal Highnesses, the Prince and Princess of Wales, and a commemorative silver dollar in honour of the 1983 University Games at Edmonton. Featuring the '83 Universiade logo, an athlete in motion and the ribbon of victory, this issue was the 18th in a series of commemorative silver dollars which began in 1935 when the Mint commemorated the Silver Jubilee of King George V.

The sales performance of the Mint's numismatic products was mixed in 1983. While the royal visit medal was an outstanding success with 73,500 sold, and the silver dollar and related issues remained strong, sales of the $100 gold coin reached only 83,200, the lowest mintage to date for any of the coins in the $100 gold series. However, with the expectation of some market recovery for gold and strong themes for both the silver and gold coins, the outlook for 1984 is good.

The above is reprinted from the Royal Canadian Mint Annual Report for 1983.

1
INTRODUCTION

HISTORICAL OUTLINE

For British North American Colonies

England was the first European power to explore the North American area, following John Cabot's discovery of the rich fishing regions of Newfoundland in 1497. The promise of good fishing drew other Europeans, including the French, into the area during the early years of the next century. The French initially concentrated on the area around the Gulf of St. Lawrence, founding settlements in Acadia (later Nova Scotia) in 1605 and Quebec City in 1608. During the next 150 years, France and England fought over the North American possessions. Gradually, England took control. The Hudson Bay region was ceded in 1713. In the 1750's most of the Acadians moved out and New Englanders moved in. Quebec and Montreal fell in 1759-60 and British control of the entire Maritimes region was confirmed by the Peace of Paris in 1763.

The area along the St. Lawrence River, formerly called New France, was re-named Quebec under English rule. The American Revolution (1775-83) had an important effect upon the northern colonies. About 50,000 Tories (English sympathizers) from the 13 colonies migrated to Canada, to the east and west of the French area. Most went to the Nova Scotia region, where the separate colony of New Brunswick was formed in 1784. Those who migrated to the west did not like the lack of democracy inherent in the old French order of Quebec and agitated for separation. This was effected by the Constitutional Act of 1791 in which Quebec became Lower Canada and the western region Upper Canada. Each was provided with its own governing body, consisting of a governor, executive council and legislative council appointed by the Home government and a legislative assembly elected by the people. The seeds were thus sown for later conflicts. Similar situations existed in the Maritime colonies.

The War of 1812 was a temporary interlude in Canadian history. It was essentially a successful defense by the British against American expansionist attempts. The battlegrounds lay in Upper Canada for the most part.

After the war, the Canadian constitutional conflicts continued to rise in intensity. The situation was the most heated in Lower Canada. There, the Catholic French-Canadians bitterly resented the tyrannical domination by a few Protestant English-speaking officials. The Lower Canadian power movement was fundamentally a "radical conservatism"; the desire was to keep life as it had always been by obtaining the power to assure it. The leader of this movement was Louis Joseph Papineau.

In Upper Canada, under William Lyon Mackenzie, the power movement was more directed toward change. In 1837 armed rebellions broke out in both the Canadas, but they were not well coordinated and were easily put down. Following the rebellions, Lord Durham was dispatched from England to examine the situation. His 1839 report is one of the most famous documents in British Imperial history. His two fundamental suggestions for correcting the causes of the uprising were to reunite the Canadas and to provide the British North American colonies with "responsible" government: the executives would hold office at the discretion of the colonial representative assemblies. Sovereignty was to be divided without disintegration of the colonial empire. This new system of responsible government was first applied in 1848 to Nova Scotia and the Province of Canada (formed from Upper and Lower Canada in 1841) and by 1855 was in operation in the other colonies.

Confederation was slow in coming. Prior to 1864 the Colonial Office did favor a union of the Maritime provinces, but feared a larger union involving Canada. They secretly backed a conference of Maritime delegates in Charlottetown, Prince Edward Island, in September 1864. Meanwhile, Canada was increasingly encumbered by its constitution dictating equal representation in the legislature for Canada West and Canada East (the new designations for what were formerly Upper and Lower Canada). Canada West wanted representation by population, and a federation of the two Canadas was sought by Canada West liberals. When word of the impending P.E.I. conference was received in Canada, the Canadians asked to be unofficially included. A formal conference to consider the union of all the provinces was then held in Quebec in October 1864 (unknown to the Colonial Office) and a series of resolu tions set forth. The resolutions were received well only in Canada West. In Canada East Nova Scotia and New Brunswick they were contested and in Newfoundland and Prince Ed ward Island they were soundly defeated in the legislatures. The union movement was saved, however, by the potential economic boons of such a union and by increasing fears o possible fresh American attempts to annex British North America. The British North America Act was passed by the English Parliament and took effect on 1, July, 1867. New foundland and Prince Edward Island did not participate in the initial union, but joined later with the more western areas.

THE PRE-CONFEDERATION COINAGES OF CANADA

One of the greatest hindrances to trade in the early days of the settlements in North America was a lack of coined money. What coins were used trickled in from all over the world. Prior to the English conquest in the 1700's, France endeavored to keep her colonies in coins with special colonial issues and some French Imperial issues, but the balance of trade always caused a net loss of coin from the colonies. The situation was not much better under the British.

One of the major coins circulating in the British North American colonies was the Spanish milled dollar, which was being produced in considerable quantities in the mints to the south. These coins gained wide acceptance and the colonial monetary systems came to be expressed in terms of them. The value of the Spanish dollar varied from colony to colony; in New York it was rated at 8 shillings and in Nova Scotia it was worth 5s. The New York rating was called York Currency and the Nova Scotia rating was called Halifax Currency. Halifax Currency was extended to old Quebec in 1777 during the American revolution and to Upper Canada, superseding York Currency, in 1822. In English money (sterling) the Spanish dollar was worth 4s, 2d.

The local non-sterling ratings of the Spanish dollar had a profound effect upon the colonial copper currency. While it was possible for British shillings to circulate at the lowered ratings (by giving them a value in local currency of 1 shilling and a certain number of pence, and then giving coppers in change), the smaller valued pieces could not pass for more than their face (sterling) value. There was no way to make change for their additional increment of value in local currency. Thus, a significant loss was incurred upon the importer and a significant profit upon the exporter of British regal coppers. Obviously, the net flow of these coins had to be out of the colonies.

As the situation grew worse, local merchants decided to import tokens from England. They were usually of halfpenny size, with a smaller number of penny pieces and a few farthings. Some were anonymously issued. Others had the name of the issue, for example, "PAYABLE AT THE STORE OF J. BROWN." Soon there were a number of attractive, generally well made, coppers in circulation.

However, the element of profit caused some to import lightweight pieces and in time the copper currency became too voluminous. New laws were passed to deal with the problem. In 1817 the Nova Scotia government forbade further importation of private copper pieces and directed that the ones already in circulation be withdrawn within three years. In the Canadas an 1825 law was passed to prohibit the private issues, but it had no clause for the withdrawal of those in circulation and was worded such that the importation of tokens dated 1825 or earlier was not illegal. And so the appearance of private coppers, many of light weight, and antedated, continued in the Canadas.

Meanwhile, the Nova Scotian government stepped in and assumed the responsibility for providing that colony's copper currency. Semi-regal pence and halfpence were issued beginning in 1823 and continued intermittently until 1856. The people were thereby spared the deluge of metallic trash that was to continue to harass the Canadas, particularly Lower Canada.

The continued and growing presence of spurious coppers, many of which were struck ocally, finally forced Lower Canada to take steps to correct the situation. In the absence of action on the part of the government the Bank of Montreal issued one sou pieces in 1835, followed in 1837 by Banque du Peuple sous. These were of mediocre quality, however, and were immediately buried under an avalanche of counterfeits.

In 1837 four major Lower Canadian banks participated in the issue of the "habitant" one and two sous. After the Canadas reunited in 1841, three banks issued copper pence and half-pence. All of these later four bank coinages were of high quality and were not counterfeited to any significant degree. Gradually, the low quality pieces disappeared from circulation.

The semi-regal and bank issues paved the way for regal issues, based upon decimal systems of dollars and cents. They were struck at the Royal Mint in London or its prime sub-contractor, Heaton's Mint in Birmingham, England. Just as there had been individual colony's currency pounds, each colony's dollar was rated in its own particular way.

The Province of Canada, New Brunswick and P.E.I. all set their dollar equal to the U.S. gold dollar, so the £ sterling was worth $4.86⅔. Nova Scotia set its currency at $5.00 to the £ sterling and Newfoundland's dollar was initially equal to the Spanish dollar, which made he £ sterling worth $4.80. The first decimals were for the Province of Canada in 1858, followed by issues for Nova Scotia and New Brunswick in 1861, Newfoundland in 1865 and Prince Edward Island in 1871.

COINAGES FOR THE DOMINION OF CANADA

Following the formation of the Dominion of Canada, decimal coins were issued in 1870. The British North American colonies which had entered into the Confederation ceased to issue their own distinctive coins and a single coinage was issued for all. Newfoundland's coinage continued until 1947 and Prince Edward Island had a single issue of cents in 1871 prior to its entry into the Dominion in 1873.

MINTS, MINT MARKS AND QUANTITIES OF COINS STRUCK

The pre-decimal colonial issues (tokens) were struck at many different mints. Most of the better quality pieces emanated from private mints in England, the foremost of which were Boulton and Watt, and Ralph Heaton and Sons. The bank tokens of 1837 (habitants) to 1857 all were struck at one or the other of these mints. Another prominent producer of tokens was Thomas Halliday of Birmingham, who struck the Tiffin pieces (Nos. 115-120), and many of the Ships, Colonies & Commerce and Wellington tokens.

The only tokens to bear mint marks are the 1846 Rutherfords (No. 4) of Newfoundland, which have RH (for Ralph Heaton) above the date. In addition some SHIPS COLONIES & COMMERCE tokens were struck with an additional incuse H (for Heaton) on the water (No. 14c). Whenever known, the maker of each token issue is indicated in the text. Prior to 1908, all decimal issues for British North America were struck in England. The matrices, punches and dies were prepared at the Royal Mint in London and, when time permitted, the coins were struck there. As the Mint's work load increased, it was necessary to sometimes send the dies to the Heaton Mint (after 1889 called The Mint, Birmingham), where the coins were struck on contract.

With the single exception of the 1871 Prince Edward Island cent, Heaton-struck coins bear a small H mint mark. The last Heaton issue for British North America was the Canadian cent of 1907. Locations of the H are as follows: *Canada:* 1¢ 1876-90, 1907: below date; 1898, 1900: below bottom leaf; 5-50¢ 1871-1903: below bow of wreath; *Newfoundland:* 1¢ 1872-1904: below bow of wreath; 5-50¢ 1872-76: below bust; 1882: below date; $2. 1882: below date.

Late in the 19th century, the Canadians began agitating for a domestic mint with the power to coin sovereigns. Such an institution was authorized by the Ottawa Mint Act of 1901. However, construction was not begun until 1905, but was finally completed in time for commencement of coinage on 2 January 1908.

The name of the new mint was The Royal Mint, Ottawa Branch, but this was changed to The Royal Canadian Mint on 1 December 1931 when it became part of the Canadian government's Department of Finance. The Mint is now a Crown Corporation (since 1969), which reports to Parliament through the Minister of Supply and Services. In November of 1973 the Mint's preparatory facility at Hull, Quebec received satellite mint status with the striking of the first Olympic coins. A completely new and separate mint at Winnipeg, Manitoba became operational in the Spring of 1975 to relieve some of the increasing demands for domestic coinage at Ottawa.

Certain of the 20th century Newfoundland coinages have been struck at the Ottawa Mint; they are designated with a C (Canada) mint mark on the reverse: 1¢ 1917-20: below bow of wreath; 1941-47: above T of CENT; 5-50¢ 1917-47: at bottom reverse below oval. In addition, Ottawa-struck British type sovereigns of 1908-19 have a raised C mint mark centered on the base of the design above the date.

In many cases mintages of the tokens are not known; when they are, it is indicated in the text. However, the reader should be cautioned that, since many of the tokens were eventually melted, mintages are not necessarily reliable guides to scarcity today.

The quantities struck for the decimal coins are known with more certainty; nevertheless, those for the period 1858-1907 must, for the most part, be considered approximate. This is because the Royal Mint often attempted to use up all good dies, even if they bore the previous year's date. Therefore, while the reported number of coins struck in a given year may be quite correct, one cannot be certain what proportion were actually of that date. A good example of the problem is the Canadian 10 cents issue for 1889. Research results have pointed to the scarcity of that date (reported mintage 600,000) as the result of 1888 dies having been used to strike most of the pieces.

The reliability of mintage figures for the decimal coins is further complicated by the fact that portions of some issues were officially melted. This has turned what would have otherwise been a readily available issue into a scarce or rare one. Where it is known or strongly suspected that such a melt has occurred, we have preceded the number struck figure with *originally:* and placed the whole in parentheses.

VARIETIES AND OTHER DIFFERENCES

Collectors have long been interested in differences between coins of the same date or in a series. There can be variations in the precise details of portraits, the style or size of lettering or date, and so on. Such items have become increasingly popular, and a study of varieties can transform an otherwise placid series into an exciting one.

Together with the rise in variety interest has come a group of terms to describe these differences. Two coins are different *types* if their designs show some *basic* difference. For example, the Elizabeth II 1953-64 vs. the 1965-obverses represent separate types. The critical distinction is the presence of a laureated bust on the former and a diademed bust on the latter. Conversely, the "broad leaves" vs. the "small leaves" Canadian 10¢ reverses of George V are of the *same* type. The designs certainly differ in fine details; however, the basic appearance was unchanged.

The above mentioned George V 10¢ examples are *major varieties,* meaning that there is an obvious and deliberate alteration without changing the basic design. Less apparent varieties are termed *minor varieties* or *variants.* When the difference was actually prepared in the dies, the resulting coins will show variations called *die varieties.* There can also be *non-die varieties.* Examples in this category include deliberate changes in planchet composition or thickness.

Not all coins that differ from each other are varieties. The latter designation is reserved for coins differing as a result of some deliberate action by the issuing mint. Any variations arising from such causes as deterioration of dies or malfunction of mint machinery are not true varieties. They are known by names such as *freaks, mint errors* or *irregularities.* The term mint error, however, is usually not appropriate and its use should in most cases be avoided.

In order to understand varieties and the place they hold in numismatics, it is important to have at least a casual knowledge of how they came into being; that is, of how coinage dies are made.

THE MANUFACTURE OF COINAGE DIES
Development of the Matrix-Punch-Die System

he usual method of making coins is to place a flat metal disc (the planchet or blank) be-
ween two *dies* bearing the designs and impart the designs to the blank with a sharp blow. A
ie has at its top the flat or slightly convex surface that will become the field of the struck
)in. The design elements (e.g., portrait), which are *cameo* (raised) on the coin are *incuse*
unken) and face the opposite direction in the die. If the reader has difficulty grasping this
)ncept, he should press a coin onto a piece of clay. The image left in the clay is a model of
·hat the top of the die which struck that side of the coin looked like.

In ancient times and for many years thereafter, dies were individually hand engraved.
his system was extremely laborious, and once any given die wore out, its precise design
/as lost for future coinages. Gradually, more complex systems arose, with the ultimate
ʒsult of preserving a design for an essentially indefinite period.

The first refinement in die-making technique was to engrave the device (e.g., the portrait)
1 the form of a *punch*. A punch is a steel intermediate that has its design in cameo, in the
ame sense as on a coin. The design of the punch would then be impressed into blocks of
·eel, each of which would become a die. All secondary details (legends, rim beads, etc.)
·ere hand engraved into each die, as previously. The effect of the punch-die system was to
xtend the life of those parts of the design borne on the punches, because each punch could
1ake ("sink") multiple dies.

Working punch and die

The transition to the period of modern die-making occurred in the 1600's with the in-
·oduction of a third kind of intermediate, the *matrix*. A matrix has its design in the same
⁻nse as a die; however, it is used to make ("raise") punches instead of to strike coins. The
ddition of the matrix step offered two advantages over the previous system. First, a design
)uld be better preserved (a matrix can be used to raise multiple punches). Second, instead of
:lding the legend and rim heads at the die stage, these details could be incorporated into
ιe matrix. With only slight modifications, the matrix-punch-die system of die making has
·ersisted to this day.

Initiation of a New Coinage Design

ι modern die-making one of the fundamental problems is how to produce matrices of new
ʒsign. The most direct way, but also the most difficult, is to engrave it by hand. After the
ιtlines are scratched on the face of a steel block, the design elements are painstakingly
and cut to the exact size they are to appear on the finished coins. Lettering and other sec-
ιdary features are often engraved as individual hand punches and punched into the

matrix. Only a highly skilled engraver is capable of hand engraving a matrix, and this once common practice has largely disappeared today. The Canadian issues produced by this method are the Victory 5¢ of 1943-45 and the Newfoundland commemorative dollar of 1949. Both were by Thomas Shingles, the Royal Canadian Mint's former chief engraver.

The alternative method for making a matrix of a new design is to use the "reducing machine." The machine was invented by a Frenchman, Contamin, around the beginning of the 19th century and was first used in London's Royal Mint in 1824. While initially rather crude, the reducing machine has gradually evolved into a very important part of the engravers' tools. Briefly, it functions as follows: An 8" diameter three dimensional model of the design is produced in some hard substance such as plastic (formerly electroplated metals). A tracer at one end of the arm is a rapidly revolving cutter that faithfully duplicates the movements of the tracer, cutting the design on a reduced scale into a steel block. The reduction from the 8" model to coin size is usually made in two steps. Using the 8" model as a pattern, a steel *intermediate model* (about 3" in diameter) is made in the machine. The intermediate model is then similarly used to make a second reduction to coin scale. The second product of the machine is almost always a punch, called the *reduction punch*. The perfected reduction punch is placed in a powerful press and its design used to sink the matrix. Any details absent from the original model are then punched into the matrix. In the Victorian period reduction punches bore only the portrait or reverse device; now only the rim denticles are lacking.

Alteration of Existing Designs

The creation of a partially new design from one already used for coinage can be accomplished by a number of methods. During the Victorian and Edwardian periods, the commonest means was to re-engrave a punch or matrix bearing the old design. In some cases the change was slight, in others very pronounced. The Victorian portrait modifications are an elegant example of such a process.

In the George VI and Elizabeth series changes have been more often made by re-engraving at some point prior to the matrix stage. For example, the famous 1953 modification of the Canadian obverses was made by re-engraving the intermediate model for the reducing machine (see above section).

Dating of Coinage Dies

The dating of dies for the decimal coins has been accomplished by two methods. During the Victorian period it was common practice to employ reverse punches which had only a portion of the date (the first two or three digits). Dies sunk from such punches would then be finished by punching in, one digit at a time, the missing portion of the date. Occasionally, the date was completed at matrix stage.

The post-Victorian dies have usually been prepared from fully dated matrices. Notable exceptions, however, are the 50¢ and dollars for part of the 1940's and the early 1950's, where the date was once again completed in the dies.

Chromium Plating of Coinage Dies

During World War II, an attempt was made to increase die life. The most important advance was the development of an electrolytic process whereby a thin layer of pure chromium was deposited on the die faces. This gave the desired increase in die life and also imparted a better finish to the coins. Following limited use in 1942-44, chromium plating was adopted for all coinage dies in 1945.

This process, for all its advantages, has also led to the creation of two kinds of trivial differences between coins. First, it sometimes happens that tiny pieces of the plating chip away, leaving pits in the die faces. Such pits are manifested on the struck coins as tiny, irregular "dots," (e.g., the 1947 "dot" coins). Second, during the late 1940's and part of the 1950's, serviceable dies with degenerated plating were replated and put back in the presses. One danger of this was the inadvertent removal of delicate design details when the dies were repolished. The 50¢ 1950 "no lines in 0" and 1955 and other so-called "Arnprior" dollars are doubtless traceable to this practice. Replating of dies is no longer done at the Mint.

COMMEMORATIVE ISSUES

Canada is a country with a rich history and many of its important events or occurances have been featured with special coinage designs.

The first commemoratives beginning with the 1935 silver dollar, were issued for general circulation. The 1935 dollar was issued to celebrate the Silver Jubilee of King George V and exhibited for the first time the symbolic "Voyageur" reverse design showing an Indian canoe containing two paddlers. This coin heralded the beginning of Canada's commemorative series. This coin also has the distinction of being Canada's first official silver dollar.

In 1939, a special design showing the centre block of the Parliament Buildings in Ottawa, was released to mark the visit of George VI to Canada. In 1949, Newfoundland became a province of the Dominion of Canada and a special commemorative coin was issued picturing the Matthew, the first ship to visit Newfoundland.

In 1951 a 5¢ piece was issued to honour the 200th anniversary of the isolation and naming of the element nickel. A nickel refinery appeared as the reverse motif. A totem pole is shown on the reverse of the 1958 dollar whose dual role extolled the centenary of the western gold rush and establishment of British Columbia as a British Crown Colony. To mark the 100th anniversary of the meetings at Charlottetown, P.E.I. and Quebec City, P.Q. which paved the way for Confederation, a special design was made for the 1964 dollar.

An entire issue from 1¢ to $1.00 in 1967 bore special wildlife reverses to honour the 100th anniversary of Confederation. In that year a $20 gold piece was also made with sets and sold to collectors even though it lacked a specific commemorative legend.

Special commemorative dollars were released for general circulation in 1970, 1971, 1973 and 1974 commemorating the Centennial of Manitoba, British Columbia, Prince Edward Island and Winnipeg (in that order). A commemorative 25¢ coin was also issued in 1973 marking the centenary of the founding of the Royal Canadian Mounted Police. The latest commemorative dollar released to the general public was the 1984 dollar to celebrate the sesquicentenial of the City of Toronto.

In 1967, the Royal Canadian Mint began a new policy of producing commemoratives as collectors pieces only. These issues were not available for general circulation. This group is listed below.

Date	Denomination	Event	Composition
1971	$1	Centennial British Columbia	Silver
1973	$1	Royal Canadian Mounted Police	Silver
1974	$1	Winnipeg Centennial	Silver
1975	$1	Calgary Centennial	Silver
1976	$1	Library of Parliament Centennial	Silver
1977	$1	Queen Elizabeth II Silver Jubilee	Silver
1977	$100	Queen Elizabeth II Silver Jubilee	Gold
1978	$1	11th Commonwealth Games	Silver
1978	$100	Canadian Unity	Gold
1979	$1	The Griffon	Silver
1979	$100	International Year of the Child	Gold
1980	$1	Arctic Territories	Silver
1980	$100	Arctic Territories	Gold
1981	$1	Trans-Canada Railway	Silver
1981	$100	"O Canada"	Gold
1982	$1	Founding of Regina	Silver
1982	$100	Canadian Constitution	Gold
1983	$1	World University Games	Silver
1983	$100	St. John's Newfoundland	Gold
1984	$1	Toronto Sesquicentennial	Silver
1984	$100	Jacques Cartier	Gold

In 1973 an ambitious fund raising endeavor to help finance the 21st Olympic Games was begun. That year saw the first of seven silver four-coin sets; by the time the Games were held in 1976 at Montreal, 28 different silver coins and $100 gold piece had been released.

The complete Canadian commemorative series, including the foregoing examples, is fully illustrated and identified in this book. Pertinent background information is provided for each issue.

CONDITIONS OF COINS

In very general terms, the condition of a coin indicates the amount of wear it has sustained since the time it was minted. Coin conditions are distinguished from each other by a series of coin grades. A coin's grade is important to know because it determines the coin's value, the better a coin's grade, the higher will be its value. Coins are classified as belonging to one of two groups, that is, as a circulated coin or an uncirculated coin. Each of these groups is further divided into many grades.

To properly understand the factors that influence a coin's grade, it is first necessary to appreciate that older coins were manufactured to be used quite simply as "money" in the world of commerce. Secondly, these business or production strike coins were made on high speed presses, run through counting machines, and dumped into bags where they were scraped with other coins as they were being shipped to various banks across the country. Needless to say they were handled with little regard to their numismatic posterity. As a result, it is the rule, not the exception, that these coins had marks and other signs of coin-to-coin contact even before they were placed into circulation for use as money. These marks show on the surface of the coin as bright spots or streaks against the soft sheen of the coin's mint lustre. They are called bagmarks or bag scratches and are easily distinguishable from ordinary wear. Once placed into circulation, all coins begin to show signs of physical wear, i.e., a gradual destruction of the fine details that were originally present on a new coin. Those coins that were used the most tend to have the fewest details remaining. Today on the contrary, the Mint makes many coins specifically for the collector. These coins are carefully handled and packaged in plastic holders by trained Mint personnel. Unless they are removed from their holders, it is unlikely their grade will change over time.

Until the mid 1970's, coin grades were described by adjectives such as Very Good, Fine and Uncirculated. Since then the industry has adopted an alternative grading scheme that uses a numerical scale that ranges from 1 to 70. This system was originally attributed to Dr Wm. Sheldon who devised it as a means of grading and relating prices for early U.S. copper cents. In this numerical scheme, the circulated grades use the range from one to 59; the un-irculated range begins with 60 and progresses to a perfect coin which is 70. In general, the igher the number assignment, the better the quality or grade of the coin. While the umerical scale is a continuous one, not all of its numbers are used. Grading simply is not nat precise, but rather a mixture of both science-like methods and human judgements. To- ay it is quite common to see coins described using both the adjectival and numerical ystems as in the example Extra Fine-40.

Uncirculated Coins

An uncirculated coin must show absolutely no signs of wear or loss of detail (due to wear) vhen examined by the naked eye. To properly grade an uncirculated coin, it is necessary to ssess three different qualities of the coin in relation to the typical mint state characteristics een on a coin of that particular type. These three factors are the quality of each of the coin's ustre, surfaces, and strike. A coin that has lustre that is dazzling and 'alive' is much to be referred to lustre that is dull and lifeless. A coin that has surfaces that are free, or nearly so, f marks is preferred to one that shows obvious marks that are very distracting to the over- ll appeal of the coin. A well struck coin that shows all of the detail intended by the coin's esigner is preferable to one that is very poorly struck with the resultant loss of detail in ome area of the coin. Each of these factors are equally important in determining the grade f an uncirculated coin. In some cases, one of the factors may be so superior to that normally een in a particular series that it can make up for a slight deficiency in the quality of one of he remaining factors which by itself would lower the grade.

There are currently five recognized grades used to describe uncirculated coins. These are, long with their numerical designations, Typical Uncirculated (Mint State-60), Choice Un- irculated (MS-63), Gem Uncirculated (MS-65), Superb Uncirculated (MS-67), and Perfect Jncirculated (MS-70). A brief description of each follows:

Perfect Uncirculated-70: The finest quality available. Such a coin under 4 power mag- uification will show no marks, lines, or other evidence of handling or contact with other oins. The lustre quality will be of the highest quality possible and without any impairment f any sort. The strike will be perfectly sharp and of a quality very unusual for that series. "he strike detail will show all of the detail intended by the coin's designer/engraver.

Superb Uncirculated-67: A more select example of a Gem Uncirculated coin by virtue of he coin's overall qualities of lustre, surfaces, and strike. To the naked eye, the coin is essen- ially perfect in all respects. Only after extensive study is there likely to be any faults or cri- icism of the coin.

Gem Uncirculated-65: This grade is reserved for coins that have an overall unquestiona- le quality look to them, Each of the factors of lustre, surfaces, and strike will be well above verage for that normally seen on a typical mintstate coin of the series. The strike will be early full except for a slight weakness in a very localized area, the lustre will be almost ompletely free of impairments, and the surfaces generally mark free except on the largest oins and those made of softer metals such as gold. Any slight imperfections present will aot be distracting in any way from the overall beauty of the coin.

Choice Uncirculated-63: A more select example of a typical uncirculated coin but not one hat has the quality appeal of a full Gem Uncirculated-65. Any faults with the lustre, sur- aces, or strike may be readily seen with the naked eye but they collectively are not a major listraction to the overall appearance of the coin.

Typical Uncirculated-60: Shows absolutely no signs of wear on any part of the coin's sur- ace. Refers to a typically seen uncirculated example. Is expected to have a moderate but not xcessive number of bagmarks or rim nicks although none of a serious nature. The coin's ustre may be somewhat impaired by spotting or dullness. The strike may be weak enough o show a generalized weakness in detail in several areas. Usually the impairments to any f these three factors will be obvious at first glance and will continue to be distracting to the verall appeal of the coin.

Circulated Coins

Once a coin enters circulation, it begins to show physical wear on its surfaces. As time goes n the coin becomes so worn until, after many decades, only a few of its original details re- nain. The extent of this wear is the primary factor that determines the grade of circulated oins. There are ten regularly used grades for circulated coins. A brief description of each, along with their numerical grade assignment, follows:

Choice About Uncirculated-55: (Abbreviation AU-55). Only a small and localized trace of wear is visible to the naked eye at the highest relief points of the coin's design.

About Uncirculated-50: (AU-50). Traces of wear on nearly all of the coin's highest areas. Much of the original mint lustre is still present.

Choice Extremely Fine-45: (EF-45). Light overall wear on the coin's highest parts. A design details are very sharp. Mint lustre is usually seen only in the sheltered areas between the letters of the inscription and around the edges.

Extremely Fine-40: (EF-40). With only slight wear but more extensive than the preceding but still with excellent overall sharpness. Traces of mint lustre may still show.

Choice Very Fine-30: (VF-30). With light even wear on the surface; design details on the highest points lightly worn, but with all lettering and major features still sharp.

Very Fine-20: (VF-20). As preceding but with moderate wear on the high parts.

Fine-12: (F-12). Moderate to considerable even wear. Entire design is bold. All lettering is visible but with some weaknesses.

Very Good-8: (VG-8). Well worn. Most of the fine details of the hair and leaves are worn nearly smooth.

Good-4: (G-4). Heavily worn. Major designs visible but faint in areas. Other major features visible only in outline form without the central details.

About Good-3: (AG-3). Very heavily worn with portions of the lettering, date, and legends being worn smooth. The date is barely readable.

While these general definitions of grades are quite useful for most coins, the exact descriptions of circulated grades vary widely from coin type to coin type. We suggest you consult "The Standard Grading Guide to Canadian Decimal Coins" by J.E. Charlton and R.C Willey. This book makes extensive use of line drawings for each coin type to indicate areas that are most likely worn at each grade level.

The use of intermediate grades such as EF-42, EF-43, and so on is not encouraged. Grading is not that precise, and using such finely split intermediate grades is imparting a degree of accuracy which probably will not be able to be verified consistently by other numismatists.

Toning

Often a coin will develop a toning or tarnish on its surfaces. This toning can be particularl colourful and attractive on uncirculated coins because they tend to be free of dirt and grime that will surround the surface of a circulated coin. Silver coins may tarnish in blues, purples reds, greens, and other colours of the rainbow. Copper or bronze coins may develop du red, purplish-brown, olive, and chocolate brown toning. However, just because a coin ha attractive toning, it should not be concluded that the coin is necessarily a strictly uncircu ated example. Numismatists have often fallen into this trap.

These toning features, while an integral part of a coin's price, do not form part of its grad assignment. That is, a coin is first graded as if it were a fully brilliant example and the quality of the toning present, if any, is described by a separate adjective. For example, Choice Uncirculated-63 coin that is fully brilliant or possibly with just a hint of toning ma be called Choice BU for Choice Brilliant Uncirculated. On the other hand, that same coi with very dark toning is referred to as being Choice Toned Uncirculated. Some tonin descriptions are prefaced by the word "Original" as in Original Toned Choice Unc. This ad ditional adjective refers to those coins that are thought to never have been cleaned (i.e., dip ped) since the time they were first minted. As a result the quality of the toning has a ver special pristine look to it which is of considerable appeal to certain connoisseur collectors

Toned coins must be considered with caution, especially if high price premiums are being demanded. Toning that is darker can obscure very fine marks on the coin's surfaces an therefore make it appear to be in better condition than it really is. Toning can also hide th fact that a coin has very slight signs of wear and in fact is not the uncirculated coin that it a first appears to be. The best protection when examining toned coins is to ensure adequat lighting, lots of study time, and use of a magnifying glass. Because collectors have begun t pay premiums for toned coins, it has spawned an increase in the number of people attempt ing to "artificially" tone coins through sped up chemical reactions. Most specialists in th colour field can tell artificial toning from that of Mother Nature. When in doubt, it would be wise to seek the opinion of one of these specialists.

Marks on Coins

There are many, many adjectives that are used to describe the various marks and other imperfections seen on coins. These descriptions tend to be confusing and make it difficult to properly describe the condition of a coin to others. The following scheme is simple and recommended for describing all marks, rim nicks, and other coin imperfections whether man made or caused by the minting process.

Major: Immediately obvious at first glance to the naked eye. Very distracting.

Minor: Still immediately noticed on first glance to the naked eye but not a major distraction considering the other qualities of the coin.

Slight: Can be seen by the naked eye but usually discovered only after a more detailed study (more than just a glance). Not distracting.

Very Slight: Really only clearly discernable when using low power magnification such as 4-5 power. Have to search to find it.

Very, Very Slight: Likely not even observable to the naked eye after the closest of study. The details will become clearly defined only under stronger magnification of 8-10 power.

SOME USEFUL GRADING CAVEATS

A grading caveat is, in simple terms, a warning of something to be sensitive to, or careful about, when evaluating the condition of a coin. A healthy respect for each of the following caveats is as important to being a consistently successful grader as is a knowledge of the rules that distinguish a VF coin from an EF and so on.

1. Scarcer dates within a coin series are not graded any differently than the more common dates of the same series.
2. There is no such grade as a 'commercial' grade. Coins are either strictly graded or they are sliders.
3. Expect the largest coins to have more and larger bagmarks than the smallest coins. Also expect to see larger and more numerous marks on coins made of softer metals such as gold.
4. The higher the grade of a coin, the greater the amount of time that should be taken to arrive at that conclusion.
5. Toned coins must always be studied more carefully in order to see what problems are being obscured.
6. Grading uncirculated coins requires an assessment of three factors. These are the qualities of the coin's lustre, surfaces, and strike. On the other hand, grading a circulated coin basically involves only one factor, that being, the amount of wear of the surfaces of the coin.
7. There is a natural human tendency for the owner of a coin to overgrade his coin and for the purchaser to undergrade someone else's coin.
8. While a coin's grade and price are inter-related, a coin can only be priced once its grade has been determined. Furthermore a coin can not be reliably graded by only knowing its price.
9. It is impossible to accurately grade an uncirculated coin of a given series without first understanding the typical mintstate characteristics for coins of that series.
10. Grading is not, and never will be, an exact science. It involves a lot of human judgement too.
11. It is the rule, not the exception, that business or production strike coins will have bagmarks and other possible manufactured imperfections.
12. Grading only by "eye appeal" is not really grading at all. Eye appeal grading can be deceptively inaccurate because the grader is tricked into forgetting about problems that may exist on the coin.

RARITY AND VALUE

When one inquires as to the rarity of a coin, it is not really sufficient to specify merely the date and denomination. Varieties exist for several issues, and where they are particularly noteworthy, they are often widely collected as distinct entities — that is, as if they were separate dates. It is also best to specify the condition of the coin. There is always a marked difference between the rarity of earlier issues in uncirculated vs. well circulated conditions. Compare values for the various conditions of the Canadian 1911 50¢. In Very Good (well circulated) it lists at $20, but in uncirculated it jumps to $3600!

Because determining rarity by the direct method of examining a large number of coins is often impractical, it is usually deduced by other means. A common practice is to compare prices. This method, while certainly a reasonable starting point, can sometimes be very misleading. For example, the Canadian 1921 50¢ in uncirculated condition lists for $50,000 while the 1870 50¢ without the designer's initials has been valued at nearly $15,000 in the same condition. Is the latter coin, then, three times commoner than the former. The mint state 1870 is in fact twice as rare as the 1921. Why the inverted price relationship? The 1870 is part of a series not widely collected by date and variety, and its rarity is much less appreciated than that of the famous 1921.

The other usual way to ascertain rarity is by comparing mintage figures. Here too, caution is in order. First, reported figures especially for the Victorian period (see above), are not always reliable. Second, in the case of varieties the mints rarely know what proportion of a given year's issue was of a particular variety. And third, mint figures tell one nothing about the number of pieces preserved in the better conditions. Example: the mintages for the Canadian 1937 and 1938 50¢ are almost identical, yet the uncirculated valuation for the 1937 is $95.00 while that for the 1938 is $370. The 1937's were saved in quantity because they were the first date of a new series. On the other hand, most of the 1938's went into circulation.

The value of a coin is determined by the law of supply and demand. Some very scarce items change little in value from year to year simply because they are not widely collected whereas commoner dates that are part of a very popular series can show great differences.

The approximate market values listed in this catalog are only indications of probable average worth. In an individual transaction a coin may sell for more or less than what is indicated here. Every attempt has been made to quote values that realistically reflect the market. These values were determined by a panel of several individuals, most of whom are in close contact with retail sales. In some instances, particularly for previously unpublished varieties, the prices are either theoretical or omitted.

THE SCOPE OF LISTINGS IN THIS CATALOGUE

Pre-decimal Colonial Issues

The well-known reference on Canadian tokens, Breton's 1894 work, is a hodgepodge of several different kinds of items which can be divided into seven basic categories:

(a) Items that are not really Canadian.
(b) Patterns.
(c) Merchant and other advertising cards, tickets, etc.
(d) Trade tokens, redeemable in goods and services only (e.g., transportation tokens) and only to a very limited extent money.
(e) Fabrications made to deceive collectors.
(f) Pieces that were used as money, with relatively unrestricted validity throughout the colony of issue.
(g) Contemporary counterfeits of (f).

The approach used in this catalog is to list only those pieces falling in classes (f) and (g). Careful note should be made of the distinction between contemporary counterfeits and those made to deceive collectors. Contemporary counterfeits, or imitations as they are often called in the listings, are of the same period as the production and circulation of the originals. They were made to circulate and serve as money along with the originals. Being of lighter weight and often of a less pure copper, the imitations brought a tidy profit to their purveyors. The contemporary counterfeits have traditionally been collected along with the originals and some can even command a higher premium today. The inclusion of contemporary imitations in this catalog is quite logical, for they, too, for a least a while served as Canada's money.

The collectors' forgeries or concoctions are another matter. They are usually made long after the originals circulated, with the intent to deceive coin collectors into paying substantial premiums for them. These items are not worthy of listing in a catalog of this kind.

Over the years, many token die varieties and freaks have been described. Men like Lees and Courteau have devoted considerable energy to the study of varieties in this series. An important reason why such studies are possible has to do with how the dies were made. Most (but not all) of the token dies, including the devices, were engraved entirely by hand. This made every such die distinct from each of the others, creating a large number of die varieties. In a general catalog it is not desirable to list every known difference, even when true die varieties are involved. Therefore, we have surveyed the varieties and have selected for separate listing those that seem to us to be the most interesting and easy for the average collector to recognize.

Decimal Issues

Although most pattern pieces are excluded from the listings (see the comments above on token patterns), two decimal coins that might be called "semi-patterns" are included: the 1965 medium beads obverse and 1967 flat dies dollars. These coins are the products of trial production runs of several thousand each and are from regular dies. True patterns are almost always proof and are struck in very small quantities.

Varieties in the decimal series have been very popular with collectors and have traditionally been included in Canadian catalogs. Unfortunately, their treatment has not always been consistent; some varieties have been listed while others, at least as important, were omitted. In this work an effort has been made to list all noteworthy varieties, regardless of how rare they might be.

It has also been deemed necessary to include a small number of items that are either trivial varieties or not varieties at all. That is because the particular items involved have been touted as differences of importance (through advertising campaigns, etc.) for so long that many collectors have been misled into thinking they really are important. At this date it would seem unwise to remove such things as the "Arnprior" dollars from the catalog. Each of these "objectionable" listings is explained in the appropriate place in the main body of the catalog.

As a final comment regarding those varieties which have been listed, it is stressed that this book is only a guide. By the inclusion of a given item the authors do not necessarily suggest that it should be part of a "complete" set. Each collector is urged to decide for himself the extent of his interest in the sub-listings.

LOCAL AND NATIONAL
NUMISMATIC ORGANIZATIONS

Throughout Canada and the U.S. are located many local coin clubs that include in their memberships those interested in any and all phases of numismatics. Becoming involved in such an organization offers important advantages to beginner and more experienced collector alike. One can acquire needed coins, dispose of extras, gain valuable knowledge and enjoy the good fellowship of others with like interests.

Similarly, anyone seriously interested in Canadian numismatics should join and support Canada's national numismatic organization, The Canadian Numismatic Association. Its members have access by mail to the association's impressive library and receive the Canadian Numismatic Journal, the official monthly periodical. The "Journal" provides a medium for publishing and disseminating numismatic knowledge, so important for progress in the hobby. Those interested in membership should contact:

> The Canadian Numismatic Association
> General Secretary
> P.O. Box 226
> Barrie, Ontario, Canada   L4M 4T2

There is also an organization for those interested in paper money:
> Canadian Paper Money Society
> P.O. Box 356
> Fredericton, N.B. Canada   E3B 4Z9

The principal national U.S. numismatic association (the largest in the world) is:
> The American Numismatic Association
> P.O. Box 2366
> Colorado Springs, Colorado   80901
> (Membership inquiries should be directed to the General Secretary.)

Weekly and bi-weekly (every two weeks) tabloid-type publications fill another need for the collector, that of providing an up-to-date view of hobby activity. Dealer advertising offering coins, paper money and related numismatic items can be found in abundance, as well as special sections devoted to features and events of interest. Many coin shops carry these informative periodicals, or subscriptions may be entered by writing directly to the publications listed below:

Canadian Coin News
P.O. Box 10,000
Bracebridge, Ontario
Canada P0B 1C0
(Bi-Weekly, sample copy $1.00)

World Coin News
700 East State Street
Iola, Wisconsin 54990
(Weekly, sample copy $1.00)

2
DECIMAL COINAGE 1858 TO DATE

Although the early 19th century coinage of commerce in all the British North American colonies was ostensibly that of England, the actual coins were scarce and issues of a number of countries were used. They were primarily those of Spain, Portugal, France, Mexico and the United States. Furthermore, as outlined in other chapters, large numbers of privately issued base metal pieces circulated for pence and halfpence. The need for unified currencies was clear-cut. The ultimate result was a distinctive decimal currency for each of the colonies.

The principal leader in the Province of Canada's struggle for its own coinage was Sir Francis Hincks, Inspector General (1848-54), Prime Minister (1851-54) and later Minister of Finance for the Dominion of Canada. Legislation establishing the Province's decimal coinage consisted of several steps that took almost a decade. Initially there was strong British opposition.

In 1850 an act was passed which empowered the provincial government to have its own distinctive coinage struck in pounds-shillings-pence denominations. The British government disallowed the act, however, partly because it was felt that the regulation of coinage was the prerogative of the Sovereign and the use of English currency facilitated trade with the Mother Country.

In a second act, passed in 1851, the Canadians continued the fight for control of their own currency. For the first time a decimal system was suggested: public accounts were to be kept in dollars, cents and mils. The English Treasury also viewed the second act with disfavour, but did not disallow it. Instead, it was proposed that the province have its own pound and that it could be divided into decimal units if necessary.

The 1851 act paved the way for an act of 1853, which established a Canadian currency consisting of pounds-shillings-pence and dollars-cents-mils, the public accounts being kept in the latter. The striking of coins was left to the Queen's prerogative and none was issued under this act.

Finally, in 1857, the dollar alone was established as the unit of money and all accounts, public and government, were to be kept in dollars and cents. The Canadian dollar was given the same intrinsic value as the U.S. dollar; the English sovereign (pound sterling) was worth $4.86⅔. An issue of decimal coins followed in 1858-59.

LARGE CENTS
Victoria, Province of Canada, 1858-1859

Diameter: 25.40 mm, weight: 4.536 grams; composition: 950 copper, .040 tin, .010 zinc; edge: plain.

G: Braid worn through
VG: No detail in braid around ear.
Fine: Segments of braid begin to merge into one another.
VF: Braid is clear but not sharp.
EF: Braid is slightly worn but generally sharp and clear.

The basic obverse design, a bust separated from the legend by a beaded circle, is said to have been copied from the Napoleon III bronze coinages of France (1853-70). The Canadian obverse shows a very youthful Victoria with a laurel wreath in her hair and was designed and engraved by the Royal Mint's famed engraver, Leonard C. Wyon.

The reverse was also by Wyon and has a serpentine vine with 16 maple leaves. There are numerous slight variations involving re-cutting of some of the leaf stems or the vine stalk.

The coins were conceived to also be used as convenient units of measure; the diameter is exactly 1 inch and 100 (unworn) pieces weigh 1 avoirdupois pound. Nevertheless, they were not very popular at first and were sometimes discounted by as much as 20% to get them into circulation.

Wide, bold 9
over 8

Early form — Late form
Narrow 9

No. 1   No. 2
Double-punched narrow 9
(No. 1 is often erroneously
called a narrow 9 over 8)

1859 date varieties. Although the Province of Canada placed its single order for cents in 1858, insufficient time forced the Royal Mint to strike the bulk of the coins in 1859. Two distinctly different 9 punches were used for dating the dies. A number of dies (at least 11) were originally dated 1858 and have the final 8 altered by overpunching with a wide, bold 9, this 9 was apparently used *only* for overdating (we cannot confirm the claims that the wide 9 occurs on a non-overdate). A second figure, used for non-overdates, is narrow and initially rather delicate. Some narrow 9 specimens have the 9 somewhat broadened; these are thought to be from dies dated late in the issue when the narrow 9 punch had distorted from extensive use (rather than two different styles of narrow 9 punches being used). Both the delicate and broadened narrow 9's are illustrated because the latter is sometimes confused with the wide, bold 9. The so-called "narrow 9 over 8" is not a true overdate but a double-punch narrow 9 with a small piece out of the die at the lower front of the 9's. A second double-punched narrow 9 has traces of the original 9 to the left of the second figure. The latter double-punchings are considered trivial by these catalogues; however, they are included because of current wide acceptance by collectors.

Date	Qty. Minted	G-4	VG-8	F-12	VF-20	EF-40	AU-50	UNC-60	BU-60
1858 421,000		$22.50	$40.00	$47.50	$62.50	$82.50	$115.00	$200.00	$450.00
1859 (incl. all varieties) . 10,000,000									
9 over 8, wide 9		18.50	35.00	45.00	60.00	80.00	105.00	185.00	475.00
narrow 9, all forms		1.25	1.75	2.50	3.75	5.25	15.00	35.00	100.00
double-punch, narrow 9 .... No. 1		50.00	100.00	160.00	225.00	325.00	425.00	650.00	1,250
double-punch, narrow 9 .... No. 2		25.00	35.00	45.00	60.00	100.00	140.00	200.00	400.00

Victoria, Dominion of Canada, 1876-1901

Diameter: 25.40 mm; weight: 5.670 grams; composition: .950 copper, .040 tin, .010 zinc; edge: plain.

G: *Hair over ear worn through.*
VG: *No details in the hair over the ear.*
Fine: *Strands of hair over the ear begin to run together.*
VF: *Hair and jewels no longer sharp but clear.*
EF: *Hair over the ear is sharp and clear. Jewels in diadem must show sharply and clearly.*

Because of the large issue of 1858-59 cents by the Province of Canada and later the Dominion of Canada governments, this denomination was not ordered again until nearly 10 years after Confederation. The Provincial cents had been unpopular because of their weight, so the Dominion cents were struck in the same weight as the British halfpenny.

The obverse type of the Dominion cents was changed to one with a diademed Queen, although a pattern piece with the 1876 reverse and 1858-59 obverse suggests that the laureated type may have been considered. The diademed obverse type is composed of four distinctive portrait varieties, differing in the facial and certain other details. The portrait for the initial obverse was created by modifying one of those for the Jamaica halfpenny. Later obverses were derived from a previously used one: Obv. 2 from Obv. 1 and Obv. 3 and 4 from Obv. 2. All designs were by L.C. Wyon except for Obv. 4, which was probably by G.W. de Saulles. The portraits are distinguished as follows:

Obverse 1: Generally youthful appearance: rounded chin and prominent lips.
Obverse 2: Somewhat aged facial features: double chin and repressed upper lip.

Obverse 3: Even more aged features: double chin with a square front and depression over the eye.

Obverse 4: Smooth chin restored, but has repressed upper lip.

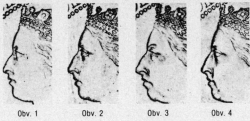

| Obv. 1 | Obv. 2 | Obv. 3 | Obv. 4 |

In addition to the portrait differences there are also several variations of lettering style, the most obvious of which occurs in association with Obv. 3. When the obverse was used in 1890, it had a normal (or nearly so) legend; however, the 1891-92 Obv. 3's *all* have a legend with more coarse style letters punched over the original.

Three major reverse varieties exist. The first (1876-82) is identical to the 1858-59 issues, except for some re-cutting of the leaf stems and vine stalk. The second has a new vine containing wider leaves with less venation. The third (1891-1901) has yet another vine containing narrow leaves with incuse venation. Each reverse was from a separate reducing machine model; the first two were by L.C. Wyon and the third is thought to be by G.W. De Saulles. There are numerous re-cuttings of the stems and stalks of the vines on the first and third reverses.

Date	Qty. Minted	G-4	VG-8	F-12	VF-20	EF-40	AU-50	UNC-60	BU-60
Provincial Leaves Reverse (1876-1882)									
1876H ....obv. 1	4,000,000	$1.00	$1.75	$2.75	$4.00	$7.00	$14.50	$37.50	$100.00
1881H ....obv. 1	2,000,000	1.75	3.25	4.50	6.50	11.50	24.50	50.00	135.00
1882H ....obv. 1,2	4,000,000	1.00	1.75	2.75	4.00	7.00	14.50	37.50	100.00

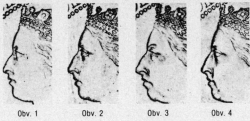

Large leaves 1884-1891

Large date

Small date

Large Leaves Reverse (1884-1891)

Date	Qty. Minted	G-4	VG-8	F-12	VF-20	EF-40	AU-50	UNC-60	BU-60
1884 ..... obv. 1,2	2,500,000	1.50	2.75	4.00	5.75	9.00	19.00	45.00	105.00
1886 ..... obv. 1,2	1,500,000	2.50	4.50	6.00	8.25	14.50	30.00	55.00	165.00
1887 ..... obv. 2	1,500,000	2.00	3.75	5.00	7.00	12.00	23.50	50.00	145.00
1888 ..... obv. 2	4,000,000	1.25	1.75	2.75	3.75	6.50	14.00	35.00	100.00
1890H ... obv. 3	1,000,000	3.50	6.00	10.00	14.00	22.50	55.00	115.00	300.00
1891 lg. dt. ... obv. 2.3 .	1,452,500	3.50	6.00	9.50	12.50	20.00	37.50	72.50	210.00
sm. date . obv. 2,3 .	incl. above	35.00	55.00	70.00	90.00	115.00	165.00	410.00	1,000

Small leaves 1891-1901

On the 1898 and 1900 Heaton issues the H mint mark is below the bottom leaf in the wreath.

Date	Qty. Minted	G-4	VG-8	F-12	VF-20	EF-40	AU-50	UNC-60	BU-60

Small Leaves Reverse (1891-1901)

Note: All small leaves coins, including those dated 1891, have a small date.

Date	Qty. Minted	G-4	VG-8	F-12	VF-20	EF-40	AU-50	UNC-60	BU-60
1891 ....obv. 2,3 ...	incl. above	$30.00	$40.00	$52.00	$65.00	$85.00	$125.00	$250.00	$650.00
1892 ....obv. 2,3,4 ..	1,200,000	2.00	3.25	6.00	8.00	12.00	25.00	50.00	140.00
1893 ....obv. 4	2,000,000	1.75	2.50	3.50	5.50	9.50	18.00	37.50	115.00
1894 ....obv. 4	1,000,000	5.00	7.00	10.50	14.50	22.50	60.00	115.00	265.00
1895 ....obv. 4	1,200,000	2.50	4.00	7.00	9.50	13.00	30.00	70.00	185.00
1896 ....obv. 4	2,000,000	1.50	2.00	3.25	4.00	5.50	14.00	37.50	105.00
1897 ....obv. 4	1,500,000	1.50	2.00	3.25	4.00	5.50	14.00	37.50	105.00
1898H ....obv. 4	1,000,000	3.50	4.75	7.25	10.00	13.50	32.00	72.00	200.00
1899 ....obv. 4	2,400,000	1.50	2.00	3.00	4.00	6.00	14.00	35.00	100.00
1900 ....obv. 4	1,000,000	5.00	7.00	10.00	15.00	20.00	37.50	75.00	215.00
1900H ....obv. 4	2,600,000	1.75	2.00	3.00	4.00	6.00	14.00	35.00	100.00
1901 ....obv. 4	4,100,000	1.25	1.75	2.50	3.50	5.50	12.00	30.00	90.00

Edward VII, Large Cents, 1902-1910

Diameter: 25.40 mm; weight: 5.670 grams; composition: .950 copper, .040 tin, .010 zinc; edge: plain.

G: Band of crown worn through.
VG: Band of crown is worn through at the highest point.
Fine: Jewels in the band of the crown will be blurred.
VF: Band of crown is still clear; no longer sharp.
EF: Band of crown slightly worn; generally sharp and clear.

A single obverse, designed and engraved by G.W. De Saulles (DES. below bust), was employed for the entire series.

The reverse was a continuation of the small leaves Victorian variety.

Date	Qty. Minted	G-4	VG-8	F-12	VF-20	EF-40	AU-50	UNC-60	BU-60
1902	3,000,000	1.00	1.50	2.00	3.00	4.50	7.50	17.50	55.00
1903	4,000,000	1.00	1.75	2.50	3.50	5.50	9.00	20.00	60.00
1904	2,500,000	1.25	2.00	3.00	4.25	6.00	10.00	22.50	65.00
1905	2,000,000	3.00	5.00	7.00	9.50	13.00	18.50	40.00	130.00
1906	4,100,000	1.00	1.75	2.50	3.50	5.50	8.50	22.50	70.00
1907	2,400,000	1.50	2.75	4.00	5.50	7.50	11.50	30.00	90.00

On the 1907 Heaton issue the mint mark is below the date.

Date	Qty. Minted	G-4	VG-8	F-12	VF-20	EF-40	AU-50	UNC-60	BU-60
1907H	800,000	6.00	10.50	14.00	20.00	37.50	50.00	100.00	300.00
1908	2,401,506	2.00	3.50	4.75	6.50	8.50	12.00	30.00	80.00
1909	3,973,339	1.00	1.50	2.00	3.00	5.00	9.00	25.00	70.00
1910	5,146,487	1.00	1.50	1.75	3.00	4.50	8.00	20.00	65.00

George V, Large Cents, 1911-1920

Diameter: 25.40 mm; weight: 5.670 grams; composition: 1911-19: .950 copper, .040 tin, .010 zinc; 1919-20: .955 copper, .030 tin, .015 zinc; edge: plain.

The original obverse, used for the 1911 issues of the 1¢ to 50¢, bore a legend lacking the words DEI GRATIA ("by the grace of God") or some abbreviation for them. The public complained, calling these coins "Godless," and in 1912 a modified legend containing DEI GRA: was introduced. Both verieties were derived from a portrait model of the King by Sir E.B. MacKennal (initials B.M on truncation).

The reverse, although resembling previous designs, is completely new. The engraver was W.H.J. Blakemore.

G: *Band of crown worn through.*
VG: *Band of crown worn through at highest point.*
Fine: *Jewels in band of crown will be blurred.*
VF: *Band of crown is still clear; no longer sharp.*
EF: *Band of crown slightly worn; generally sharp and*
        clear.

Date	Qty. Minted	G-4	VG-8	F-12	VF-20	EF-40	AU-50	UNC-60	BU-60
Godless Obverse (1911)									
1911	4,663,486	$1.00	$1.75	$2.25	$3.25	$5.75	$11.50	$24.00	$70.00

Modified Obverse Legend (1912-1920)									
1912	5,107,642	.50	1.00	1.50	2.75	4.75	8.00	20.00	62.00
1913	5,735,405	.50	1.00	1.50	2.75	4.75	7.00	18.00	60.00
1914	3,405,958	1.00	1.75	2.25	3.50	6.00	12.50	30.00	85.00
1915	4,932,134	.75	1.25	1.75	3.00	5.00	10.50	22.50	70.00
1916	11,022,367	.50	.90	1.25	2.00	4.00	7.00	16.50	50.00
1917	11,899,254	.35	.60	1.00	1.50	2.75	5.50	12.50	42.00
1918	12,970,798	.35	.60	1.00	1.50	2.75	5.50	12.50	42.00
1919	11,279,634	.35	.60	1.00	1.50	2.75	5.50	12.50	42.00
1920	6,762,247	.35	.85	1.10	1.75	3.00	6.50	15.00	50.00

SMALL CENTS
George V, Small Cents, 1920-1936

Diameter: 19.05 mm; weight: 3.240 grams; composition: .955 copper, .030 tin, .015 zinc; edge: plain.

G: *Band of crown worn through.*
VG: *Band of crown worn through at highest point.*
Fine: *Jewels in band of crown will be blurred.*
VF: *Band of crown is still clear but no longer sharp.*
EF: *Band of crown slightly worn but generally sharp
and clear.*

In order to conserve copper, the large cent was replaced in 1920 with one of smaller size, like that of the United States. The obverse bust was MacKennal's familiar design and the reverse was a new design by Fred Lewis. The master matrices were prepared in London by W.H.J. Blakemore.

Date	Qty. Minted	G-4	VG-8	F-12	VF-20	EF-40	AU-50	UNC-60	BU-60
1920	15,483,923	.20	.35	.75	2.00	3.75	5.50	14.00	37.50
1921	7,601,627	.50	.85	1.50	3.50	8.00	12.00	18.00	55.00
1922	1,243,635	10.00	15.00	20.00	25.00	45.00	75.00	135.00	375.00
1923	1,019,002	15.00	25.00	30.00	35.00	50.00	100.00	250.00	600.00
1924	1,593,195	5.00	6.50	8.50	12.00	18.50	40.00	90.00	250.00
1925	1,000,622	15.00	18.50	25.00	30.00	42.50	80.00	200.00	550.00
1926	2,143,372	1.75	3.00	4.50	6.00	13.50	32.00	75.00	200.00
1927	3,553,928	1.00	1.75	3.00	5.00	12.00	20.00	36.00	100.00
1928	9,144,860	.20	.35	.50	1.50	3.50	6.00	13.50	36.00
1929	12,159,840	.20	.35	.50	1.25	3.00	5.00	12.00	32.00
1930	2,538,613	1.50	2.50	3.25	4.50	10.00	20.00	45.00	120.00
1931	3,842,776	1.25	1.75	2.50	3.50	8.00	15.00	35.00	90.00

Date	Qty. Minted	G-4	VG-8	F-12	VF-20	EF-40	AU-50	UNC-60	BU-60
1932	21,316,190	$ .20	$ .25	$ .35	$ .75	$2.75	$5.00	$14.00	$40.00
1933	12,079,310	.20	.30	.40	1.00	3.00	5.00	14.00	40.00
1934	7,042,358	.25	.35	.60	2.00	3.50	5.00	14.00	40.00
1935	7,526,400	.25	.35	.60	2.00	3.50	5.00	14.00	40.00
1936	8,768,769	.25	.35	.60	2.00	3.50	5.00	14.00	40.00

George VI Issue Struck in Name of George V

King George V died early in 1936 and was succeeded by his son Edward VIII, whose portrait was planned for introduction on 1937 coinage. Edward abdicated late in 1936, however, and his younger brother was crowned as George VI. The Royal Mint in London did not have time to prepare new Canadian George VI obverse matrices and punches for shipment to Ottawa by the beginning of 1937. This led to an emergency situation because of a pressing demand for 1, 10 and 25 cents, and in order to meet the emergency, coins were struck using George V dies dated 1936. To denote that the coins were actually struck in 1937 a small round depression was punched into each die, causing a raised dot to appear in that position on the coins. On the cent the dot is centered below the date.

Of the three denominations thus made, only the 25¢ is readily available (in circulated condition), while the two others are known only in mint state and are very rare. Obviously if all had been released they would be known in greater quantity today; therefore it seems reasonable to explain the situation in one of two ways: (a) the 1¢ and 10¢ were not struck with the dots (it has often been suggested that the depressions in these dies filled with extraneous matter or that they were never punched into the dies in the first place), or (b) they were made with dots but not issued. The first explanation is quite doubtful because (1) a former mint employee who worked in the press room in early 1937 maintains that all three denominations were struck with dots; (2) the known 10¢ specimens have a dot larger than that on the 25¢, yet the "clogging" theory would require that the 25¢ dies did not fill up while all the rest did; (3) one of the dot cents was found in the Pyx box, a container where coins taken at random from production runs are reserved for assay.

In view of the above, these authors suggest serious consideration of the possibility that the dot 1¢ and 10¢ pieces were struck but never issued (i.e., melted).

The physical specifications are as on the George V issues.

Date	Qty. Minted		
1936 raised dot below date	(Originally: 678,823)	Rare	5 known

George VI, Small Cents, 1937-1952

Diameter: 19.05 mm; weight: 3.240 grams; composition 1937-42: .955 copper, .030 tin, .015 zinc; 1942-52: .980 copper, .015 tin, .005 zinc; edge: plain.

VG: No detail in hair above ear.
Fine: Only slight detail in hair above ear.
VF: Where not worn, hair is clear but not sharp.
EF: Slight wear in hair over ear.

The obverses of the George VI issues are unique in that the monarch is bareheaded. The initial obverse variety has a legend containing the phrase ET IND : IMP : (for ET INDIAE IMPERATOR, meaning "and Emperor of India"). Beginning with coins dated 1948, the phrase was omitted from the King's titles, due to India having gained independence from England in the previous year. Both varieties were derived from a portrait model by T.H. Paget (H.P. under bust).

In keeping with a Government decision to modernize the designs, the simple but compelling "maple twig" design by G.E. Kruger-Gray (K·G under the right leaf) was adopted for the cent.

1947 maple leaf. Some specimens of this and all the other denominations dated 1947 have a tiny maple leaf after the date, to denote that they were actually struck in 1948. In that year, while the Royal Canadian Mint was awaiting the new obverse matrices and punches bearing the modified legend (see above) from the Royal Mint in London, a pressing demand for all denominations arose. In order to meet the demand, coins were struck with 1947 obverse and reverse dies, with the leaf added to indicate the incorrect date. After the new obverse matrices and punches arrived later in the year, normal 1948 coins were put into production.

Date	Qty. Minted	VG-8	F-12	VF-20	EF-40	AU-50	UNC-60	BU-60
ET IND : IMP : Obverse (1937-1947)								
1937	10,040,231	$ .40	$ .60	$2.00	$3.00	$4.00	$4.50	$7.00
1938	18,365,608	.25	.40	.60	1.25	2.75	5.00	10.00
1939	21,600,319	.25	.40	.60	1.25	2.75	4.00	7.50
1940	85,740,532	.15	.20	.40	.85	1.25	2.50	5.50
1941	56,335,011	.15	.25	.50	1.00	5.00	15.00	50.00
1942	76,113,708	.15	.25	.50	1.00	5.00	13.00	40.00
1943	89,111,969	.15	.25	.50	1.00	3.00	6.00	15.00
1944	44,131,216	.30	.50	.75	1.25	5.00	14.00	45.00
1945	77,268,591	.15	.20	.35	.75	1.00	2.00	6.00
1946	56,662,071	.15	.20	.35	.75	1.00	2.00	6.00
1947	31,093,901	.30	.40	.60	1.00	1.50	3.00	7.50
1947 maple leaf	43,855,448	.15	.20	.35	.75	1.00	1.75	4.50

Modified Obverse Legend (1948-1952)

1948	25,767,779	.20	.35	.65	1.00	1.50	3.00	7.50
1949	33,128,933	.10	.20	.30	.50	.75	2.00	3.50
1950	60,444,992	.10	.20	.30	.50	.75	2.00	3.50
1951	80,430,379	.10	.15	.25	.50	.75	1.00	3.00
1952	67,631,736	.10	.15	.25	.50	.75	1.00	3.00

Elizabeth II, Laureate Bust Cents, 1953-1964

Diameter: 19.05 mm; weight: 3.240 grams; composition: .980 copper, .015 tin, .005 zinc; edge: plain.

Fine: *Leaves worn almost through; shoulder fold indistinct.*
VF: *Leaves considerably worn; shoulder fold must be clear*
EF: *Laurel leaves on head somewhat worn.*

No shoulder fold
1953-55

Note style of letters, relation to denticles.
The "I" points between two denticles.

The initial obverse for the 1953 issue had a high relief, laureate portrait of the Queen by Mrs. Mary Gillick (M.G. on truncation) which did not strike up well on the coins. Later in the year, the relief was lowered and the hair and shoulder detail re-engraved by Thomas Shingles, the Royal Canadian Mint's chief engraver. Two lines at the shoulder, representing a fold in the gown, are clear on the second variety but almost missing on the first. (There has been a tendency to erroneously term them "shoulder strap" and "no shoulder strap," respectively, but even on the original portrait the ridge representing the top of the gown

With shoulder fold
1953-1964

Note style of letters, relation to denticles.
The "I" points to a denticle.

can be seen high above the shoulder.) The two varieties also differ in the positioning of the legend relative to the rim denticles and in the styles of some of the letters.

The reverse throughout the 1953-64 period remained basically the same as that for George VI.

1954-5 No shoulder fold. Through an oversight a small number of the 1954 prooflike sets included cents struck from the rejected no shoulder fold obverse. An even smaller number of regular 1955 cents were also struck with this obverse.

Date	Qty. Minted	F-12	VF-20	EF-40	AU-50	UNC-60	BU-60
1953 no sh. fold	67,806,016	$ .15	$ .30	$ .50	$ .75	$1.25	$3.00
shoulder fold	incl. above	2.00	3.00	5.00	10.00	20.00	42.00
1954 no sh. fold	22,181,760			Prooflike Only		175.00	350.00
shoulder fold	incl. above	—	.50	1.00	2.00	3.00	7.00
1955 no sh. fold	56,403,193	15.00	40.00	65.00	150.00	300.00	700.00
shoulder fold	incl. above	.15	.25	.35	.50	.75	2.00
1956	78,685,535	.15	.25	.35	.50	.75	1.25
1957	100,601,792	.15	.25	.35	.50	.75	1.25
1958	59,385,679	.15	.25	.35	.50	.75	1.25
1959	83,615,343	.10	.20	.30	.40	.50	1.00
1960	75,772,775	.10	.20	.30	.40	.50	1.00
1961	139,598,404	.10	.20	.30	.40	.50	.85
1962	227,244,069	.10	.15	.25	.30	.40	.70
1963	279,076,334	.10	.15	.20	.25	.35	.50
1964	484,655,322	.10	.15	.20	.25	.35	.50

Elizabeth II, Tiara Obverse, 1965-1978

In 1965 an obverse with a new style portrait by Arnold Machin was introduced. The Queen has more mature facial features and is wearing a tiara. Two obverse varieties exist for 1965: the first has a flat field and small rim beads, while the second has a concave field (it slopes up toward the edge) and large rim beads. The second obverse was instituted because unacceptable die life was being obtained with the first. The large beads obverse, however, also had to be replaced because of a tendency for the rim detail in the dies to wear too rapidly. So, starting in 1966, the obverse has a less concave field and small rim beads. As with the 1953 issues, the 1965-66 varieties can be distinguished by the positioning of the legend relative to the rim beads.

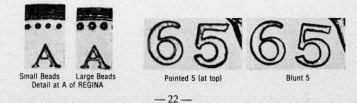

Small Beads   Large Beads
Detail at A of REGINA

Pointed 5 (at top)   Blunt 5

1965 date and combinational varieties. Coupled with the two 1965 obverses in all combinations were two reverses, having trivially different 5's in the dates. The varieties of 5 have become popular, but the authors of this catalog do not consider them significant.

Date		Qty. Minted	UNC-60	BU-60
1965	small beads, pointed 5 (Var. 1)	304,441,082	$ .75	$1.75
	small beads, blunt 5 (Var. 2)	incl. above	.15	.35
	large beads, blunt 5 (Var. 3)	incl. above	.25	.60
	large beads, pointed 5 (Var. 4)	incl. above	18.00	36.00
1966		183,644,388	.15	.30

Confederation Centennial 1967

All denominations for 1967 bore special reverses to commemorate the 1867 confederation of the provinces of Canada, Nova Scotia and New Brunswick to form the Dominion of Canada. The designer was Alex Colville, the device being a rock dove in flight.

1967	Confederation commemorative	345,140,645	.20	.35

Maple Twig Reverse Resumed 1968-

1968		329,695,772	.10	.25
1969		335,240,929	.10	.25
1970		311,145,010	.10	.25
1971		298,228,936	.10	.20
1972		451,304,591	.10	.20
1973		457,059,852	.10	.20
1974		692,058,489	.10	.20
1975		642,318,000	.10	.20
1976		701,122,890	.10	.15
1977		453,050,666	.10	.15
1978		911,170,647	.10	.15

Elizabeth II, Modified Tiara Obverse, 1979-

Beginning with 1979, the portrait of the Queen was made smaller. This was done to standardize our coinage, making the size of the portrait proportional to the diameter of the coin, regardless of denomination.

1979		754,394,064	.10	.15

Reduced Weight 1980-
Pattern pieces dated 1979 were struck in 1978 with a reduced weight and a diameter of 16mm. This action was in response to the rising cost of copper which was causing the 1-cent coin to be produced at a loss. However, the 16mm cent was cancelled when it was found that this was the same diameter used for tokens by the Toronto Transit Commission. The 1979 cent was of the old weight and diameter. In 1980, a new decreased diameter coin was introduced with a decreased thickness and weight.

Diameter: 19 mm; weight: 2.8 grams; thickness: 1.38 mm; composition: .980 copper, .005 tin, .015 zinc; edge: plain.

Date	Qty. Minted	UNC-60	BU-60
1980	912,052,318	$ .10	$ .15
1981	1,209,468,500	10	.15

New Design 1982

Diameter: 19.1 mm; weight: 2.5 grams; thickness: N/A; edge: plain.

Beginning in 1982 the 1-cent coin shape was changed from a round to a 12-sided coin in order to make it easier for the blind to identify. The new size also meant a reduction in weight of 10.7%

1982	876,029,450	.10	.15
1983	997,820,210	.10	.15
1984		.10	.15

5 CENTS

Victoria, 5 Cents Silver, 1858-1901

Diameter: 15.49 mm; weight 1858: 1.162 grams; 1870-1901: 1.166 grams; composition: .925 silver, .075 copper; edge: reeded.

G: *Braid around ear worn through.*
VG: *No details in braid around the ear.*
Fine: *Segments of braid begin to merge into one another.*
VF: *Braid is clear but not sharp.*
EF: *Braid is slightly worn but generally sharp and clear.*

Five different portraits of Victoria were employed for this denomination, each differing from the other in some of the facial features and in certain other respects. Except for the initial portrait, all subsequent varieties were created by re-engraving a previous design. The first and probably all later varieties were designed and engraved by L.C. Wyon. None of these was a serious attempt to accurately portray Victoria as she looked at the time.

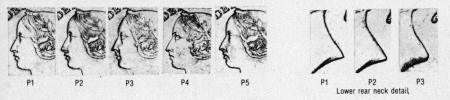

P1   P2   P3   P4   P5   P1   P2   P3
                                        Lower rear neck detail

In some years two busts were coupled with a given date reverse. These are most easily distinguished as follows:

P1 vs P2: P1 has a convex lower rear neck profile and an incuse hairline above the eye, while P2 has a straight lower rear neck profile and lacks the incuse hairline.

P2 vs P3: P2 has a prominent forehead, a smooth chin and a slightly rounded point at the lower right corner of the neck, while P3 has a recessed forehead, a slight double chin and a very blunted lower right neck corner.

P2 vs P5: P2 has a prominent upper lip and a smooth chin, while P5 has a repressed upper lip, generally "droopy" mouth and an irregular chin.

The basic reverse device consists of crossed maple boughs, tied at the bottom by a ribbon, and separated at the top by St. Edward's crown. Three major reverse varieties exist. The first (1858, 1870) has an unusually wide rim, long denticles and a crown with both bottom corners protruding. The second (1870-81, 1890-1901), derived from the first, has some-what altered leaves, a narrow rim, short rim denticles and a crown on which only the left lower corner protrudes. The third design (1882-89) has an extra (22nd) maple leaf added to the lower right of the wreath of the second variety. Sub-varieties of all three reverses are known; for example, the 22nd leaf on the 1882 issue differs from and was added independently of that on the 1883-89 issues. The major and most of the minor varieties were designed and engraved by L.C. Wyon.

Wide rim
long denticles

Small date

Large date over small date

Date		Qty. Minted	G-4	VG-8	F-12	VF-20	EF-40	AU-50	BU-60	CH-63
Wide Rim Reverse (1858, 1870)										
1858	small dt. P1	500,000	$8.00	$12.00	$20.00	$27.50	$45.00	$125.00	$325.00	$575.00
	lg. over sm. dt. P1	incl. above	100.00	140.00	200.00	300.00	400.00	650.00	1,500	2,400
1870	. . . . P1	2,800,000	5.50	10.00	15.00	25.00	50.00	150.00	300.00	550.00

Narrow rim
short denticles

21 leaves
1870-81, 1890-1901

Date		Qty. Minted	G-4	VG-8	F-12	VF-20	EF-40	AU-50	BU-60	CH-63
Narrow Rim, 21-Leaf Reverse (1870-1881)										
1870	. . . . P2	incl. above	$7.00	$11.50	$17.50	$30.00	$55.00	$175.00	$350.00	$600.00
1871	. . . . P2	1,400,000	5.00	10.00	15.00	25.00	45.00	150.00	300.00	600.00
1872H	. . P2	2,000,000	4.00	8.00	12.00	20.00	35.00	125.00	275.00	525.00

Plain 4, small date

Crosslet 4, large date

Small date

Large date

Date		Qty. Minted	G-4	VG-8	F-12	VF-20	EF-40	AU-50	BU-60	CH-63
1874H	plain 4 . . . P2 . . .	1,800,000	10.00	20.00	30.00	50.00	110.00	275.00	600.00	1,200
	crosslet 4 . P2 . .	incl. above	8.00	12.00	18.00	30.00	50.00	200.00	425.00	850.00
1875H	small dt. . P2 . .	incl. above	55.00	100.00	150.00	225.00	400.00	650.00	1,350	2,400
	large date . P2 . .	incl. above	60.00	125.00	175.00	275.00	550.00	1,000	2,000	3,400
1880H	. . . . P2,3 . .	3,000,000	2.75	5.00	9.00	12.00	25.00	125.00	275.00	475.00
1881H	. . . . P3 . . .	1,500,000	3.50	6.00	10.00	17,50	32.00	125.00	275.00	550.00

*Note: 1874H and 1875H mintage figures were combined through a mint error.

22nd leaf added
1882-89

Date		Qty. Minted	G-4	VG-8	F-12	VF-20	EF-40	AU-50	BU-60	CH-63
Narrow Rim, 22-Leaf Reverse										
1882H	. . P4	1,000,000	4.50	7.00	11.00	18.50	35.00	150.00	300.00	550.00
1883H	. . P5	600,000	7.50	13.50	24.00	35.00	60.00	225.00	550.00	1,100
1884	. . . . P5	200,000	60.00	100.00	150.00	225.00	400.00	750.00	2,000	3,000

Large tail 5   Small tail 5   Small 6   Large 6

Date		Qty. Minted	G-4	VG-8	F-12	VF-20	EF-40	AU-50	BU-60	CH-63
1885	large tail 5 . . P5 . . .	1,000,000	4.50	8.00	12.00	20.00	40.00	175.00	450.00	1,000
	small tail 5 . P5 . . .	incl. above	4.50	8.00	12.00	20.00	40.00	175.00	450.00	1,000
1886	small 6 . . . . P5 . . .	1,700,000	3.50	6.00	10.00	15.00	30.00	150.00	350.00	650.00
	large 6 . . . . . P5 . . .	incl. above	3.50	6.00	10.00	15.00	30.00	150.00	350.00	650.00
1887	. . . . P5 . . .	500,000	10.00	16.50	25.00	40.00	65.00	200.00	500.00	1,000
1888	. . . . P5 . . .	2,200,000	2.50	5.00	8.00	12.00	25.00	100.00	260.00	425.00
1889	. . . . P5 . . .	incl. above	13.50	25.00	35.00	55.00	110.00	300.00	700.00	1,200

Date	Qty. Minted	G-4	VG-8	F-12	VF-20	EF-40	AU-50	BU-60	CH-63
21-Leaf Reverse Resumed (1890-1901)									
1890H .. P5	1,000,000	3.75	6.00	8.50	15.00	30.00	150.00	325.00	500.00
1891 .... P5,2	1,800,000	2.50	4.00	6.50	12.00	20.00	100.00	250.00	400.00
1892 .... P5,2	860,000	4.50	6.50	11.00	17.50	32.50	175.00	375.00	600.00
1893 .... P2	1,700,000	2.75	4.25	7.00	12.00	20.00	100.00	275.00	425.00
1894 .... P2	500,000	8.00	15.00	22.50	37.50	65.00	225.00	450.00	900.00
1896 .... P2	1,500,000	3.00	5.00	7.50	12.00	20.00	100.00	250.00	400.00
1897 .... P2	1,319,283	3.00	5.00	7.50	12.00	20.00	100.00	250.00	400.00
1898 .... P2	580,717	6.00	12.00	18.00	30.00	50.00	140.00	325.00	625.00
1899 .... P2	3,000,000	2.00	3.25	5.00	7.50	15.00	100.00	200.00	325.00

Large date, wide 0's   Small date, narrow 0's

1900 large date P2	1,800,000	$12.50	$22.50	$36.00	$45.00	$75.00	$250.00	$525.00	$1,000
small date P2	incl. above	2.00	3.25	5.00	7.50	15.00	100.00	200.00	325.00
1901 ....P2	2,000,000	2.00	3.25	4.00	6.00	12.00	100.00	200.00	325.00

Edward VII, 5 Cents Silver, 1902-1910

Diameter: 15.49 mm; weight: 1.166 grams; composition: .925 silver, .075 copper; edge: reeded.

G: Band of crown worn through.
VG: Band of crown is worn through at the highest point.
Fine: Jewels in the band of the crown will be blurred.
VF: Band of crown is still clear, no longer sharp.
EF: Band of crown slightly worn but generally sharp and clear.

A single obverse, designed and engraved by G.W. De Saulles (DES. below bust), was used for the entire reign.

With the initiation of a new series, two basic changes were to be made in the reverse designs. First, the word CANADA was to be transferred from the obverse to the reverse legend. Second, the heraldic St. Edward's crown (depressed arches), used on the English coinages throughout most of the 19th century and on the Victorian Canadian issues, was to be replaced with the Imperial State crown (raised arches). These objectives were realized on all silver denominations except the 5 cents, where a shortage of time at the Royal Mint forced a compromise. The 1902 design (London & Heaton) utilized the unaltered crown and wreath from the second variety Victorian reverse with the date and modified legend added. The presence of the out-moded St. Edward's crown caused the public to surmise that an error had been made; the 1902 coinage was consequently hoarded.

With the 1903 Heaton issue the Imperial State crown was incorporated into the 5 cent reverse. Again the wreath was derived from the second variety Victorian reverse, in this instance with slight retouching of some of the leaves. The designer and engraver for the 1902 and probably the 1903H reverses was G.W. De Saulles.

A third major reverse variety, introduced for the 1903 London issue, is from a new reducing machine model, and as such represents the first completely new reverse since 1858. The designer is presumably W.H.J. Blakemore. The maple wreath contains 22 leaves. This reverse was used every year from 1903 through the conclusion of the reign; however, in 1909-10 a major variety derived therefrom was also employed. This modification is characterized by the presence of a "+" cross *cut over* the original bow tie cross atop the crown and by sharp points along the leaf edges. The fourth variety is presumably by Blakemore, modifying his previous design.

| Large H | Small H |

Date	Qty. Minted	G-4	VG-8	F-12	VF-20	EF-40	AU-50	BU-60	CH-63
St. Edward's Crown Reverse (1902)									
1902	2,120,000	1.50	2.50	4.00	5.00	10.00	32.00	90.00	150.00
1902H large H	2,200,000	1.75	3.50	5.00	7.50	14.00	45.00	100.00	165.00
small H	incl. above	5.00	10.00	15.00	25.00	50.00	135.00	285.00	425.00

Imperial crown,
21 leaves
1903H only

Imperial Crown, 21-Leaf Reverse (1903 Heaton)

| 1903H . . . . | 2,640,000 | $1.75 | $3.00 | $5.00 | $8.00 | $15.00 | $80.00 | $185.00 | $325.00 |

| Imperial crown, 22 leaves 1903-1910 | Leaves with rounded edges 1903-1910 | Leaves with pointed edges 1909-1910 |

Rounded Leaves Reverse (1903-1910)

1903	1,000,000	2.75	5.00	8.00	15.00	25.00	150.00	400.00	650.00
1904	2,400,000	2.00	3.50	5.50	8.50	16.00	70.00	175.00	300.00
1905	2,600,000	2.00	3.50	5.50	8.50	16.00	70.00	150.00	275.00
1906	3,100,000	1.75	2.50	3.75	5.50	10.00	60.00	150.00	275.00
1907	5,200,000	1.50	2.50	3.75	5.50	10.00	60.00	150.00	250.00

| Large 8 | Small 8 | "Bow tie" cross | "+" cross |
| Note shape of inner circles | | Cross at top of crown | |

1908 varieties: The normal reverse (bow tie cross atop the crown — see above) for 1908 has a large 8; a second variety has a "+" cross cut over the bow tie (as on the 1909-1910 reverse with sharp leaf points) and a small date.

1908 large 8	1,197,780	3.50	7.00	11.00	18.00	30.00	100.00	250.00	400.00
small 8	incl. above	3.50	7.00	11.00	18.00	30.00	100.00	250.00	400.00
Pointed Leaves Reverse (1909-1910)									
1909 round leaves	1,890,865	2.00	3.00	4.00	7.50	15.00	90.00	250.00	400.00
pointed leaves	incl. above	2.00	3.00	4.00	7.50	15.00	90.00	250.00	400.00
1910 round leaves	5,850,325	1.50	2.00	3.00	5.00	10.00	50.00	120.00	185.00
pointed leaves	incl. above	1.50	2.00	3.00	5.00	10.00	50.00	120.00	185.00

George V, 5 Cents Silver, 1911-1921

Diameter: 15.49 mm; weight: 1.166 grams; composition; 1911-19: .925 silver, .075 copper; 1920-21: .800 silver, .200 copper; edge: reeded.

G: *Band of crown worn through.*
VG: *Band of crown worn through at highest point.*
Fine: *Jewels in band of crown will be blurred.*
VF: *Band of crown still clear, no longer sharp.*
EF: *Band of crown slightly worn but generally sharp and clear.*

Two obverse varieties exist; the first (1911) lacks the phrase DEI GRATIA or an abbreviation for it and the second (1912-21) has DEI GRA: incorporated into the legend. Both obverses were derived from a portrait model by Sir E.B. MacKennal (B.M. on truncation). See text on the 1 cent for more details.

The reverse is identical to Blakemore's rounded leaves design introduced in the Edward VII series. On 3 May 1921 the Canadian Government passed an act authorizing the substitution of a larger nickel 5 cent piece for the small silver coin. Consequently, almost the entire coinage of the silver five cents dated 1921 was melted. About 400 specimens of this date are known, most or all of which were (a) regular strikes sold by the Mint in 1921 to visitors or (b) specimen strikes sold or given to individuals as part of 1921 specimen sets.

Date	Qty. Minted	G-4	VG-8	F-12	VF-20	EF-40	AU-50	BU-60	CH-63
"Godless" Obverse (1911)									
1911	3,692,350	$1.75	$3.00	$5.00	$7.50	$15.00	$75.00	$200.00	$325.00
Modified Obverse Legend (1912-1921)									
1912	5,863,170	1.25	2.00	3.00	5.00	7.50	40.00	95.00	150.00
1913	5,588,048	1.25	2.00	3.00	5.00	7.50	35.00	85.00	130.00
1914	4,202,179	1.50	2.00	3.00	5.50	8.50	42.00	115.00	190.00
1915	1,172,258	5.00	10.00	15.00	25.00	55.00	220.00	450.00	725.00
1916	2,481,675	2.00	4.00	7.50	12.00	20.00	90.00	200.00	325.00
1917	5,521,373	1.50	2.50	3.50	4.00	6.50	30.00	85.00	130.00
1918	6,052,289	1.50	2.50	3.50	4.00	6.50	30.00	85.00	125.00
1919 .... (Orig.: 7,835,400)		1.50	2.50	3.50	4.00	6.50	30.00	85.00	125.00
1920 .... (Orig.: 10,649,851)		1.50	2.50	3.50	4.00	6.50	30.00	85.00	130.00
1921 .... (Orig.: 2,582,495)		1,650	2,000	3,000	4,200	6,000	11,500	22,000	32,000

George V, 5 Cents Nickel, 1922-1936

Diameter: 21.21 mm; weight: 4.536 grams; composition: 1.000 nickel; edge: plain.

G: *Band of crown worn through.*
VG: *Band of crown is worn through at the highest point.*
Fine: *Jewels in band of crown will be blurred.*
VF: *Band of crown is still clear but no longer sharp.*
EF: *Band of crown slightly worn but generally sharp and clear.*

In order to provide a 5 cent piece of more manageable size, and "because nickel was essentially a Canadian metal" the Canadian Government introduced in 1922 a coin of pure nickel, similar in size to the United States 5 cents.

The obverse was derived from the MacKennal portrait model (initials B.M. on truncation); the reverse was engraved by W.H.J. Blakemore. Mint records do not clearly specify the designer; it was either Blakemore or Fred Lewis.

Date	Qty. Minted	G-4	VG-8	F-12	VF-20	EF-40	AU-50	BU-60	CH-63
1922	4,763,186	.30	.50	.85	3.00	8.00	25.00	85.00	135.00
1923	2,475,201	.40	.75	1.75	4.00	12.00	50.00	125.00	225.00
1924	3,066,658	.30	.60	1.25	3.75	10.00	35.00	100.00	200.00
1925	200,050	30.00	40.00	50.00	75.00	200.00	425.00	950.00	1,600

"Near 6", tip near leaf   "Far 6", tip far from leaf

1926 date varieties. Most of the 1926 issue was derived from a matrix in which the tip of the 6 is very close to the right-hand maple leaf. A second matrix (or perhaps individual die) had the 6 punched in lower, so that it was farther from the leaf. Such digit spacing and position differences are considered trivial by these cataloguers; the 1926 varieties are included only because their listing in previous catalogues has led to their widespread acceptance by collectors.

1926 Near 6	933,577	$2.50	$4.00	$6.00	$20.00	$75.00	$150.00	$325.00	$600.00
Far 6	incl. above	75.00	125.00	150.00	225.00	400.00	800.00	1,800	2,800
1927	5,285,627	.30	.50	1.00	3.50	8.50	32.50	85.00	145.00
1928	4,558,725	.30	.50	1.00	3.50	10.00	28.00	75.00	135.00
1929	5,562,262	.30	.50	1.00	3.50	10.00	32.50	85.00	145.00
1930	3,685,991	.30	.50	1.00	3.50	10.00	35.00	95.00	175.00
1931	5,100,830	.30	.50	1.00	3.50	10.00	32.50	95.00	175.00
1932	3,198,566	.30	.50	1.00	3.50	11.00	37.50	100.00	180.00
1933	2,597,867	.40	.75	1.50	4.00	12.00	55.00	135.00	300.00
1934	3,827,303	.30	.50	1.00	3.50	10.00	35.00	110.00	210.00
1935	3,891,151	.30	.50	1.00	3.50	10.00	35.00	110.00	230.00
1936	4,400,450	.30	.50	1.00	3.50	10.00	32.50	85.00	165.00

George VI, Beaver Reverse, 1937-1942

Diameter 1937-42: 21.21 mm; 1942 tombac: 21.23-21.29 mm (opposite corners), 20.88-20.93 mm (opposite sides); weight: 4.536 grams; composition 1937-42: 1.000 nickel; 1942 tombac: .880 copper, .120 zinc; edge: plain.

VG: *No detail in hair above the ear.*
Fine: *Only slight detail in hair above the ear.*
VF: *Where not worn the hair is clear but not sharp.*
EF: *Slight wear in the hair over the ear.*

Both obverses (for the round and 12-sided issues) have a bare-headed portrait of the King designed by T.H. Paget (H.P. below bust).

In keeping with a decision to modernize the new George VI reverses, the now-familiar beaver motif was chosen for the 5 cents (it was first considered for the 10 cents). The 1937 issue has a period after the date to balance the design, but after 1937 the period was omitted. The original design was by G.E. Kruger-Gray (K·G left of the log).

Because nickel was needed for World War II, its use for coinage was suspended late in 1942. The substitute first used was a brass alloy commonly called "tombac." This metal quickly tarnishes to the brownish hue acquired by bronze, so the new coins were made 12-sided to avoid their confusion with the cents. Due to lack of time, the new matrices (obverse and reverse) were made without the conventional rim denticles.

Period after date 1937 only	1937.	1940	No period 1938-1942				
Date	**Qty. Minted**	**VG-8**	**F-12**	**VF-20**	**EF-40**	**AU-50**	**BU-60**	**CH-63**
Nickel Issues (1937-1942)								
1937 (period after date) . . .	4,593,263	.40	.75	2.75	5.00	10.00	25.00	35.00
1938	3,898,974	.40	1.50	3.75	12.50	35.00	110.00	200.00
1939	5,661,123	.30	.85	3.00	7.50	25.00	80.00	135.00
1940	13,920,197	.25	.60	1.75	4.50	12.00	35.00	50.00
1941	8,681,785	.25	.60	1.75	5.00	14.00	40.00	60.00
1942	6,847,544	.25	.60	1.75	4.50	13.50	35.00	60.00

"Tombac" (Brass) Issue (1942)								
1942 12-sided	3,396,234	75	1.00	1.50	2.25	3.00	4.50	10.00

Victory Reverse 1943-1945

Composition 1943: .880 copper, .120 zinc; 1944-1945: steel coated with .0127 mm layer of nickel and .0003 mm plating of chromium. Other specifications as for 1942 tombac issue.

This design was introduced with the aim of furthering the war efforts. The obverse is as the 1942 tombac issue, except that rim denticles were added.

The torch and V on the reverse symbolize sacrifice and victory (the V also indicates the denomination, the idea coming from the U.S. Liberty 5 cents of 1883-1912). Instead of rim denticles is a dot-dash pattern forming the International code message, "We win when we work willingly." The designer was the Royal Canadian Mint's chief engraver, Thomas Shingles (T.S. at right of torch). who cut the master matrix entirely by hand — a feat few present-day engravers can accomplish.

The 1943 issue was struck in tombac, however, the alloy was replaced with chromium-plated steel in 1944-45 because copper and zinc were needed for the war effort. The other specifications are as on the 1942 tombac issue.

Date	Qty. Minted	VG-8	F-12	VF-20	EF-40	AU-50	BU-60	CH-63
"Tombac" Issue (1943)								
1943	24,760,256	$ .40	$ .50	$ .75	$1.00	$2.50	$5.00	$8.00
Chromium-Plated Steel (1944-1945)								
1944	11,532,784	.20	.35	.60	1.00	2.00	3.50	7.50
1945	18,893,216	.20	.35	.60	1.00	2.00	3.50	7.50

Beaver Reverse Resumed 1946-1952

Composition 1946-50, 1951 commem.: nickel 1.000; 1951-52 beaver: steel, coated with a .0127 mm layer of nickel and plated with a .0003 mm layer of chromium. Other specifications as for 1942 tombac issue.

Small beaver
1946-1950

After the conclusion of World War II the 5 cents was again struck in nickel, but the 12-sided shape had become popular and was retained. The initial obverse is identical to that of the 1943-45 issues. A second variety, introduced in 1948, incorporates the modified titles of the King (see 1 cent text). This second obverse was used for the 1948-50, 1951 commemorative, and a portion of the 1951 beaver issues. A third variety was coupled with most of the 1951 beaver and all of the 1952 issues. It is distinguished by the lower relief of its portrait and the different positioning of the legend relative to the rim denticles.

Two major reverse varieties are known. The first (1946-50) differs from the 1942 tombac issue only in having rim denticles. A second variety (1951-52) was introduced simultaneously with the change to steel composition (see below). The beaver is slightly larger and perhaps slightly lower in relief.

1947 "dot"
(deteriorated die)

1947 maple leaf
(official issue)

1947 "dot." This item is apparently the product of a deteriorated die and hence not a true die variety. Some have suggested that this was an official issue because of the fact that 25 cents and dollars (pointed 7) dated 1947 are also known with a "dot" after the date. The alternative, currently favored by most students of the decimal coins, is that the "dots" are the result of small pieces chipping out of the chromium plating of individual dies, leaving pits that would become "dots" on the struck coins. It is conceded, however, that if the latter were true it would be a remarkable coincidence. In any case the 1947 "dot" coins are probably not official because (a) the dots are irregular and of poor quality and (b) the engravers who would have officially prepared such dies are quite certain that they did not do so.

1947 maple leaf variety. This was an official issue struck in 1948, which is explained in the text for the 1 cent.

Small Beaver Reverse (1946-1950)

		VG-8	F-12	VF-20	EF-40	AU-50	BU-60	CH-63
1946	6,952,684	$ .25	$ .40	$1.00	$3.50	$6.00	$15.00	$30.00
1947 normal date	7,603,724	.20	.35	.75	2.75	5.00	14.00	25.00
"dot"	incl. above	18.00	22.50	35.00	65.00	350.00	600.00	1,100
1947 maple leaf	9,595,124	.20	.35	.75	2.25	4.50	12.50	20.00

Modified legend,
high relief portrait
1948-1951

High Relief
Last A of
GRATIA points
to denticle

Date	Qty. Minted	VG-8	F-12	VF-20	EF-40	AU-50	BU-60	CH-63
Modified Legend (1948-1952)								
1948	1,810,789	.75	1.00	2.00	5.00	12.50	35.00	50.00
1949	13,037,090	.20	.25	.50	1.00	2.50	7.00	12.00
1950	11,970,520	.20	.25	.50	1.00	2.50	7.00	12.00

Isolation of Nickel, Bicentennial 1951

Low relief
portrait 1951-1952

As Canada is the world's largest single producer of nickel, it seemed appropriate to issue a commemorative piece upon the 200th anniversary of the isolation and naming of the element by the Swedish chemist A.F. Cronstedt. The obverse is as on the 1948-50 issues; the reverse, showing a nickel refinery, was designed by Stephen Trenka (ST monogram at lower right).

1951 commemorative	9,028,507	.20	.25	.45	.70	1.00	3.00	5.50

Beaver Reverse Resumed, Steel Coinage 1951-1952

Low Relief
Last A of
GRATIA points
between denticles

Large beaver
reverse

Because nickel was needed for the Korean War, the use of nickel was suspended near the end of 1951. The Beaver reverse was resumed for the balance of 1951 5-cent pieces but the substitute used was steel. New lower relief dies had to be prepared for both the obverse and reverse since the harder steel surface did not strike well with the higher relief dies the Mint had been using. By mistake, a small quantity of 1951 pieces were struck with a High Relief obverse die creating two varieties for 1951. As mentioned above, the two varieties are distinguished by the difference in relief in the portraits as well as in the different positioning of the legend relative to the rim denticles.

Large Beaver Reverse (1951-1952)								
1951 high relief obv	4,313,410	20.00	30.00	60.00	125.00	175.00	400.00	650.00
low relief obv	incl. above	.25	.50	1.00	2.00	3.00	6.00	10.00
1952 (low relief obv.)	10,891,148	.20	.40	.75	2.00	3.00	5.00	8.00

Elizabeth II, Laureate Bust, 1953-1964

Diameter 1953-62: 21.23-21.29 mm (opposite corners), 20.88-20.93 mm (opposite sides); 1963-64: 21.21 mm; weight: 4.536 grams; composition 1953-54: steel, coated with a .0127 mm layer of nickel and plated with a .0003 mm layer of chromium; 1955-64: 1.000 nickel; edge: plain.

No shoulder fold 1953

Large beaver 1953-1954

VF: *Leaves considerably worn.*
EF: *Laurel leaves on the head somewhat worn.*

The initial obverse for the 1953 issue had a high relief, laureate portrait of the Queen by Mrs. Mary Gillick (M.G. on truncation) which did not strike up well on the coins. Later in the year, the relief was lowered and the hair and shoulder detail re-engraved. The latter included sharpening two lines which represent a fold in, not a shoulder strap on, the Queen's gown. The two varieties also differ in the positioning of the legend relative to the rim denticles and the styles of some of the letters (see the 1 cent text for more details). The second portrait was not modified when the shape of the 5 cents returned to round in 1963.

No Shoulder Fold 1953

Note style of letters, relation to denticles

Date	Qty. Minted	F-12	VF-20	EF-40	AU-50	BU-60	CH-63
"No Shoulder Fold" Obverse (1953)							
1953 (no fold)	16,635,552	$ .25	$ .65	$1.25	$2.50	$5.00	$7.50

With shoulder fold 1953-1962

Note style of letters, relation to denticles

"Shoulder Fold" Obverse (1953-1962)							
1953 (with fold)	Incl. above	.25	.75	1.75	3.50	7.00	12.00
1954	6,998,662	.50	1.00	2.00	4.50	9.00	13.50

Four noteworthy reverse varieties appeared during the 1953-64 period. The first is associated with the 1953 "no shoulder fold" obverse and is identical to the 1951-52 George VI beaver design. The second reverse has the design elements placed closer to the rim denticles than before. It was used for the 1953 "shoulder fold" and 1954 issues. With the resumption of coinage in nickel in 1955, the smaller beaver, last used in 1950, was restored. It continued without significant modification until 1963, when it was re-adapted to a round motif because of continuing difficulties with the 12-sided collars.

Design far from rim 1953

Design near rim 1953-1954

Small beaver 1955-1962

Small Beaver Reverse (12-sided) (1955-1962)

1955	5,355,028	.25	.65	1.25	2.50	5.00	7.50
1956	9,399,854	.10	.25	.75	1.50	2.50	4.50
1957	7,387,703	.10	.25	.75	1.50	2.50	4.50
1958	7,607,521	.10	.25	.75	1.50	2.50	4.50
1959	11,552,523	—	.20	.25	.60	1.00	2.00
1960	37,157,433	—	—	—	.25	.50	1.00
1961	47,889,051	—	—	—	—	.20	.50
1962	46,307,305	—	—	—	—	.20	.50

Round Coinage Resumed (1963-1964)

1964
"Extra waterline"

Date	Qty. Minted	EF-40	AU-50	BU-60	CH-63
1963	43,970,320	—	—	$ .15	$ .35
1964	78,075,068	—	—	.15	.25
1964 (extra waterline)	(incl. above)	10.00	15.00	45.00	60.00

Elizabeth II, Tiara Obverse, 1965-1978

Diameter: 21.21 mm; weight: 4.54 grams; composition: (1965-1981) 1.00 nickel (1982-   ) .75 copper, .25 nickel; edge: plain.

In 1965 an obverse with a new style portrait by Arnold Machin was introduced. The Queen has more mature facial features and is wearing a tiara.

The reverses and physical specifications during 1965-66 are as for the 1963-64 issues.

Date	Qty. Minted	BU-60	CH-63
1965	84,876,018	$ .15	$ .25
1966	27,976,648	.15	.25

Confederation Centennial 1967

All denominations for 1967 bore special reverses to commemorate the 1967 confederation of the province of Canada, Nova Scotia and New Brunswick to form the Dominion of Canada. The 5 cents reverse device depicts a hopping rabbit. Designer: Alex Colville. The obverse and physical specifications are as for the 1956-66 issues.

Date	Qty. Minted	BU-60	CH-63
1967 Confederation commemorative	36,876,574	.25	.30

Beaver Reverse Resumed 1968-

The obverse, reverse and physical specifications are as or the issues of 1965-66.

Date	Qty. Minted	CH-63
1968	99,253,330	$ .20
1969	27,830,229	.20
1970	5,726,010	.80
1971	27,312,609	.20
1972	62,417,387	.20
1973	53,507,435	.20
1974	94,704,645	.20
1975	138,882,000	.20
1976	55,140,213	.20
1977	89,120,791	.20
1978	137,079,273	.20

Modified Obverse 1979-

Beginning with 1979 the portrait of the Queen was made smaller. This was done to standardize our coinage, making the size of the portrait proportional to the diameter of the coin, regardless of denomination. In 1982, the five-cent piece was first coined in cupro-nickel, an alloy of 75% copper and 25% nickel. This is the same alloy used in United States coinage.

Date	Qty. Minted	CH-63
1979	186,706,667	.20
1980	135,247,457	.20
1981	99,107,900	.20
1982	105,532,450	.20
1983	33,220,210	.20
1984		.20

10 CENTS
Victoria, 10 Cents Silver, 1858-1901

Diameter: 18.00 mm; weight 1858: 2.324 grams, 1870-1901, 2.333 grams; composition: .925 silver, .075 copper; edge: plain.

G: *Braid near ear worn through.*
VG: *No details in braid around ear.*
Fine: *Segments of braid begin to merge into one another.*
VF: *Braid is clear but not sharp.*
EF: *Braid is slightly worn but generally sharp and clear.*

In all, six different portrait varieties of Victoria were used for this denomination. Each differs from the other in some of the facial features and in certain other respects. Except for the initial portrait, all subsequent varieties were created by re-engraving a previous design; these modifications were probably the work of the original designer, L.C. Wyon. None of them represented a serious attempt to accurately portray Victoria as she looked at the time.

In some years two busts were coupled with a given date reverse. Such varieties are most easily distinguished as follows:

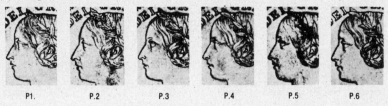

| P1. | P.2 | P.3 | P.4 | P.5 | P.6 |

P.1 vs. P.2: P.1 has a smooth chin and a narrow truncation, extending almost the entire length of the lower neck, while P.2 has a slightly "double" chin and a wide truncation, restricted to the rear half of the lower neck.
P.4 vs. P.5: P.4 has a rounded forehead, smooth chin and much hairline detail above the eye, while P.5 has a flat forehead, slightly double chin and very little hair detail above the eye.
P.5 vs. P.6: P.5 is as described above, while P.6 has the general characteristics of P.4.

The basic reverse device consists of crossed maple boughs tied at the bottom by a ribbon. At the top is St. Edward's crown. Two major device varieties exist; the first has a wreath with 21 leaves and the second, derived from the first, has a 22nd leaf added to the lower right. Numerous sub-varieties of both reverses are known; for example, the 22nd leaf on the 1882 issue differs and was added independently to that on the 1883-1901 issues. Both of the major and most of the minor varieties were designed and engraved by L.C. Wyon.

1871H Newfoundland/Canada mule. See page 96.

| | 21 leaves
1858-1881, 1891 | | | 22 leaves
1882-1901 |

Date	Qty. Minted	G-4	VG-8	F-12	VF-20	EF-40	AU-50	BU-60	CH-63
21-Leaf Reverse (1858-1881,1891)									
1858 . . . . P1	1,250,000	$7.50	$15.00	$25.00	$50.00	$100.00	$200.00	$425.00	$700.00
1870 . . . . P1	1,600,000	7.00	12.50	22.50	50.00	125.00	225.00	500.00	800.00
1871 . . . . P1	800,000	10.00	15.00	27.50	60.00	135.00	300.00	600.00	900.00
1871H P1	1,870,000	12.00	21.00	40.00	75.00	150.00	325.00	750.00	1,150
1872H P1	1,000,000	40.00	75.00	140.00	240.00	475.00	800.00	2,000	3,000
1874H P1	1,600,000	5.00	9.00	18.00	40.00	75.00	210.00	450.00	700.00
1875H . . . . P1 . . . incl. above		125.00	200.00	350.00	550.00	1,150	2,000	3,500	7,000
1880 . . . . P1,2 . .	1,500,000	4.50	9.00	15.00	30.00	75.00	210.00	450.00	700.00
1881H P1,2	950,000	5.50	10.00	20.00	40.00	90.00	250.00	575.00	850.00

22-Leaf Reverse (1882-1901)

Date			Qty. Minted	G-4	VG-8	F-12	VF-20	EF-40	AU-50	BU-60	CH-63
1882H	P3		1,000,000	$4.50	$9.00	$17.50	$35.00	$80.00	$240.00	$550.00	$800.00
1883H	P3		300,000	12.00	20.00	40.00	80.00	175.00	465.00	1,150	1,750
1884	P4		150,000	75.00	135.00	250.00	525.00	1,150	1,850	4,500	7,250
1885	P4,5		400,000	7.50	15.00	30.00	70.00	175.00	375.00	850.00	2,000

Small 6	Large over small 6	Large knobbed 6

1886 small 6... P4,5		800,000	7.00	13.00	25.00	55.00	110.00	265.00	600.00	950.00
lg. over sm. 6. P5		incl. above	8.00	15.00	30.00	70.00	175.00	375.00	800.00	1,250
lg. pointed 6.. P5		incl. above	8.00	15.00	30.00	70.00	175.00	375.00	800.00	1,250
lg. knobbed 6. P5		incl. above	8.00	15.00	30.00	70.00	175.00	375.00	800.00	1,250
1887	P5	350,000	10.00	20.00	40.00	100.00	250.00	700.00	1,600	2,400
1888	P5	1,100,000	4.00	6.00	12.00	30.00	65.00	185.00	425.00	650.00
1889	P5	incl. above	250.00	475.00	800.00	1,500	2,500	4,500	10,000	14,000
1890H	P5	450,000	7.00	13.00	22.50	50.00	110.00	275.00	600.00	900.00

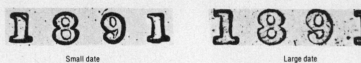

Small date	Large date

2 over 1, large 9   Normal date, small 9

1891 21 lvs., sm. dt. . P5	800,000	7.50	13.50	25.00	60.00	135.00	350.00	650.00	1,100	
22 lvs., lg dt . P5	incl. above	7.00	12.50	22.50	55.00	120.00	285.00	675.00	1,150	
1892 2 over 1, lg. 9 . P5	520,000	5.00	10.00	20.00	40.00	100.00	250.00	650.00	1,000	
nor. dt., sm. 9 P5,6	incl. above	5.00	10.00	20.00	40.00	100.00	250.00	650.00	1,000	

Flat top 3	Round top 3

1893 flat top 3. . P5,6		500,000	7.00	15.00	30.00	70.00	140.00	375.00	850.00	1,250
round top 3... P5,6		incl. above	275.00	475.00	850.00	1,600	3,750	6,000	10,500	20,000
1894	P5,6		500,000	5.00	10.00	20.00	40.00	80.00	200.00	650.00	1,050
1896	P5,6		650,000	4.00	7.50	13.50	27.50	60.00	175.00	425.00	675.00
1898	P6		720,000	4.00	7.50	13.50	27.50	60.00	200.00	475.00	725.00

Small 9's	Large 9's

1899 small 9's.. P6		1,200,000	3.50	6.00	10.00	20.00	50.00	175.00	400.00	675.00
large 9's.. P6		incl. above	5.50	10.00	20.00	40.00	100.00	300.00	625.00	1,000
1900	P6		1,100,000	3.00	4.00	8.00	17.50	50.00	125.00	300.00	525.00
1901	P6		1,200,000	3.00	4.00	8.00	17.50	50.00	125.00	300.00	525.00

Edward VII, 10 Cents Silver, 1902-1910

Diameter: 18.00 mm; weight: 2.333 grams; composition: .925 silver, .075 copper; edge: reeded.

G: *Band of crown worn through.*
VG: *Band of crown worn through at highest point.*
Fine: *Jewels in band of crown will be blurred.*
VF: *Band of crown still clear but no longer sharp.*
EF: *Band of crown slightly worn but generally sharp and clear.*

Only a single obverse, designed and engraved by G.W. De Saulles (initials DES. below bust), was employed. The initial reverse was partially by De Saulles; the wreath was taken unaltered from Wyon's 22-leaf Victorian variety and a new legend and the Imperial State crown added. The leaves of the wreath have moderate venation, with all of the veins raised. A second variety, from a new reducing machine model, has broader leaves with extensive, incuse venation. It was designed and engraved by W.H.J. Blakemore (copying the previous design).

Victorian leaves 1902-1909   Broad leaves 1909-1910

Date	Qty. Minted	G-4	VG-8	F-12	VF-20	EF-40	AU-50	BU-60	CH-63
Victorian Leaves Reverse (1902-1909)									
1902	720,000	$3.00	$4.00	$8.00	$17.50	$50.00	$125.00	$350.00	$600.00
1902H	1,100,000	2.00	3.25	6.50	12.50	32.00	90.00	200.00	325.00
1903	500,000	4.00	8.00	16.00	42.50	110.00	250.00	700.00	1,300
1903H	1,320,000	2.00	4.00	8.00	17.50	50.00	150.00	350.00	550.00
1904	1,000,000	3.50	7.00	14.00	32.00	85.00	200.00	450.00	750.00
1905	1,000,000	3.00	5.50	11.00	25.00	70.00	200.00	465.00	800.00
1906	1,700,000	2.00	3.25	7.00	15.00	40.00	125.00	350.00	600.00
1907	2,620,000	2.00	3.00	5.50	13.50	35.00	100.00	275.00	450.00
1908	776,666	3.00	6.00	12.50	30.00	75.00	200.00	575.00	1,050
1909 Vict. lvs	1,697,200	3.00	4.25	9.00	22.00	60.00	150.00	450.00	750.00
Broad Leaves Reverse (1909-1910)									
1909 brd. lvs	inc. above	4.00	7.00	12.50	32.00	75.00	225.00	500.00	850.00
1910	4,468,331	2.00	3.00	5.00	10.00	30.00	100.00	250.00	400.00

George V, 10 Cents Silver, 1911-1936

Diameter: 18.034 mm; weight: 2.333 grams; composition 1911-19: .925 silver, .075 copper; 1920-36: .800 silver, .200 copper; edge: reeded.

Obverse 1911

G: *Band of crown worn through.*
VG: *Band of crown worn through at highest point.*
Fine: *Jewels in band of crown will be blurred.*
VF: *Band of crown still clear but no longer sharp.*
EF: *Band of crown slightly worn but generally sharp and clear.*

Two obverse varieties exist; the first (1911) lacks the phrase DEI GRATIA or an abbreviation for it and the second (1912-36) has DEI GRA: incorporated into the legend. Both obverses were derived from a portrait model by Sir. E.B. MacKennal (B.M. on truncation). See the 1 cent text for more details.

The series began with the broad leaves design introduced late in the Edward VII series.

However, this was replaced in 1913 with another Blakemore design (from a new model) in which the maple leaves are distinctly smaller and have less venation.

Obverse
1912-1936

Broad leaves 1911-1913

Date	Qty. Minted	G-4	VG-8	F-12	VF-20	EF-40	AU-50	BU-60	CH-63
Broad Leaves Reverse (1911-1913)									
1911 (no DEI GRA:)	2,737,584	6.00	10.00	18.50	32.00	90.00	150.00	400.00	575.00
1912	3,235,557	2.00	3.00	4.00	10.00	25.00	125.00	325.00	575.00
1913 broad leaves	3,613,937	70.00	120.00	200.00	400.00	750.00	1,500	4,500	6,500

Small leaves 1913-1936

Small Leaves Reverse (1913-1936)									
1913 (small leaves) (incl. above)		$1.50	$2.50	$3.50	$7.50	$20.00	$100.00	$275.00	$450.00
1914	2,549,811	1.50	2.50	3.50	7.50	20.00	100.00	275.00	450.00
1915	688,057	5.00	8.00	15.00	42.50	165.00	425.00	1,100	1,600
1916	4,218,114	*	2.00	3.00	5.50	13.50	80.00	225.00	300.00
1917	5,011,988	*	2.00	3.00	5.50	12.00	60.00	150.00	225.00
1918	5,133,602	*	2.00	3.00	5.50	12.00	60.00	150.00	225.00
1919	7,877,722	*	2.00	3.00	5.50	12.00	60.00	150.00	225.00
1920	6,305,345	*	2.00	3.00	5.50	12.00	60.00	150.00	225.00
1921	2,469,562	*	2.50	4.00	7.00	17.50	100.00	200.00	375.00
1928	2,458,602	*	2.00	3.50	6.50	14.00	70.00	175.00	250.00
1929	3,253,888	*	2.25	4.00	6.50	14.00	70.00	175.00	250.00
1930	1,831,043	*	2.50	4.00	7.00	17.50	80.00	190.00	300.00
1931	2,067,421	*	2.25	4.00	6.50	14.00	70.00	175.00	250.00
1932	1,154,317	1.50	2.75	5.00	8.50	20.00	100.00	225.00	350.00
1933	672,368	2.25	4.00	6.00	10.00	40.00	100.00	250.00	375.00
1934	409,067	3.00	5.50	9.00	18.00	65.00	250.00	650.00	1,100
1935	384,056	3.50	6.00	9.50	20.00	70.00	300.00	775.00	1,250
1936	2,460,871	1.50	2.25	3.00	5.00	10.00	60.00	150.00	225.00

George VI Issue Struck in Name of George V

A portion of the 1, 10 and 25 cents dated 1936 have a small raised dot on the reverse, denoting that they were actually struck in 1937 for George VI. On the 10 cents the dot is below the bow in the wreath. There is some question whether all of the dot 1 and 10 cents reported to have been struck exist today (see the 1 cent text for more details). The grading and physical specifications are as for the George V issues.

1936 raised dot below wreath .... (Originally: 191,237)   4 known

George VI, 10 Cents Silver, 1937-1952

Diameter: 18.034 mm; weight: 2.333 grams; composition: .800 silver, .200 copper; edge: reeded.

Obverse
1937-1947

VG: *No detail in hair above ear.*
Fine: *Only slight detail in hair above ear.*
VF: *Where not worn, hair is clear but not sharp.*
EF: *Slight wear in hair over ear.*

The first obverse for this series has a legend containing the phrase ET IND: IMP: (for *Et Indiae Imperator,* "and Emperor of India"). Beginning with coins dated 1948 the phrase was omitted from the King's titles, as India had gained independence from England the previous year. Both varieties were derived from a portrait model by T.H. Paget (initials H.P. under bust). The obverses of this series are unique in that the monarch is bare-headed.

A Government decision was made to modernize the reverse designs for the George VI series, and the popular fishing schooner motif was selected for this denomination. At first the design was considered for the 25 cents, with the beaver design to be used for the 10 cents. Although the Government proclamation states that a "fishing schooner under sail" is shown, it is clear that the designer, Emanuel Hahn, in fact used the famous Canadian racing yacht *Bluenose* as the source for his model. Hahn's initial H appears above the waves to the left. The small date on the 1937 issue proved to wear badly in circulation, so beginning in 1938 the date was enlarged and placed higher in the field. Some of the coins dated 1947 have a tiny maple leaf after the date. This denotes that they were actually struck in 1948. For more information see text on the 1 cent.

Small
low date
1937 only

Large
high date
1938-1952

Date	Qty. Minted	VG-8	F-12	VF-20	EF-40	AU-50	BU-60	CH63
ET IND : IMP : Obverse (1937-1947)								
1937 (small date)	2,500,095	3.00	4.00	5.00	10.00	17.50	32.50	50.00
1938	4,197,323	3.00	4.00	5.00	12.50	55.00	135.00	225.00
1939	5,501,748	3.00	4.00	5.00	12.50	55.00	130.00	210.00
1940	16,526,470	1.50	2.00	3.00	8.50	20.00	40.00	60.00
1941	8,716,386	1.50	2.00	5.00	12.00	40.00	100.00	175.00
1942	10,214,011	1.50	2.00	3.50	10.00	30.00	80.00	135.00
1943	21,143,229	1.50	2.00	3.50	7.00	15.00	30.00	50.00
1944	9,388,582	1.50	2.00	3.50	8.00	30.00	65.00	110.00
1945	10,979,570	1.50	2.00	3.50	6.50	15.00	30.00	45.00
1946	6,300,066	1.75	2.50	4.00	8.00	25.00	60.00	90.00
1947	4,431,926	1.75	2.50	5.00	12.00	40.00	85.00	125.00
1947 maple leaf	9,638,793	1.50	2.00	3.50	6.00	15.00	30.00	45.00

Obverse
1948-1952

Modified Obverse Legend (1948-1952)								
1948	422,741	5.50	7.50	13.50	32.50	65.00	175.00	225.00
1949	11,336,172	1.50	2.00	2.50	3.50	6.00	15.00	25.00
1950	17,823,075	1.50	2.00	2.50	3.50	6.00	13.00	18.00
1951	15,079,265	1.50	2.00	2.50	3.50	5.00	12.00	18.00
1952	10,474,455	1.50	2.00	2.50	3.50	5.00	12.00	18.00

Elizabeth II, Laureate Bust, 1953-1964

Diameter: 18.034 mm; weight: 2.333 grams; composition: .800 silver, .200 copper; edge: reeded.

Fine: *Leaves worn almost through; shoulder fold indistinct.*
VF: *Leaves worn considerably; shoulder fold must be clear.*
EF: *Laurel leaves on head somewhat worn.*

The initial obverse for the 1953 issue had a high relief, laureate portrait of the Queen by Mrs. Mary Gillick (M.G. on truncation) which did not strike up well on the coins. Later in the year, the relief was lowered and the hair and shoulder detail re-engraved. The latter included sharpening two lines which represented a fold in the Queen's gown. The two varieties also differ in the positioning of the legend relative to the rim denticles and the styles of some of the letters. See text on the 1 cent for more details.

The reverse used during this period remained basically the same as that introduced in the previous series.

With shoulder fold 1953-1964

Note style of letters, relation of I to denticles

No shoulder fold 1953

Date	Qty. Minted	VG-8	F-12	VF-20	EF-40	AU-50	BU-60	CH-63
"No Shoulder Fold" Obverse (1953)								
1953 (no fold)	17,706,395	*	$1.50	$2.00	$2.50	$4.00	$8.00	$12.00
"Shoulder Fold" Obverse (1953-1964)								
1953 (with fold)	Incl. above	*	2.00	2.50	3.00	4.50	10.00	15.00
1954	4,493,150	*	2.00	2.50	3.00	6.50	15.00	25.00
1955	12,237,294	*	1.50	2.00	2.50	3.50	7.50	10.00
1956	16,732,844	*	1.50	2.00	2.50	3.50	6.00	8.00
1956 Dot	(incl. above)	2.50	4.00	6.00	8.00	12.00	20.00	35.00
1957	16,110,229	*	*	1.50	2.00	2.25	3.00	4.00
1958	10,621,236	*	*	1.50	2.00	2.25	3.00	4.00
1959	19,691,433	*	*	*	1.50	2.00	3.00	4.00
1960	45,446,835	*	*	*	*	1.50	2.00	3.00
1961	26,850,859	*	*	*	*	1.50	2.00	2.50
1962	41,864,335	*	*	*	*	1.50	2.00	2.50
1963	41,916,208	*	*	*	*	1.50	2.00	2.50
1964	49,518,549	*	*	*	*	1.50	2.00	2.50

Elizabeth II, Tiara Obverse, 1965-1978

In 1965 an obverse with a new style portrait by Arnold Machin was introduced. The Queen has more mature facial features and is wearing a tiara. The reverse and physical specifications for the 1965-66 period remain as before.

1965	56,965,392	1.75	2.00
1966	34,330,199	1.75	2.00

Confederation Centennial 1967

All denominations for 1967 bore special reverses to commemorate the 1867 confederation of the provinces of Canada, Nova Scotia and New Brunswick to form the Dominion of Canada. The design for this denomination, by Alex Colville, shows a mackerel. During the issue, the alloy was changed to .500 silver, .500 copper. The alloy varieties are not distinguishable by eye, so only a single catalog value is given below.

Date	Qty. Minted	BU-60	CH-63
1967 .800 silver	32,309,135	$1.75	$2.00
.500 silver	30,689,080	1.75	2.00

Schooner Reverse Resumed 1968-

Diameter: 18.034 mm; weight: 2.333 grams (silver), 2.074 grams (nickel); composition 1968: .500 silver, .500 copper; 1968-: 1.000 nickel; edge: reeded.

Two major reverse varieties have appeared since the 1968 resumption of the fishing schooner design. The first is as the previous issue; the second, by Myron Cook (but still bearing Emanuel Hahn's initial H), has the size of the device reduced and a smaller date placed lower in the field.

1968 varieties. The earlier portion of the 1968 issue was in silver. Later, the composition was changed to nickel. The nickel specimens are slightly darker in color and are attracted to a magnet. Due to lack of time, the Royal Canadian Mint made arrangements with the United States Mint at Philadelphia to strike many of the nickel 10 cents for 1968. The Ottawa and Philadelphia strikings differ only in the number of reeds on the edge and shape of the slots between them.

Large high date
1968-1969

Ottawa Mint
V-shaped grooves

Philadelphia Mint
flat-bottomed grooves

Large Schooner Reverse (1968-1969)

1968 .500 silver	70,460,000		2.00
nickel, Ottawa	87,412,930		.35
nickel, Philadelphia	85,170,000		.35
1969 (large date)*	(incl. below)		Rare

* Rarity not yet known.

Small schooner
small low date 1969-

Date	Qty. Minted	CH-63
Small Schooner Reverse (1969-)		
1969 (small date)	55,833,929	$ .35
1970	5,249,296	1.00
1971	41,016,968	.30
1972	60,169,387	.30
1973	167,715,435	.30
1974	210,566,565	.30
1975	207,680,000	.30
1976	95,018,533	.30
1977	128,452,206	.30
1978	170,366,431	.30

Modified Obverse 1979-

Beginning with 1979, the portrait of the Queen was made smaller. This was done to standardize our coinage, making the size of the portrait proportional to the diameter of the coin, regardless of denomination.

1979	237,321,321	.30
1980	170,111,533	.30
1981	123,912,900	.30
1982	93,953,450	.30
1983	111,920,210	.30
1984		.30

20 CENTS
Victoria, 20 Cents Silver, 1858

Diameter: 23.27 mm; weight: 4.648 grams; composition: .925 silver, .075 copper; edge: reeded.

G: *Braid around ear worn through.*
VG: *No details in braid around the ear.*
Fine: *Segments of braid begin to merge into one another.*
VF: *Braid is clear but not sharp.*
EF: *Braid is slightly worn but generally sharp and clear.*

The English shilling being valued at slightly over 24 cents and the Halifax currency shilling valued at 20 cents (there was no actual coin in the latter instance), the Province of Canada decided to issue a 20 cent instead of a 25 cent coin.

This move proved unpopular because of the ease of confusion of the coin with U.S. and later Canadian 25 cent pieces. Consequently, the 20 cents was never again issued for circulation.

In 1870, when the Dominion of Canada issued its first coins, the 25 cent piece was selected and by a proclamation dated 9 September, 1870, the old 20 cent pieces were withdrawn. Over half the issue was returned to the Royal Mint at various times between 1885 and 1906, melted and the silver recoined into 25 cent pieces.

Date	Approx. Qty. Minted.	G-4	VG-8	F-12	VF-20	EF-40	AU-50	BU-60	CH-63
1858	(Originally: 750,000)	$45.00	$65.00	$85.00	$125.00	$250.00	$700.00	$1,400	$2,500

25 CENTS

Victoria, 25 Cents Silver, 1870-1901

Diameter: 23.62 mm; weight: 5.810 grams; composition: .925 silver, .075 copper; edge: reeded.

G: *Hair over ear worn through.*
VG: *No details in the hair over the ear and the jewels in the diadem are partly worn away.*
Fine: *Strands of the hair over the ear begin to merge together and jewels slightly blurred.*
VF: *Hair and the jewels clear but not sharp.*
EF: *Hair over the ear and jewels of the diadem slightly worn, but generally sharp and clear.*

A total of five minor varieties of the Queen's portrait were used for this denomination, each differing in some of the facial features and in certain other respects. Each successive variety after the initial one was created by re-engraving one of those used previously. The initial and probably all later portraits were designed and engraved by L.C. Wyon; only on the final variety was he probably attempting to portray Victoria as she appeared in real life.
In some instances two portraits are coupled with a given date reverse. Such portraits are most easily differentiated as follows:

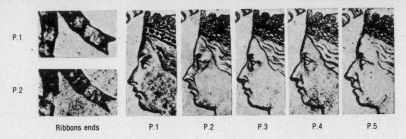

P.1					
P.2					
Ribbons ends	P.1	P.2	P.3	P.4	P.5

P.1 vs. P.2: The ribbon end extending toward the rear has a relatively constant width on P.1 but gradually narrows on P.2.

P.4. vs. P.5: The P.5 face has much more aged features and a larger nose.

The reverse device shows crossed boughs of maple, tied at the bottom with a ribbon and separated at the top by St. Edward's crown. Although there were several modifications of the design, the most noteworthy came in 1886. This second design, derived from the first, has longer cut ends to the maple boughs, slight re-cutting of other portions of the wreath and the design elements generally closer to the rim denticles. Both of these reverses were by L.C. Wyon.

Short bough ends 1870-1886

1 8 7 0 7 0

Narrow 0   Wide 0

Date		Qty. Minted	G-4	VG-8	F-12	VF-20	EF-40	AU-50	BU-60	CH-63
Short Bough Ends Reverse (1870-1886)										
1870 narrow 0	P1	900,000	$7.50	$13.50	$25.00	$60.00	$135.00	$450.00	$1,200	$1,750
wide 0	P2	incl. above	—	—	—	—	—	—	—	—
1871	P1,2	400,000	8.50	16.50	30.00	75.00	250.00	725.00	1,700	2,400
1871H	P1,2	748,000	9.00	20.00	35.00	80.00	250.00	750.00	1,550	2,250
1872H	P1,2	2,240,000	5.00	8.50	15.00	30.00	85.00	400.00	1,000	1,500
1874H	P2	2,600,000	5.00	8.50	15.00	30.00	85.00	400.00	1,000	1,500
1875H	P2	incl. above	150.00	225.00	500.00	1,150	2,500	4,000	8,000	12,500

8 0   8 0   8 0

Wide 0   Wide over narrow 0   Narrow 0

1880H wide 0	P2	400,000	55.00	90.00	175.00	385.00	725.00	1,650	3,750	5,500
nar. over wide 0	P2	incl. above	30.00	45.00	100.00	225.00	500.00	1,400	3,000	4,000
narrow 0	P2	incl. above	20.00	40.00	75.00	200.00	450.00	800.00	1,800	3,000
1881H	P2	820,000	8.00	12.50	25.00	70.00	200.00	550.00	1,350	2,000
1882H	P3	600,000	9.00	17.50	30.00	75.00	250.00	600.00	1,500	2,250
1883H	P4	960,000	7.00	12.00	20.00	55.00	185.00	450.00	1,250	2,000
1885	P2	192,000	50.00	100.00	175.00	350.00	900.00	2,000	4,200	6,500
1886 short b. ends	P2,4,5	540,000	7.50	15.00	27.50	75.00	250.00	675.00	1,800	2,500

Long bough ends 1886-1901

Large Bough Ends Reverse (1886-1901)										
1886 long b. ends	P5	incl. above	7.50	15.00	27.50	75.00	250.00	675.00	1,800	2,500
1887	P5	400,000	50.00	90.00	165.00	350.00	850.00	1,750	4,000	6,000

Narrow 8's **1888**   **1888** Wide 8's

Date		Qty. Minted	G-4	VG-8	F-12	VF-20	EF-40	AU-50	BU-60	CH-63
1888 narrow 8's...	P5 ...	400,000	7.00	13.00	25.00	65.00	175.00	500.00	1,150	1,700
wide 8's.....	P5 .	incl. above	9.00	16.00	35.00	75.00	200.00	600.00	1,300	2,100
1889	P5 ...	66,324	60.00	100.00	185.00	375.00	1,000	2,000	4,250	6,500
1890H	P5 ...	200,000	10.00	20.00	37.50	85.00	250.00	800.00	2,000	3,000
1891	P5 ...	120,000	35.00	65.00	125.00	250.00	500.00	1,000	2,500	3,600
1892	P5 ...	510,000	6.50	12.00	20.00	50.00	125.00	500.00	1,200	1,800
1893	P5 ...	100,000	40.00	80.00	150.00	325.00	625.00	1,250	3,000	4,600
1894	P5 ...	220,000	9.00	16.50	30.00	75.00	200.00	700.00	1,500	2,500
1899	P5 ...	415,580	4.50	7.50	12.00	30.00	100.00	400.00	1,000	1,500
1900	P5 .	1,320,000	4.00	6.00	9.00	20.00	65.00	325.00	750.00	1,150
1901	P5 ...	640,000	4.50	6.50	10.00	25.00	75.00	350.00	850.00	1,300

Edward VII, 25 Cents Silver, 1902-1910

Diameter: 23.62 mm; weight: 5.810 grams; composition: .925 silver, .075 copper; edge: reeded.

G: *Band of crown worn through.*
VG: *Band of the crown is worn through at the highest point.*
Fine: *Jewels in the band of crown will be blurred.*
VF: *Band of the crown is still clear but no longer sharp.*
EF: *Band of the crown slightly worn but generally sharp and clear.*

A single obverse, designed and engraved by G.W. DeSaulles (DES. below bust), was used for the entire series.

For the first reverse, De Saulles used the almost unaltered wreath from the second Victorian reverse and coupled it with the Imperial State crown and a new legend. A major modification, presumably by W.H.J. Blakemore, appeared in 1906. It has a larger crown and many of the leaves are re-engraved. A specimen dated 1906 with the small crown reverse has been documented. The issues of 1908-10 have thickened stems.

Small Crown Reverse (1902-1906)

	Qty. Minted	G-4	VG-8	F-12	VF-20	EF-40	AU-50	BU-60	CH-63
1902	464,000	$4.00	$6.00	$12.50	$30.00	$85.00	$350.00	$650.00	$1,000
1902H	800,000	3.50	4.50	8.50	22.00	65.00	200.00	500.00	750.00
1903	846,000	4.50	6.50	13.00	35.00	95.00	375.00	900.00	1,400
1904	400,000	6.00	10.50	25.00	65.00	175.00	600.00	1,500	2,400
1905	800,000	4.50	7.00	15.00	35.00	125.00	500.00	1,250	2,100
1906	incl. below	—	—	—	—	—	—	—	—

Large Crown Reverse (1906-1910)

	Qty. Minted	G-4	VG-8	F-12	VF-20	EF-40	AU-50	BU-60	CH-63
1906	1,237,843	3.50	5.00	10.00	22.50	75.00	300.00	750.00	1,100
1907	2,088,000	3.50	5.00	10.00	22.50	75.00	275.00	700.00	1,000
1908	495,016	5.00	8.50	20.00	45.00	130.00	450.00	1,100	1,600
1909	1,335,929	3.50	6.50	12.00	32.50	100.00	400.00	1,000	1,500
1910	3,577,569	3.00	5.00	8.00	20.00	65.00	200.00	550.00	725.00

George V, 25 Cents Silver, 1911-1936

Diameter: 23.62 mm; weight: 5.832 grams; composition 1911-19: .925 silver, .075 copper; 1920-36: .800 silver, .200 copper; edge: reeded.

G: *Band of crown worn through.*
VG: *Band of crown worn through at highest point.*
Fine: *Jewels in band of crown will be blurred. (CAN of CANADA worn but readable on 1936 dot.)*
VF: *Band of crown is still clear but no longer sharp.*
EF: *Band of crown slightly worn but generally sharp and clear.*

As in the case of all other Canadian denominations, the 1911 legend did not include the phrase DEI GRATIA ("by the grace of God"). Public objection to this break with tradition resulted in the addition of the abbreviation DEI GRA: the following year. Both varieties were based on the design of Sir E.B. MacKennal, whose initials B.M. appear on the truncation of the bust. The reverse is identical to that for 1908-10.

Date	Qty. Minted	G-4	VG-8	F-12	VF-20	EF-40	AU-50	BU-60	CH-63
"Godless" Obverse (1911)									
1911	1,721,341	$9.00	$13.50	$27.50	$70.00	$165.00	$350.00	$900.00	$1,250

Modified Obverse Legend (1912-1936)

Date	Qty. Minted	G-4	VG-8	F-12	VF-20	EF-40	AU-50	BU-60	CH-63
1912	2,544,199	*	5.00	7.00	15.00	50.00	200.00	650.00	1,100
1913	2,213,595	*	5.00	7.00	15.00	45.00	160.00	500.00	750.00
1914	1,215,397	*	5.50	8.00	20.00	65.00	300.00	850.00	1,250
1915	242,382	7.50	15.00	35.00	150.00	400.00	1,000	3,250	5,250
1916	1,462,566	*	4.50	7.00	15.00	40.00	150.00	450.00	650.00
1917	3,365,644	*	4.00	5.00	12.50	35.00	100.00	325.00	500.00
1918	4,175,649	*	4.00	5.00	12.50	35.00	100.00	325.00	500.00
1919 .... (Orig.:	5,852,262)	*	4.00	5.00	12.50	35.00	100.00	325.00	500.00
1920	1,975,278	*	4.00	6.00	12.00	40.00	120.00	400.00	600.00
1921	597,337	6.50	12.00	25.00	75.00	200.00	900.00	2,100	3,200
1927	468,096	17.50	35.00	65.00	150.00	350.00	1,000	2,250	3,500
1928	2,114,178	*	4.00	5.00	12.50	40.00	120.00	400.00	600.00
1929	2,690,562	*	4.00	5.00	12.50	40.00	120.00	400.00	600.00
1930	968,748	3.00	5.00	6.00	16.00	45.00	135.00	500.00	750.00
1931	537,815	3.00	5.00	7.00	17.50	50.00	175.00	550.00	800.00
1932	537,994	3.00	5.00	7.00	17.50	50.00	175.00	550.00	800.00
1933	421,282	3.00	5.50	8.00	20.00	60.00	185.00	650.00	950.00
1934	384,350	3.00	7.00	12.00	30.00	80.00	275.00	850.00	1,250
1935	537,772	3.00	7.00	10.50	25.00	70.00	250.00	750.00	1,100
1936	972,094	*	4.00	5.50	12.50	40.00	100.00	350.00	500.00

George VI Issue, Struck in Name of George V

A portion of the 1, 10 and 25 cents dated 1936 have a small raised dot on the reverse, denoting that they were actually struck in 1937 for George VI. On the 25 cents the dot is below the ribbon of the wreath. See text on the 1 cent for more details.

This issue seems to be particularly liable to "ghosting," thus the CAN of CANADA often will be much weaker than the rest of the legend. Nevertheless, the entire CANADA must still be readable for any specimen to grade at least Very Good. Otherwise, the grading and physical specifications are exactly as for the regular George V issues.

Date	Qty. Minted	G-4	VG-8	F-12	VF-20	EF-40	AU-50	BU-60	CH-63
1936 raised dot under wreath............	153,685	20.00	40.00	85.00	300.00	650.00	1,100	2,500	3,600

George VI, 25 Cents Silver, 1937-1952

Diameter: 23.62 mm; weight: 5.832 grams; composition: .800 silver, .200 copper; edge: reeded.

VG: No detail in hair above the ear.
Fine: Only slight detail in hair above the ear.
VF: Hair above ear and side of head is clear but not sharp.
EF: Slight wear in the hair over the ear.

Three obverse varieties are known for this series. The first two have in common a high relief bust of the King by T.H. Paget (H.P. below); the second variety has the ET IND: IMP: omitted from the legend (see the 1 cent text). The third has a low relief modification of the original portrait. The latter variety, the work of Thomas Shingles, was made to improve the overall appearance and the clarity with which the design could be struck up. In addition to the relief of the portraits, the second and third varieties can be differentiated by the position of the legend relative to the rim denticles and by the style of some of the letters.

In keeping with a Government decision to modernize the reverse designs the caribou motif was selected for the 25 cents. At one time the fishing schooner was considered for this denomination. The designer was Emanuel Hahn (H under caribou's neck).

1947 "dot." This item is apparently the product of a deteriorated die (see text on the 5 cent for more details).

1947 maple leaf variety. This is an official issue struck in 1948. See text on the 1 cent for details.

"dot" after date
(deteriorated die)

1947 maple leaf
(official issue)

Date	Qty. Minted	VG-8	F-12	VF-20	EF-40	AU-50	BU-60	CH-63
ET IND : IMP : Obverse (1937-1947)								
1937	2,689,813	$3.00	$5.00	$6.50	$10.00	$15.00	$32.50	$50.00
1938	3,149,245	3.00	5.00	7.50	15.00	70.00	175.00	275.00
1939	3,532,495	3.00	5.00	7.50	15.00	70.00	150.00	250.00
1940	9,583,650	*	4.00	5.00	8.50	20.00	45.00	70.00
1941	6,654,672	*	4.00	5.00	8.50	25.00	50.00	80.00
1942	6,935,871	*	4.00	5.00	8.50	25.00	50.00	80.00
1943	13,559,575	*	3.50	4.50	7.50	17.50	45.00	65.00
1944	7,216,237	*	4.00	5.00	10.00	30.00	75.00	110.00
1945	5,296,495	*	3.50	4.50	7.50	17.50	45.00	65.00
1946	2,210,810	*	4.00	6.50	12.50	50.00	120.00	165.00
1947 normal date	1,524,544	*	4.00	7.00	15.00	60.00	140.00	195.00
"dot"	incl. above	32.50	65.00	115.00	235.00	400.00	1,000	1,500
1947 maple leaf	4,393,938	*	3.00	4.00	6.00	15.00	35.00	50.00

High relief
1948-1952

Low relief
1951-1952

GRA   GRA

High relief   Low relief

Note style of letters, relation of A
to denticles.

Modified Legend, High Relief Bust (1948-1952) Low Relief Bust (1951-1952)								
1948	2,564,424	*	$4.00	$6.50	$12.50	$45.00	$125.00	$175.00
1949	7,988,830	*	3.00	4.00	5.00	10.00	25.00	35.00
1950	9,673,335	*	3.00	4.00	5.00	8.00	20.00	30.00
1951 high relief bust	8,290,719	*	3.00	4.00	5.00	7.00	15.00	25.00
low relief bust	incl. above	*	3.00	4.00	5.00	7.00	15.00	25.00
1952 high relief bust	8,859,642	*	3.00	4.00	5.00	7.00	15.00	25.00
low relief bust	incl. above	*	3.00	4.00	5.00	7.00	15.00	25.00

Elizabeth II, Laureate Bust, 1953-1964

Diameter 1953 large date: 23.62 mm; 1953 small date to 1964: 23.88 mm; weight: 5.832 grams; composition: .800 silver, .200 copper; edge: reeded.

Fine: Leaves worn almost through; shoulder fold indistinct.

VF: Leaves considerably worn; shoulder fold must be clear.

EF: Laurel leaves on the head somewhat worn.

The initial obverse for the 1953 issue had a high relief, laureate portrait of the Queen by Mrs. Mary Gillick (M.G. on truncation) which did not strike up well on the coins. Later in the year, the rim width and coin diameter were increased, the obverse relief lowered and the hair and shoulder detail re-engraved. The latter included sharpening two lines which represented a fold in, not a shoulder strap on, the Queen's gown. The two varieties also differ in the positioning of the legend relative to the rim denticles and the styles of some of the letters.

The reverse coupled with the "no shoulder fold" obverse in 1953 is exactly as that for the George VI issues. Together with the obverse change, however, came a new reverse with a smaller date, wider rim and modified caribou (note the change in the contour of the lower neck). After 1953, the reverse design was not significantly altered until 1967.

No shoulder fold, high relief, narrow rim 1953

Large date, narrow rim 1953

Date	Qty. Minted	F-12	VF-20	EF-40	AU-50	BU-60	CH-63
Large Date, No Shoulder Fold (1953)							
1953 large date	10,456,769	*	3.00	4.00	6.00	10.00	15.00

With shoulder fold, low relief, wide rim 1953-1964

Small date, wide rim, modified caribou 1953-1964

Small Date, With Shoulder Fold (1953-1964)							
1953 small date................	incl. above	*	$3.00	$4.00	$7.50	$15.00	$20.00
1954	2,318,891	*	6.50	13.50	25.00	60.00	80.00
1955	9,552,505	*	*	3.00	5.00	10.00	15.00
1956	11,269,353	*	*	*	4.00	6.00	8.50
1957	12,770,190	*	*	*	4.00	6.00	8.00
1958	9,336,910	*	*	*	3.00	5.00	7.00
1959	13,503,461	*	*	*	3.00	4.00	5.50
1960	22,835,327	*	*	*	3.00	5.00	6.00
1961	18,164,368	*	*	*	3.00	5.00	6.00
1962	29,559,266	*	*	*	3.00	4.00	5.50
1963	21,180,652	*	*	*	3.00	4.00	5.50
1964	36,479,343	*	*	*	3.00	4.00	5.50

Elizabeth II, Tiara Obverse, 1965-1978

In 1965 an obverse with a new style portrait by Arnold Machin was introduced. The Queen has more mature facial features and is wearing a tiara. The reverse was continued as before, and physical specifications are as on the previous issues.

Date	Qty. Minted	BU-60	CH-63
1965	44,708,869	$4.00	$5.00
1966	25,388,892	4.00	5.00

Confederation Centennial 1967

All denominations for 1967 bore special reverses to commemorate the 1867 confederation of the provinces of Canada, Nova Scotia and New Brunswick to form the Dominion of Canada. The design for this denomination, by Alex Colville, shows a bobcat as its device. During 1967 the alloy was changed to .500 silver, .500 copper.

1967 .800 silver	48,855,500	3.00	4.00
.500 silver	incl. above	3.00	4.00

Elizabeth II, 25 Cents Nickel, 1968-

Diameter: 23.88 mm; weight: 5.832 grams (silver), 5.054 grams (nickel); composition 1968: .500 silver, .500 copper; 1968-1.000 nickel.

During 1968, the composition was changed to pure nickel. The nickel specimens are slightly darker in color and are attracted to a magnet.

1968 .500 silver	71,464,000	$3.00	$4.00
pure nickel	88,686,931	—	1.00
1969	133,037,929	—	1.00
1970	10,302,010	—	4.00
1971	48,170,428	—	1.00
1972	43,743,387	—	1.00

Royal Canadian Mounted Police Centennial 1973

Large bust   Small bust

The 25 cent pieces for 1973 bore a special reverse designed by Paul Cedarberg (PC behind horse) marking the centenary of the founding of the Royal Canadian Mounted Police. The initial circulation strikes were made with obverse dies left over from 1972. However, it was found necessary to change to a second obverse bearing a smaller portrait engraved from Patrick Brindley's modification of the Machin bust of Elizabeth. Aside from having a smaller portrait with more hair detail, Brindley's obverse has fewer beads, pulled in farther from the edge. To date the Brindley obverse has been used only in 1973.

Date	Qty. Minted	F-12	VF-20	EF-40	AU-50	BU-60	CH-63
1973 small bust	134,958,589	—	—	—	—	—	$1.00
large bust	incl. above	$125.00	$150.00	$200.00	$300.00	$350.00	450.00

Caribou Reverse Resumed 1974-

Date	Qty. Minted	CH-63
1974	192,360,598	$1.00
1975	141,486,838	1.00
1976	86,898,261	1.00
1977	99,634,555	1.00
1978	176,475,408	1.00

Modified Obverse 1979-

Beginning with 1979, the portrait of the Queen was made smaller. This was done to standardize our coinage, making the size of the portrait proportional to the diameter of the coin, regardless of denomination.

1979	231,453,747	1.00
1980	77,547,645	.75
1981	131,583,900	.75
1982	167,414,450	.75
1983	13,920,210	.75
1984		.75

*Note: Common silver coins (marked with *) are worth a premium only for their silver content. This price may vary according to prevailing market value of silver bullion.

50 CENTS
Victoria, 50 Cents Silver, 1870-1901

Diameter: 29.72 mm; weight:11.620 grams; composition: .925 silver, .075 copper; edge: reeded.

G: *Hair over ear worn through.*
VG: *No details in the hair over the ear and the jewels in the diadem are partly worn away.*
Fine: *Strands of hair over the ear begin to merge together; jewels slightly blurred.*
VF: *Hair and jewels clear but not sharp.*
EF: *Hair over ear and jewels of diadem slightly worn but generally sharp and clear.*

In all, four portraits were used for this denomination. Except for the first two varieties, which have the same face, the portraits differ in the facial features as well as certain other respects. Each successive variety after the first was created by re-engraving an earlier one. The first and probably all later portraits were designed and engraved by L.C. Wyon; only on the final one or two varieties could he have been attempting to portray Victoria as she appeared at the time. In some instances two portraits were coupled with a given date reverse. These are most easily differentiated as follows:

| P.1 | P.2 | P.1,2 | P.3 | P.4 |

P.1 vs. P.2: P.1 has no initials on the truncation, a blank space immediately behind the front cross in the crown and a break in the left-hand ribbon end; while P.2 has L.C.W. on the truncation, a shamrock behind the front cross in the crown and no breaks in the ribbon ends.

P.3 vs. P.4: P.3 has a rounded chin front, and the lower front corner of the crown is in front of the forehead; while P.4 has a flat chin front and the lower front corner of the crown even with the forehead.

The reverse device consists of crossed maple boughs, tied at the bottom by a ribbon and separated at the top by St. Edward's crown. Although there were several slight modifications, the most noteworthy came in 1871. The second design (1871-1901), derived from the first, has parts of both the crown and the wreath re-engraved. Both reverse varieties were by L.C. Wyon.

Date	Qty. Minted	G-4	VG-8	F-12	VF-20	EF-40	AU-50	BU-60	CH-63
First Reverse Design (1870)									
1870 no LCW.... P1	450,000	$175.00	$300.00	$750.00	$2,750	$4,000	$9,000	$15,000	$20,000
1870 LCW on obv. P2 ..	incl. above	25.00	50.00	120.00	210.00	400.00	1,500	5,000	7,500

Date	Qty. Minted	G-4	VG-8	F-12	VF-20	EF-40	AU-50	BU-60	CH-63
Modified Reverse Design (1871-1901)									
1871 . . . . P2	200,000	$35.00	$65.00	$150.00	$325.00	$700.00	$1,600	$4,700	$7,600
1871H P2	45,000	55.00	110.00	200.00	475.00	1,100	2,400	6,500	9,500

Normal 2　　　　　　　　Short base 2

Specimens of the 1872H issue often have part or all
of the reverse legend repunched.

1872H, inverted A over V

1872H normal 2 . P2	80,000	25.00	50.00	125.00	250.00	500.00	1,500	4,800	7,500
short base 2 . . P2	incl. above	25.00	50.00	125.00	250.00	500.00	1,500	4,800	7,500
inv. A over V . . P2	incl. above	50.00	85.00	175.00	400.00	1,000	2,200	6,400	9,500
1881H P3	150,000	25.00	50.00	100.00	250.00	550.00	1,650	4,800	7,000
1888 . . . . P3	60,000	70.00	125.00	250.00	500.00	1,000	2,000	5,500	8,000
1890H P3,4	20,000	450.00	800.00	1,500	3,000	6,500	15,000	35,000	50,000
1892 . . . . P4	151,000	30.00	55.00	110.00	250.00	525.00	1,600	5,200	8,200
1894 . . . . P4	29,036	125.00	225.00	425.00	1,000	2,500	6,500	15,000	18,500
1898 . . . . P4	100,000	30.00	55.00	100.00	250.00	500.00	1,650	4,500	7,000
1899 . . . . P4	50,000	60.00	110.00	200.00	500.00	1,250	2,800	8,000	13,500
1900 . . . . P4	118,000	25.00	45.00	100.00	200.00	500.00	1,400	4,000	5,500
1901 . . . . P4	80,000	30.00	50.00	100.00	250.00	600.00	1,500	4,250	6,250

Edward VII, 50 Cents Silver, 1902-1910

Diameter: 29.72 mm; weight: 11.620 grams; composition: .925 silver, .075 copper; edge: reeded.

G: *Band of crown worn through.*
VG: *Band of crown worn through at highest point.*
Fine: *Jewels blurred in band of crown.*
VF: *Band of crown still clear but no longer sharp.*
EF: *Band of crown slightly worn; generally sharp and clear.*

A single obverse, designed and engraved by G.W. De Saulles (DES below bust), was used for the entire series.

For the initial reverse variety (1902-10) De Saulles utilized the unmodified wreath from the later Victorian reverse with a new legend and the Imperial State crown. A modification of the first variety (probably by W.H.J. Blakemore) appeared in 1910; several leaves and the cross atop the crown differ. The most noticeable change is in the two leaves at the far right opposite CANADA. On the first variety the leaves have long, pointed corners, whereas they are much shorter on the second.

Victorian leaves
1902-1910

Edwardian leaves
1910

Note 3 leaf tips near rims.

Victorian Leaves Reverse (1902-1910)									
1902	120,000	13.50	22.50	50.00	175.00	350.00	900.00	2,250	3,500
1903H	140,000	18.00	35.00	70.00	225.00	425.00	1,150	3,600	5,200
1904	60,000	60.00	100.00	210.00	525.00	1,100	3,000	7,500	12,000
1905	40,000	65.00	125.00	250.00	600.00	1,350	3,500	8,500	17,500

Date	Qty. Minted	G-4	VG-8	F-12	VF-20	EF-40	AU-50	BU-60	CH-63
1906	350,000	$10.50	$17.50	$45.00	$120.00	$325.00	$1,000	$2,200	$3,600
1907	300,000	10.50	18.50	45.00	110.00	300.00	800.00	2,000	3,300
1908	128,119	16.00	30.00	70.00	175.00	425.00	1,350	3,000	4,500
1909	203,118	10.50	18.50	55.00	140.00	400.00	1,200	2,500	4,500
1910 (Victorian leaves)	649,521	10.50	18.00	45.00	110.00	300.00	800.00	2,000	3,100
Edwardian Leaves Reverse (1910)									
1910 (Edwardian leaves) incl. above		10.50	18.00	45.00	110.00	300.00	800.00	2,000	3,100

George V, 50 Cents Silver, 1911-1936

Diameter: 29.72 mm; weight: 11.664 grams; composition 1911-19: .925 silver, .075 copper; 1920-36: .800 silver, .200 copper; edge: reeded.

G: *Band of crown worn through.*
VG: *Band of crown worn through at highest point.*
Fine: *Jewels blurred in band of crown.*
VF: *Band of crown clear; no longer sharp.*
EF: *Band of crown slightly worn; generally sharp and clear.*

Two obverse varieties exist; the first (1911) lacks the phrase DEI GRATIA or an abbreviation for it and the second (1912-36) has DEI GRA incorporated into the legend. Both obverses were derived from a portrait model by Sir E.B .MacKennal (B.M. on truncation). See the 1 cent text for more details. The reverse is identical to the Edwardian leaves variety, introduced in the previous series.

1921. During the late teens and early 1920's far more 50 cent pieces were struck than were needed. Many of them remained unissued in the Mint with only about 24,000 pieces being issued in 1921-28. In 1929 a sizable demand for this denomination arose. The Mint, however, fearing the public would doubt the authenticity of new coins bearing "old" dates, melted the 500,000 50 cent pieces in stock and struck new ones with the current date (1929). It seems very likely that most of the original 1921 mintage of 206,398 was included in this melt. Only about 100 1921's survive today; most are business strikes, but a few specimen strikes (originally issued as part of specimen sets) are known.

"Godless" Obverse (1911)

1911	209,972	12.50	20.00	100.00	550.00	1,100	1,850	3,500	5,500

Modified Obverse Legend (1912-1936)

1912	285,867	6.00	11.00	25.00	100.00	350.00	1,300	2,800	5,000
1913	265,889	6.00	11.00	25.00	100.00	325.00	1,250	2,500	5,200
1914	160,128	20.00	40.00	100.00	300.00	600.00	1,800	4,500	7,500
1916	459,070	6.00	10.00	22.50	75.00	225.00	700.00	1,500	2,500
1917	752,213	6.00	10.00	17.50	45.00	175.00	450.00	1,000	1,750
1918	854,989	6.00	9.50	17.50	42.00	160.00	425.00	900.00	1,750
1919	1,113,429	6.00	9.50	17.50	40.00	140.00	375.00	850.00	1,700

Date	Qty. Minted	G-4	VG-8	F-12	VF-20	EF-40	AU-50	BU-60	CH-63
1920 .... (Originally: 584,691)		$6.00	$10.00	$18.50	$55.00	$200.00	$500.00	$1,250	$2,600
1921 .... (Originally: 206,328)		5,000	7,500	10,500	20,000	30,000	40,000	50,000	75,000
1929 228,328		6.00	10.50	20.00	50.00	175.00	550.00	1,250	2,500
1931 57,581		7.50	15.00	25.00	85.00	350.00	1,050	2,250	3,600
1932 19,213		42.50	70.00	135.00	400.00	900.00	2,000	3,800	5,500
1934 39,539		10.00	18.00	40.00	125.00	425.00	1,100	2,600	4,400
1936 38,550		9.00	16.50	35.00	110.00	375.00	900.00	1,800	2,850

George VI, 50 Cents Silver, 1937-1952

Diameter: 29.72 mm; weight: 11.664 grams; composition: .800 silver, .200 copper, edge: reeded.

VG: No detail in hair above the ear.
Fine: Only slight detail in hair above the ear.
VF: Where not worn, hair is clear but not sharp.
EF: Slight wear in hair over the ear.

There are two obverses, both of which have the bare-headed portrait of the King by T.H. Paget (H.P. below). The varieties differ in that the second (1948-52) incorporated the change in the King's titles which ensued when India was granted independence from England (see text on the 1 cent).

In keeping with a Government decision to modernize all reverses, a simplified Canadian coat of arms was chosen for this denomination. The simplification involved omission of the crest, helmet and mantling, motto and floral emblems; in addition, no attempt was made to heraldically color the shield and banners. The shield consists of the arms of England (three lions), Scotland (rearing lion), royalist France (three fleurs-de-lis) and Ireland (a harp) and is surmounted by a stylized Imperial crown. At the left is the English lion holding a lance with the Union flag; on the right is a Scottish unicorn holding a lance with the flag of royalist France. The whole is resting upon a layer of serried clouds. The initials KG flanking the crown indicate the designer, George Kruger-Gray.

The position of the final digit in the date varies because during most of the 1940's it was punched separately into each die. Such varieties are too minor to include in a catalog of this kind.

Date	Qty. Minted	VG-8	F-12	VF-20	EF-40	AU-50	BU-60	CH-63
ET IND : IMP : Obverse (1937-1947)								
1937 192,016		$7.00	$10.50	$15.00	$22.00	$45.00	$85.00	$125.00
1938 192,018		7.50	13.00	25.00	65.00	145.00	365.00	625.00
1939 287,976		7.50	11.50	20.00	40.00	110.00	300.00	500.00
1940 1,996,566		*	7.50	11.50	15.00	25.00	50.00	85.00
1941 1,714,874		*	7.50	11.50	15.00	25.00	50.00	85.00
1942 1,974,165		*	7.50	11.50	15.00	25.00	50.00	85.00
1943 3,109,583		*	7.50	11.50	14.00	22.00	45.00	80.00
1944 2,460,205		*	8.00	12.00	16.00	30.00	60.00	90.00
1945 1,959,528		*	7.50	11.50	14.00	22.00	45.00	80.00

"Hoof" in 6 | Tall 7 | Short 7 | Tall 7 | Short 7
(deteriorated die) | Without maple leaf | | With maple leaf after date |

1946 and 1949 "hoof." These items are apparently the products of damaged dies and as such are not true die varieties. For further comments on such items, see page 6.

1947 maple leaf and 7 varieties. The 1947 (no maple leaf) issue comes with two styles of 7 in the date. One is a rather tall figure, the bottom of which points to the left and the other is a shorter 7 with the bottom curving back to the right. Both 7's were also used for the maple leaf issue (see 1 cent text) struck in 1948.

Date		Qty. Minted	VG-8	F-12	VF-20	EF-40	AU-50	BU-60	CH-63
1946	normal 6	950,235	*	$8.00	$12.50	$22.00	$50.00	$140.00	$175.00
	"hoof" in 6	incl. above	25.00	40.00	70.00	200.00	1,000	2,000	3,500
1947	tall 7	424,885	6.50	8.50	12.00	25.00	85.00	200.00	325.00
	short 7	incl. above	6.50	8.50	12.00	25.00	85.00	200.00	325.00
1947	maple leaf, tall 7 ..	38,433	35.00	50.00	75.00	125.00	225.00	425.00	625.00
	maple leaf. short 7 .	incl. above	1,500	2,000	2,500	3,000	4,000	6,000	8,000

Obverse 1948-1952

"Hoof" over 9
(deteriorated die)

Modified Obverse Legend (1948-1952)

Date	Qty. Minted	VG-8	F-12	VF-20	EF-40	AU-50	BU-60	CH-63
1948	37,784	65.00	85.00	125.00	175.00	250.00	375.00	550.00
1949 normal 9	858,991	6.00	8.00	12.50	17.50	35.00	75.00	120.00
"hoof" over 9	incl. above	15.00	25.00	45.00	100.00	250.00	850.00	1,500

1950 no lines in 0. In 1950 the 50 cents dies were derived from a single, fully dated matrix in which the 0 of the date had 4 horizontal lines in its centre. Depending upon the amount of polishing or re-polishing (see page 7) of each individual die, the lines in the 0 ranged from completely present to partially missing to entirely absent. Previous cataloguers have chosen to list as a separate entry those pieces that lack the lines. For further comments on such items see page 13.

Lines in 0

No lines in 0
(overpolished die)

Date	Qty. Minted	VG-8	F-12	VF-20	EF-40	AU-50	BU-60	CH-63
1950 lines in 0	2,384,179	6.00	7.50	10.00	12.50	15.00	25.00	35.00
1950 no lines in 0	incl. above	12.00	18.00	25.00	45.00	110.00	500.00	750.00
1951	2,421,730	6.00	7.50	10.00	12.50	15.00	20.00	30.00
1952	2,596,465	6.00	7.50	10.00	12.50	15.00	20.00	30.00

Elizabeth II, Laureate Bust, 1953-1964

Diameter: 29.72 mm; weight: 11.664 grams; composition: .800 silver, .200 copper; edge: reeded.

VF: *Leaves considerably worn, shoulder fold must show.*
EF: *Laurel leaves on head somewhat worn.*
AU: *Trace of wear on laurel leaves.*

The initial obverse for the 1953 issue had a high relief portrait by Mrs. Mary Gillick (M.G. on truncation) which did not strike up well on the coins. Later in the year, the relief was lowered and the hair and shoulder detail re-engraved. On the second variety two lines at the shoulder, representing a fold in the Queen's gown, are clear, while on the first variety they are almost missing. The obverses also differ in the shape of some letters and in positioning of the legend relative to the rim denticles (see the 1 cent text for more details).

The first reverse for the 1953 issue, used only with the high relief "no shoulder fold" obverse, is identical to that used for the 1950-52 George VI coinages, both in the device and the style and size of the date. Later in the year a new reverse with a larger date and with design elements positioned closer to the rim denticles was introduced. The second reverse is associated with both the high and low relief obverses, the former combination being a mule.

In an attempt to reduce the "ghosting" that had been so common in the past, a third modification was introduced in 1955. It is characterized by smaller design elements.

No shoulder fold 1953   Small date 1953

Date	Qty. Minted	F-12	VF-20	EF-40	AU-50	BU-60	CH-63
Small Date Reverse (1953)							
1953 no shoulder fold ...	1,630,429	*	$7.50	$10.00	$13.50	$18.00	$30.00

With shoulder fold 1953-1964   Large date 1953-1954

Large Date Reverse (1953-1954)							
1953 no shoulder fold ...	incl. above	*	30.00	50.00	125.00	300.00	425.00
with shoulder fold .	incl. above	*	11.00	15.00	30.00	60.00	85.00
1954	506.305	*	11.00	17.50	32.00	60.00	85.00

Modified Reverse, 1955-1958

Smaller Coat of Arms (1955-1958)							
1955	753,511	*	10.00	13.50	22.00	40.00	55.00
1956	1,379,499	*	6.00	8.00	9.50	13.50	20.00
1957	2,171,689	*	*	6.00	7.50	10.00	13.50
1958	2,957,266	*	*	6.00	7.50	10.00	13.50

Complete Coat of Arms Reverse 1959-1964

The obverse for the 1959-64 issues continued to be the shoulder fold variety.

In 1957 the Canadian coat of arms as described by the Royal proclamation of 21 November, 1921 (except for the replacement of the Imperial crown with the St. Edward's crown, which Elizabeth preferred) was approved for all government purposes. A representation of the complete coat of arms was consequently modeled and engraved by Thomas Shingles (TS flanking lower part of the shield) for this denomination. As far as was practical, considering the size of the coins, heraldic coloring of the arms and the flags was attempted: blue is represented by horizontal lines, while white or silver is plain with no symbols. On the 1959 issue the background of the lower section (the Canadian emblem) in the shield was inadvertently colored blue, instead of the correct white or silver. The lines were removed beginning with the 1960 issue and no further changes were made in the reverse until 1967. Physical specifications remained as for the previous issues.

Horizontal lines in lower shield 1959

No lines in lower shield 1960-1966

Date	Qt. Minted	EF-40	AU-50	BU-60	CH-63
"Blue Lower Panel" Reverse (1959)					
1959	3,095,535	*	$6.00	$8.00	$10.00
"White Lower Panel" Reverse (1960-1966)					
1960	3,488,897	*	6.00	8.00	10.00
1961	3,584,417	*	*	7.50	9.00
1962	5,208,030	*	*	7.50	9.00
1963	8,348,871	*	*	7.00	8.00
1964	9,377,676	*	*	7.00	8.00

Elizabeth II, Tiara Obverse, 1965-

In 1965 an obverse with a new style portrait by Arnold Machin was introduced. The Queen has more mature facial features and is wearing a tiara.

The reverse and physical specifications continued as previously.

Date	Qty. Minted	AU-50	BU-60	CH-63
1965	12,629,974	*	$7.00	$8.00
1966	7,683,228	*	7.00	8.00

Confederation Centennial 1967

All denominations for 1967 bore special reverses to commemorate the 1867 confederation of the provinces of Canada, Nova Scotia and New Brunswick to form the Dominion of Canada. The design, by Alex Colville, shows a howling wolf.

1967 Confederation commemorative	4,211,395	*	8.00	10.00

Elizabeth II, 50 Cents Nickel, 1968-

Diameter: 27.13 mm; weight: 8.100 grams; composition: 1.000 nickel; edge: reeded.

With the resumption of the regular reverse design in 1968, two significant changes were made. The diameter and weight were reduced, and the composition changed to nickel.

Date	Qty. Minted	CH-63
1968	3,966,932	$1.00
1969	7,113,929	1.00
1970	2,429,516	1.50
1971	2,166,144	1.00
1972	2,515,632	1.00
1973	2,546,096	1.00
1974	3,436,650	1.00
1975	3,710,000	1.00
1976	2,940,719	1.00

Modified Obverse and Reverse, 1977

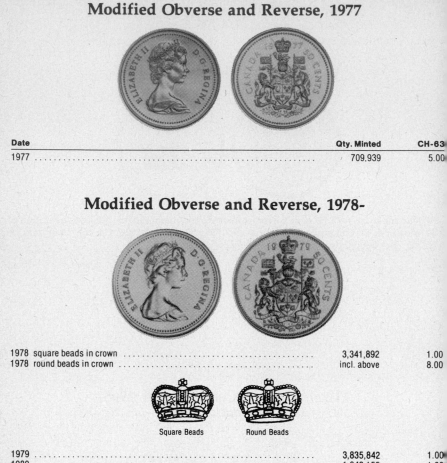

Date	Qty. Minted	CH-63
1977	709.939	5.00

Modified Obverse and Reverse, 1978-

1978 square beads in crown	3,341,892	1.00
1978 round beads in crown	incl. above	8.00

Square Beads   Round Beads

1979	3,835,842	1.00
1980	1,943,155	1.00
1981	2,588,900	1.00
1982	2,877,124	1.00
1983	1,920,210	1.00
1984		1.00

---

*Note: Common silver coins (marked with *) are worth a premium only for their silver content. This price may vary according to prevailing market value of silver bullion.

1 DOLLAR

George V, Silver Jubilee Dollar, 1935

Diameter: 36.00 mm; weight: 23.327 grams; composition: .800 silver, .200 copper; edge: reeded.

Fine: *Jewels in the band of crown will be blurred.*
V.F.: *Band of the crown still clear but no longer sharp.*
EF: *Band of the crown slightly worn but generally sharp and clear.*
AU: *Trace of wear in band of crown.*

The first Canadian dollar issued for circulation had a special obverse to mark the 25th anniversary of the accession of George V. The portrait was from a model by Percy Metcalfe, used previously for the obverses of certain Australian and New Zealand coinages of 1933-35. The Latin legend is translated: "George V, King, Emperor; Regnal year 25."

The reverse device consists of a canoe manned by an Indian and a *voyageur* (travelling agent of a fur company), behind which is an islet with two trees. In the sky are lines representing the northern lights. On the front bundle in the canoe are the incuse initials HB; these signify Hudson's Bay Co., which played an important role in Canada's early history. The designer was Emanuel Hahn (EH at left under canoe).

Date	Qty. Minted	VG-8	F-12	VF-20	EF-40	AU-50	BU-60	CH-63
1935	428,707	*	$15.00	$20.00	$25.00	$30.00	$65.00	$100.00

George V, Silver Dollar, 1936

The obverse for 1936 had the regular design for George V, first seen on the 1 through 50 cent business strikes in 1912. The designer was Sir E.B. MacKennal (B.M. on truncation). The master matrix from which the 1936 obverse dies were prepared was that made in 1911 for the dollar proposed at that time.

The reverse design, physical specifications and grading are as for the 1935 issue.

| 1936 .... | 306,100 | * | 15.00 | 20.00 | 25.00 | 35.00 | 70.00 | 120.00 |

George VI, Silver Dollar, 1937-1952

Diameter: 36.00 mm; weight: 23.327 grams; composition: .800 silver, .200 copper; edge: reeded.

The obverse has the conventional bare-headed portrait of the King by T.H. Paget (H.P. under rear of neck) as used for the lower denominations.

The reverse remains unchanged from the George V issues.

Fine: Only slight detail in hair above
     ear.
VF: Where not worn, hair is clear
     but not sharp.
EF: Slight wear in hair over ear.
AU: Trace of wear in hair.

Date	Qty. Minted	VG-8	F-12	VF-20	EF-40	AU-50	BU-60	CH-63
1937	241,002	*	$15.00	$20.00	$25.00	$35.00	$70.00	$125.00
1938	90,304	*	30.00	40.00	55.00	85.00	185.00	325.00

Royal Visit Commemorative 1939

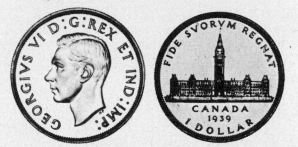

In 1939 a special reverse was used on the dollar to mark the visit of George VI and Queen
Elizabeth to Canada. The design shows the center block of the Parliament buildings in Ottawa. Above is the Latin phrase FIDE SUORUM REGNAT, meaning "He reigns by the faith of his
people." The designer was Emanuel Hahn; his initials EH flanked the building on the original model, but were removed by government decision prior to the manufacture of the dies.
Because of lack of demand, about 150,000 specimens were returned to the Mint and melted
in 1940.

The obverse design and physical specifications are as for the 1937-38 issues.

| 1939 .... | 1,363,816 | * | 10.00 | 12.50 | 15.00 | 17.50 | 25.00 | 35.00 |

Voyageur Reverse Resumed 1945-1948

During 1945-48 two major obverse varieties appeared on this and all lower denominations. The first has the usual legend containing ET IND: IMP: ("and Emperor of India") and the second has that phrase deleted (see text on the 1 cent for more details).

The reverse design and physical specifications are as on the 1937-38 issues.

1947 varieties. The 1947 issue of the dollar has two styles of 7 which differ mainly in the lower tip of the 7 in the date. The 1947 maple leaf coins of 1948 (see the 1 cent text) have only one of these 7's.

	Pointed 7		Blunt 7		Maple leaf —(blunt 7 only)			
Date	Qty. Minted	VG-8	F-12	VF-20	EF-40	AU-50	BU-60	CH-63
ET IND : IMP : Obverse (1945-1947)								
1945	38,391	*	$80.00	$125.00	$165.00	$240.00	$425.00	$600.00
1946	93,055	*	25.00	40.00	60.00	80.00	190.00	300.00
1947 pointed 7	65,595	*	125.00	175.00	225.00	325.00	725.00	950.00
blunt 7 .... incl. above		*	45.00	70.00	90.00	125.00	240.00	335.00
1947 maple leaf	21,135	*	165.00	210.00	275.00	375.00	575.00	800.00

Modified Obverse Legend 1948-1952

| 1948 .... | 18,780 | | 650.00 | 750.00 | 900.00 | 1,050 | 1,500 | 2,000 |

Newfoundland Commemorative 1949

On 31 December 1949 Newfoundland became a province of the Dominion of Canada. To mark this event a special reverse appeared on the dollar for that year. The *Matthew,* the

ship in which John Cabot is thought to have discovered Newfoundland, is depicted. Below is the Latin phrase FLOREAT TERRA NOVA, "May the new found land flourish." Thomas Shingles was the designer and engraver (T.S. above horizon at right); he engraved the master matrix entirely by hand. The obverse is as the 1948 issue, and the physical specifications remain unchanged.

Date	Qty. Minted	VG-8	F-12	VF-20	EF-40	AU-50	BU-60	CH-63
1949	672,218	*	$15.00	$20.00	$25.00	$30.00	$45.00	$70.00

Voyageur Reverse Resumed 1950-1952

The obverse for the final George VI Voyageurs is as on the 1948-49 issues. There are two noteworthy reverse varieties. The first is the usual "water lines" variety, used for all Voyageurs prior to 1950. The second is the so-called "no water lines" reverse of 1952. On this interesting variety the water lines on both sides of the canoe have been removed and the right-hand tip of the islet re-engraved so that it is both wider and longer than before. There can be no question that the "no water lines" was a deliberate issue; furthermore, unlike the "Arnpriors" (see next page) it was created by the alteration of a matrix — not simply an individual die or dies. For some reason the modification was apparently not acceptable because it was used only during the one year.

"Arnprior" dollars of 1950 and 1955. In 1955 a firm in Arnprior, Ontario ordered and received 2,000 silver dollars for use as Christmas bonuses. It was later discovered that these coins had only 1½ water lines (instead of the normal 3) to the right of the canoe. This difference became popular and was collected separately from the "normal" counterpart. Further study revealed that some dollars of 1950, 1951 and perhaps 1952-53 have a similar water line configuration. Only the 1950 and 1955's are currently included in the major listings. These items are the result of inadvertent overpolishing of individual dies and as such are *not* true die varieties. In fact, for 1950, 1955 and certain other years there is a whole gamut of water line differences, ranging from 3 full lines to parts of all 3 to 1½. Collectors and cataloguers have tended to deem all partial water lines greater than 1½ as normal. Whether items like this have any place in a more general catalogue is very questionable; they are included here only because of their current popularity. For further comments on such issues, see page 13.

Physical specifications are as on the previous issues.

| 3 water lines, small islet tip (normal 1935-1952) | 1½ water lines 1950 | No water lines 1952 |

Date	Qty. Minted	VG-8	F-12	VF-20	EF-40	AU-50	BU-60	CH-63
"Water Lines" Reverse (1950-1952)								
1950 normal water lines	261,002	*	$12.00	$15.00	$18.00	$22.50	$35.00	$50.00
1½ lines "Arnprior"	incl. above	*	25.00	30.00	40.00	60.00	100.00	150.00
1951 normal water lines	416,395	*	12.50	14.00	15.00	20.00	25.00	37.50
1½ lines "Arnprior"	incl. above	*	30.00	40.00	65.00	100.00	165.00	275.00
1952	406,148	*	12.00	14.00	18.00	20.00	25.00	37.50
"No Water Lines" Reverse (1952)								
1952	incl. above	*	14.00	18.00	20.00	30.00	35.00	55.00

Elizabeth II, Laureate Bust 1953-1964

Diameter 1953 narrow rim: 36.00 mm; 1953 wide rim - 1964: 36.07 mm; weight: 23.327 grams; composition: .800 silver, .200 copper; edge: reeded.

VF: *Leaves considerably worn, shoulder fold must show.*
EF: *Laurel leaves on head somewhat worn.*
AU: *Trace of wear on laurel leaves.*

The first obverse for 1953 had a high relief, laureate portrait of the Queen by Mrs. Mary Gillick (M.G. on truncation) which did not strike up well on the coins. Later in the year the rim width and coin diameter were increased, the relief lowered and the hair and shoulder detail re-engraved. The latter included sharpening two lines which represented a fold in the Queen's gown. The two varieties also differ in position of the legend relative to rim denticles and the styles of some letters.

The reverse used with the "no shoulder fold" obverse on 1953 was the "water lines" George VI variety. It has a very narrow rim and the triangular islet tip extending to the canoe's right ends about halfway to the rim denticles. Together with the obverse change came a slightly modified reverse, the most distinctive of which are a wider rim and a right-hand islet tip that extends almost to the rim denticles.

1955 Arnprior. See previous page.

1957 1 water line. This item had the same cause as the "Arnpriors" (see above and is therefore not a true die variety.

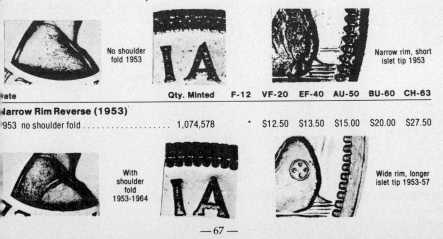

Date	Qty. Minted	F-12	VF-20	EF-40	AU-50	BU-60	CH-63
Narrow Rim Reverse (1953)							
1953 no shoulder fold	1,074,578	*	$12.50	$13.50	$15.00	$20.00	$27.50

No shoulder fold 1953

Narrow rim, short islet tip 1953

With shoulder fold 1953-1964

Wide rim, longer islet tip 1953-57

Wide Rim Reverse (1953-1957)

Date	Qty. Minted	F-12	VF-20	EF-40	AU-50	BU-60	CH-63
1953 with shoulder fold	incl. above	*	$12.50	$13.50	$15.00	$18.00	$22.50
1954	246,606	*	15.00	18.00	20.00	25.00	35.00
1955 normal water lines	268,105	*	15.00	18.00	20.00	25.00	35.00
"Arnprior"	incl. above	*	125.00	150.00	190.00	225.00	300.00
1956	209,092	*	18.00	22.00	25.00	37.00	55.00
1957 normal water lines	496,389	*	12.50	13.50	15.00	18.00	25.00
one water line	incl. above	*	15.00	20.00	25.00	30.00	45.00

"Arnprior" water lines (overpolished die) 1955

1 water line (overpolished die) 1957

British Columbia Commemorative 1958

To commemorate the gold rush centenary and establishment of British Columbia as an English Crown colony, a special reverse by Stephen Trenka (ST at right bottom of totem) was employed. British Columbia is the only area in Canada where the Indians constructed totem poles, so the design is very appropriate. It was rumored that the issue was unpopular with the coastal Indians because it contained an element which to them signified death. The physical specifications remained unchanged.

Date	Qty. Minted	EF-40	AU-50	BU-60	CH-63
1958	3,039,630	*	$15.00	$16.50	$20.00

Voyageur Reverse Resumed 1959-1963

There are two major varieties of the Voyageur reverse during this period. The first is the wide rim design, introduced in late 1953. The second has re-engraved water lines and northern lights.

Date	Qty. Minted	EF-40	AU-50	BU-60	CH-63
Reverse of 1953-1957 (1959)					
1959	1,443,502	*	$12.50	$15.00	$16.00
Recut Water Lines and Northern Lights (1960-1963)					
1960	1,420,486	*	12.50	15.00	16.00
1961	1,262,231	*	12.50	15.00	16.00
1962	1,884,789	*	12.50	15.00	16.00
1963	4,179,981	*	12.50	15.00	16.00

Confederation Meetings Commemorative 1964

To make the 100th anniversary of the meetings at Charlottetown, Prince Edward Island and Quebec, P.Q. which paved the way for Confederation, a special reverse was used for the dollar in 1964. The device is a circle within which are the conjoined French fleur-de-lis, Irish shamrock, Scottish thistle and English rose. Although Dinko Vodanovic was the designer, the Royal Canadian Mint's chief engraver, Thomas Shingles, actually prepared the model based on Vodanovic's sketch. The initials of both men (D.V. and T.S.) appear along the inner circle.

The obverse of this issue has a re-engraved portrait. It is by Myron Cook, modifying Shingles' alteration of the original Gillick design. The new features consist mostly of sharpened gown details. Physical specifications remained unchanged.

1964	7,296,832	*	12.50	15.00	16.00

Elizabeth II, Tiara Obverse, 1965-

In 1965 a new obverse portrait by Arnold Machin was introduced. The Queen has more mature features and is wearing a tiara. Three obverse varieties exist for 1965. The first has a flat field and small rim beads, and was replaced because of unacceptable die life. The second variety has a slightly concave field, medium sized rim beads and slight changes in the portrait. Most distinctive is a very thin support to the rearmost jewel. This variety was struck from a single "test die," made to determine whether a concave field would give better die life. The experiment was successful and a new matrix, punches and dies were prepared. Coins from these dies have the concave field and rim beads even larger than on the "test" variety. In addition, the medium and large beads varieties differ in the positioning of the legend relative to the rim beads.

The 1965-66 reverse is very similar but not identical to earlier Voyageurs. Physical specifications remain unchanged.

1965 date and combinational varieties. Coupled with the small and large beads obverses were two reverses, having trivially different 5's in the dates. The medium beads obverse is coupled with only one of the 5's.

Small beads   Medium beads   Large beads
Details of NA in REGINA; note bead size and position
relative to apex of A.

Pointed 5   Blunt 5

Detail of rear jewel in tiara

Small and large   Medium bead
bead obverse   obverse

Date		Variety	Qty. Minted	AU-50	BU-60	CH-63
1965	small beads, pointed 5	var. 1	10,768,569	*	$14.00	$16.00
	small beads, blunt 5	var. 2	incl. above	*	14.00	16.00
	med. beads, pointed 5	var. 5	incl. above	*	22.00	25.00
	large beads, pointed 5	var. 4	incl. above	*	14.00	16.00
	large beads, blunt 5	var. 3	incl. above	*	14.00	16.00
1966	large beads obverse		9,912,178	*	14.00	16.00
	small beads obverse		incl. above	*	1,750	2.000

Confederation Centennial 1967

All denominations for 1967 bore Confederation commemorative reverses designed by Alex Colville. During 1966, trial production runs were made with dies of the new designs. Those for the dollar had flat fields; the coins did not strike up well, so new dies with convex fields (giving concave or dished fields to the coins) were prepared. Almost all of the flat fields dollars were apparently melted. Apart from the fields, the initial designs can be distinguished from the adopted ones by the position of the legends relative to the rim beads.

| Flat fields | Concave fields |

Note size and spacing of beads.

Date	Qty. Minted	AU-50	BU-60	CH-63
1967 flat fields*	6,767,496**	—	—	
concave fields	incl. above	*	$16.00	$20.00

*Rarity not yet known.
**Note: 141,741 pieces were melted down in 1967.

Elizabeth II, Nickel Dollars, 1968-

Diameter: 32.13 mm; weight: 15.616 grams; composition: 1.000 nickel; edge: reeded.

With the resumption of the regular reverse design in 1968, two significant changes were made. The diameter and weight were reduced and the composition changed to nickel.

Date	Qty. Minted	CH-63
1968	5,579,714	$1.75
1969	4,809,313	1.75

Manitoba Centennial 1970

This denomination bore a special reverse in 1970 to mark the 100th anniversary of Manitoba's entrance into the Dominion of Canada. Raymond Taylor was the designer (RT to the right of the centre stem); the device depicts the prairie crocus, Manitoba's flower. Physical specifications are as for the 1968-69 issues.

1970	4,140,058	2.00

British Columbia Centennial 1971

In 1971 two different dollars, one in nickel and the other in silver, were struck in honour of the 100th anniversary of British Columbia's becoming part of the Dominion of Canada. The reverse of the nickel piece was designed by Thomas Shingles (TS below shield) and incorporates the Provincial arms and its flower, dogwood. Physical specifications and obverse are as for 1968-70. The .500 silver coin is a special collectors' issue and is listed in a section exclusively for such items (see page 78).

Date	Qty. Minted	CH-63
1971	4,260,781	$2.00

Voyageur Reverse Resumed 1972

1972	2,193,000	2.50

Prince Edward Island Centennial 1973

Prince Edward Island's entry into the Dominion of Canada in 1873 is commemorated in this nickel dollar for 1973. The obverse features Patrick Brindley's modification of the Machin bust of Queen Elizabeth, first used for the collectors' silver dollar in 1971. Walter Ott (wo at right) working from a sketch by Terry Manning (TM at left), modelled the reverse which shows the P.E.I. Provincial Legislature building.

1973 P.E.I. Commemorative	3,196,452	2.50

Winnipeg Centennial 1974

This nickel dollar for 1974 marks the centenary of the city of Winnipeg Manitoba. The obverse is the same as the 1973 dollar. Based on a sketch by Paul Pederson (PP at bottom). Patrick Brindley (B at top) modelled the reverse. It features a large "100" with an 1874 scene of Winnipeg's Main Street in the first "0" and a corresponding modern scene in 1974 in the second "0"). Size: 32 mm. (See page 79 for a slightly larger .500 silver special collectors' dollar depicting this same design.)

Date	Qty. Minted	CH-63
1974 Winnipeg commemorative (nickel)	2,799,363	$3.00

Voyageur Reverse Resumed 1975-1976

1975	3,685,615	2.00
1976	3,256,000	2.75

Modified Reverse 1977

The device for the 1977 reverse was reduced in size as was the legend. The legend is farther from the rim of the coin and the rim denticles were replaced with beads.

1977	1,393,745	3.00

Modified Obverse and Reverse 1978

In 1978 both sides of the nickel dollar were modified to appear more like the issues prior to 1977. The unmodified Machin portrait was restored to the obverse and the reverse returned to the pre-1977 voyageur design, with rim denticles. The northern lights were depicted as raised lines.

Date	Qty. Minted	CH-63
1978	2,948,488	$2.00
1979	2,954,842	2.00
1980	3,291,221	2.00
1981	2,778,900	2.00
1982	3,391,624	2.00

Constitution 1982

To commemorate the new Canadian Constitution almost twelve million pure nickel dollars were struck. The reverse features the well-known painting of the Fathers of Confederation.

1982 Constitution	11,812,000	2.00
1982 Constitution in deluxe case	107,353	10.00

Voyageur Reverse Resumed 1983

1983	2,720,210	2.00

Jacques Cartier Commemorative 1984

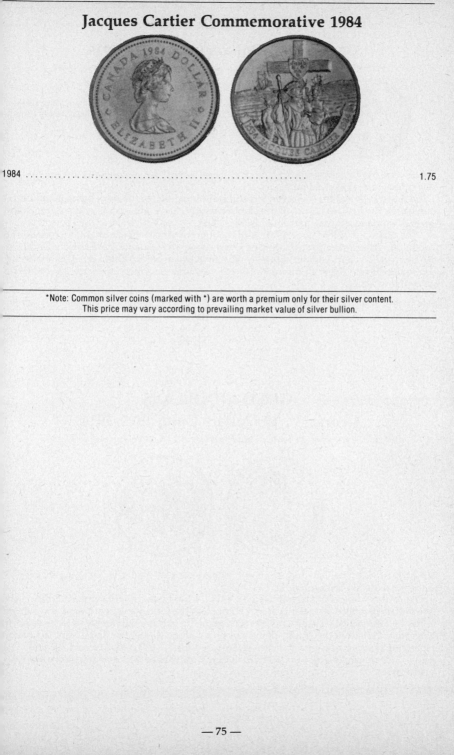

1984 . . . . : 1.75

---

*Note: Common silver coins (marked with *) are worth a premium only for their silver content. This price may vary according to prevailing market value of silver bullion.

GOLD 5 DOLLARS
George V, 5 Dollars Gold, 1912-1914

Diameter: 21.59 mm; weight: 8.359 grams; composition: .900 gold, .100 copper; edge: reeded.

VF: *Band of crown is still clear, but no longer sharp*
EF: *Band of crown slightly worn but generally sharp and clear*
AU: *Trace of wear on band of crown*

The obverse of this brief series was derived from the portrait model of the King by Sir E.B. MacKennal (B.M. on truncation).

The design selected for the reverse is still considered one of the most beautiful on Canadian coins. The device consists of the shield from the Canadian coat of arms as granted by Queen Victoria in a Royal Warrant of 26 May 1868, behind which are crossed boughs of maple. The quartered shield has the arms of the four provinces which originally formed the Dominion. These arms are: St. George's Cross above, three maple leaves below (Ontario); two fleurs-de-lis above, lion in centre, three maple leaves below (Quebec); a lion above, ancient galley below (New Brunswick); two thistles above, salmon in centre, single thistle below (Nova Scotia).

Date	Qty. Minted	VF-20	EF-40	AU-50	BU-60	CH-63
1912	154,745	$225.00	$275.00	$350.00	$500.00	$725.00
1913	93,791	225.00	275.00	350.00	550.00	775.00
1914	29,078	675.00	850.00	1,000	1,350	2,000

GOLD 10 DOLLARS
George V, 10 Dollars Gold, 1912-1914

Diameter: 26.92 mm; weight: 16.718 grams; composition: .900 gold, .100 copper; edge: reeded.

The obverse was derived from the well known portrait model of the King by Sir E.B. MacKennal (B.M. on truncation).

The reverse, designed and engraved by W.H.J. Blakemore, is very similar to that on the five dollars described above. It is worth noting that the Canadian government also wanted to have additional gold denominations for George V. This is evidenced by a letter dated 10 November 1910 from the Master of the Royal Canadian Mint to the Royal Mint in London requesting that matrices and punches be prepared for "... $20 gold, $10 gold, $5 gold, $2½ gold ..." Obviously, plans were altered and only the $5 and $10 denominations were actually issued.

1912	70,752	625.00	725.00	825.00	1,150	1,700
1913	141,994	650.00	775.00	875.00	1,250	1,850
1914	135,292	750.00	925.00	1,125	1,400	2,050

OTTAWA MINT GOLD SOVEREIGNS

Like other branches of the Royal Mint, the Ottawa Mint was authorized to strike gold sovereigns, and did so during the period 1908-19. The designs and physical specifications were identical to those of the corresponding English issues, except for the presence of the C mint mark for Canada just above the date on the Ottawa strikings. Sovereigns struck in London had no mint mark while pieces with mint marks I, M, P, S and SA were from mints in India, Australia and South Africa.

During the First World WAr, these coins were used to help pay for war materials that England purchased from the United States. England was thus saved the risk of sending London-minted gold across the Atlantic.

Such "branch mint" sovereigns are generally considered to form part of the coinage of the country in which they were struck, and so are included here.

Edward VII Sovereigns, 1908-1910

Diameter: 22.05 mm; weight: 7.988 grams; composition: .917 gold, .083 copper; edge: reeded.

Position of C mint mark
for Ottawa Mint

The obverse was derived from a portrait model by G.W. De Saulles (DES below neck) and the reverse is a slight modification of the original 1816 St. George and the dragon design by Benedetto Pistrucci (B.P. at lower right).

Date	Qty. Minted	VF-20	EF-40	AU-50	BU-60	CH-63
1908C*	636	$2,000	$2,750	$3,800	$5,000	$7,000
1909C	16,273	450.00	550.00	650.00	1,300	2,000
1910C	28,012	425.00	525.00	600.00	1,300	2,000

*Originally struck in specimen only; however, some circulated.

George V, Sovereigns, 1911-1919

Diameter: 22.05 mm; weight: 7.988 grams; composition: .917 gold, .083 copper; edge: reeded.

VF: *Wear on the head spreads nearer the ear and slight wear develops on the beard*
EF: *Hair over the ear is only slightly worn. Beard is still sharp.*

The obverse was derived from a portrait model by Sir E.B. MacKennal (B.M. on truncation) and the reverse is as on the Edward VII issues.

1916C. Despite the reported mintage of over 6,000, specimens of this date are rare, with only about 10 known today. Most were probably melted, as undoubtedly happened with the 1917 London issues and some Australian issues.

Date	Qty. Minted	VF-20	EF-40	AU-50	BU-60	CH-63
1911C	256,946	175.00	190.00	215.00	250.00	350.00
1913C	3,715	725.00	1,050	1,350	1,750	2,500
1914C	14,891	400.00	500.00	700.00	1,100	1,600
1916C	6,111	20,000	30,000	35,000	40,000	50,000
1917C	58,845	175.00	200.00	225.0C	275.00	375.00
1918C	105,516	175.00	200.00	225.00	275.00	375.00
1919C	135,889	175.00	200.00	225.00	275.00	375.00

3
CANADIAN COLLECTORS' ISSUES

In recent years the Royal Canadian Mint has struck a group of special issues that have no counterpart in regular circulation strikes. The first of these was the 1967 $20 gold, followed by a 1971 silver dollar. Most noteworthy is the extensive series of $5 and $10 Olympic silver pieces and the Companion $100 gold. All of these are specifically intended for distribution to collectors, and not for use in normal everyday commerce. These special collector's issues are generally of "specimen" quality (double struck and prepared from special planchets and dies) but many are also available in "proof" condition.

In addition to these popular collector's issues, the Mint has a long history of producing sets of coins which are usually offered to the public in special packaging. Quality of these sets ranges from "uncirculated" to "proof".

CASED .500 FINE SILVER DOLLARS

Diameter: 36.01 mm; weight: 23.33 grams; composition: .500 silver, .500 copper; edge: reeded.

Beginning in 1971, the Mint began to once again offer collectors silver dollars (.500 fine). Quality was "Specimen," although the Mint began also to offer "Proof" dollars beginning in 1981. All of these coins have been issued in special black leather cases. Beginning in 1974 the cased silver dollars have been enclosed in clear plastic capsules for protection.

British Columbia Centennial 1971

In addition to the small British Columbia commemorative dollar a .500 fine silver dollar, of the same size and weight as the pre-1968 dollars, was struck for collectors. Its reverse was adapted from the arms of the Province and was designed and engraved by Patrick Brindley. The coin also features a new obverse, which is a modification of the original Machin design.

Date	Issue Price	Qty. Minted	Specimen
1971 silver.............................	$3.00	585,674	$20.00

Voyageur Reverse 1972

The special collectors' .500 silver dollar issues continued in 1972 with a resumption of the Voyageur design, although the reverse is from a new model by Patrick Brindley.

Date	Issue Price	Qty. Minted	Specimen
1972 silver	$3.00	341,598	$28.00

Royal Canadian Mounted Police Centennial 1973

In addition to the 25¢ circulation pieces, a special collectors' .500 silver RCMP commemorative dollar was struck in 1973. The reverse design was modelled and engraved by Paul Cedarberg.

Date	Issue Price	Qty. Minted	Specimen
1973 silver	$3.00	1,031,271	$15.00

Winnipeg Centennial 1974

The obverse and reverse designs of this .500 fine silver commemorative are the same as the 1974 dollar struck in nickel (see page 73) except that the diameter was increased to 36 mm.

Date	Issue Price	Qty. Minted	Specimen
1974 silver	$3.50	728,947	$13.50

Calgary Centennial 1975

The 100th anniversary of the founding of the city of Calgary, Alberta was commemorated by this issue. Donald D. Paterson designed the reverse depicting a rider on a bucking horse, with oil wells and city skyline in the background.

Date	Issue Price	Qty. Minted	Specimen
1975 silver	$3.50	930,956	$14.00

Library of Parliament Centennial 1976

The 100th anniversary of the completion of the Library of Parliament building was commemorated by this issue. The reverse was modelled principally by Walter Ott. The obverse motif for this, as well as all preceding silver dollar commemoratives in this section, remained unchanged.

Date	Issue Price	Qty. Minted	Specimen
1976 silver........	$4.00	578,708	$20.00

Queen Elizabeth II Silver Jubilee 1977

The silver dollar issue for 1977 commemorates the 25th anniversary of Queen Elizabeth's accession to the throne. The reverse design by Raymond Lee depicts the throne of the Senate of Canda used for ceremonial events.

Date	Issue Price	Qty. Minted	Specimen
1977 silver........	$4.25	742,332	$16.00

11th Commonwealth Games 1978

The 11th Commonwealth Games, held in Edmonton, Alberta, August 3-12, were commemorated by this dollar issue. Featured on the reverse, designed by Raymond Taylor, are the Games' symbol and the symbols of the ten games involved.

Date	Issue Price	Qty. Minted	Specimen
1978 silver........	$4.50	787,000	$15.00

Griffon Commemorative 1979

Recognition of the first voyage of the Great Lakes by a commercial ship was the intent of this commemorative issue. The reverse, depicting the Griffon, was designed by Walter Schluep.

Date	Issue Price	Qty. Minted	Specimen
1979 silver........	$5.50	826,695	$24.00

Arctic Territories 1980

This issue commemorated the centenary of the transfer of the Arctic Islands to the government of the Dominion of Canada by the British government. The reverse features a polar bear and was designed by Donald D. Paterson.

Date	Issue Price	Qty. Minted	Specimen
1980 silver	$22.00	552,439	$32.00

Trans-Canada Railway 1981

The 100th anniversary of the construction of the Trans-Canada Railway is commemorated by this issue. The reverse was designed by Christopher Gorey and depicts a steam locomotive and a map of Canada in the background.

Date	Issue Price	Qty. Minted	Value
1981 Uncirculated .	$14.00	695,400	$19.00
1981 Proof	18.00	incl. above	60.00

Founding of Regina 1982

The 100th anniversary of the founding of Regina was commemorated by this issue. The reverse was designed by Huntley Brown.

Sate	Issue Price	Qty. Minted	Value
1982 Uncirculated .		903,888	$15.00
1982 Proof		incl. above	23.00

World University Games, Edmonton 1983

This issue commemorated the World University Games held in Edmonton in July, 1983. The reverse was designed by Carola Tietz.

Date	Issue Price	Qty. Minted	Value
1983 Uncirculated .	$10.85	667,784	$15.00
1983 Proof	16.15	incl. above	23.00

Toronto Sesquicentennial 1984

The 150th anniversary of the incorporation of the City of
Toronto is commemorated by this issue. The reverse
design by David Craig depicts a voyageur with the City of
Toronto skyline in the background.

Date	Issue Price	Qty. Minted	Value
1984 Uncirculated		—	$15.00
1984 Proof...............		—	23.00

GOLD 20 DOLLARS

Diameter: 27.05 mm; weight: 18.274 g; composition: .900 gold, .100 copper; edge: reeded.

Elizabeth II, Confederation Centennial 1967

This denomination was struck only for the special proof sets of Confederation Centennial coins, which were originally sold in a black leather box to the public for $40. It is the only coin of the set that does not have the commemorative dates "1867-1967." The obverse is Arnold Machin's design, introduced on regular denominations in 1965, and the reverse is an adaption of the Canadian coat of arms by Myron Cook, using Thomas Shingles' model for the 50 cents type of 1959.

Date	Qty. Minted	Specimen
1967 Confederation commemorative	337,512	$280.00

GOLD 100 DOLLARS

Olympic Commemorative 1976

Specimen (with beads): diameter: 27.00 mm; weight: 13.338 g; composition: .583 gold, .417 copper alloy; edge: reeded.
Proof (without beads): diameter: 25.00 mm; weight: 16.966 g; composition: .917 gold, .083 copper alloy; edge: reeded.

Two separate $100 gold coins were issued in 1976 to commemorate the XXI Olympiad. The arnold Machin obverse is similar to that of the $5 and $10 dollar olympic issues. The reverse device shows an athlete of ancient Greece being crowned with a laurel wreath. The uncirculated edition was struck in 14 k gold and has beads around the perimeter of both sides. The 22 k version of the coin was struck in proof only and has no beads. The proof issue is smaller than the uncirculated issue.

Date	Issue Price	Qty. Minted	Value
1976 Olympic, Unc. 14k, with beads.................................	$105.00	650,000	$150.00
1976 Olympic, Proof 22k, without beads.............................	150.00	350.000	285.00

Elizabeth II, Silver Jubilee Commemorative 1977

Diameter: 27.00 mm; weight: 16.965 g; composition: .917 gold, .083 silver; edge: reeded.

The obverse design is by Arnold Machin. The reverse, a bouquet of the official flowers of the provinces and territories, is by Ramond Lee.

Date	Issue Price	Qty. Minted	Specimen
1977 Silver Jubilee	$140.00	180,396	$375.00

Canadian Unity 1978

The obverse again is by Arnold Machin. The reverse, 12 Canada Geese flying in formation, is by Roger Savage and represents the unity of the 10 provinces and 2 territories of Canada.

Date	Issue Price	Qty. Minted	Specimen
1978 Unity	$150.00	200,000	$275.00

International Year of the Child 1979

The 1979 $100 proof commemorates the International Year of the Child with a reverse motif of playing children beside a globe. The reverse design is by Carala Tietz, the obverse by Arnold Machin.

Date	Issue Price	Qty. Minted	Specimen
1979 Year of the Child	$185.00	250,000	$275.00

Arctic Territories Commemorative 1980

The obverse again is by Arnold Machin. The reverse design by Arnoldo Marchetti bears no legend and depicts an Inuit in a kayak with an iceberg nearby. The issue commemorated the centenary of the transfer of the Arctic islands from Britain to Canada.

Date	Issue Price	Qty. Minted	Specimen
1980 Arctic Territories	$430.00	130,000	$320.00

"O Canada" Commemorative 1981

This proof issue commemorates the adoption of "O Canada" as the Canadian national anthem on July 1, 1980. The reverse design is by Roger Savage and the obverse by Arnold Machin.

Date	Issue Price	Qty. Minted	Specimen
1981 "O Canada"	$300.00	100,950	$350.00

Canadian Constitution 1982

This issue commemorates the patriation of the Canadian Constitution. Obverse by Arnold Machin. The reverse, depicting an
open book with the coat of arms of Canada and a maple leaf is by
Friedrich Peter.

Date	Issue Price	Qty. Minted	Specimen
1982 Constitution	$285.00	121,706	$335.00

St. John's Newfoundland 1983

The 400th anniversary of Sir Humphrey Gilbert's landing in
Newfoundland is commemorated by this issue. The obverse is by
Arnold Machin with a reverse designed by John Jaciw.

Date	Issue Price	Qty. Minted	Specimen
1983 St. John's Nfld.	$310.00	83,200	$325.00

Jacques Cartier Commemorative 1984

Date	Issue Price	Qty. Minted	Specimen
1984 Jacques Cartier		—	$325.00

PROOF-LIKE MINT SETS AND DOLLARS

In 1949 the Royal Canadian Mint's numismatic section was established. Prior to this date, the Ottawa branch of the Bank of Canada looked after orders for Uncirculated coin sets at face value plus postage. During the period 1949 to 1953, it was possible to obtain mint sets of the current year and sometimes those of previous years as well. These coins initially came in cellophane envelopes and later in a white punched card wrapped in cellophane. Prices charged for these sets were the face value of the coins, plus the cost of packaging and postage. The coins in these sets were almost all *regular production strikes* of the same quality as those placed in bags and sent out for general use. However a *few* of the sets and dollars for at least the period 1951-1953 had a markedly superior finish but these were not of specimen quality. This could be due to a minimum of handling and possibly some careful selection but complete sets of this superior quality are rare. In 1954 dealer J.E. Charlton introduced the term "proof-like" to describe one such 1953 set. These special coins represented the modest beginning of the Mint's attempts to produce higher quality strikings in quantity for collectors.

Beginning in 1954, all sets and dollars sold to collectors by the mint have been the specially prepared "proof-like" coins. The term is used because these coins are most like proofs in terms of their mirror-like finish and lack of handling abrasions. Selected dies and planchets are used and the coins are struck on slow-moving presses. The operators wear clean gloves and the coins are carefully checked before packaging. It should be noted that "proof-like" is not an official term. The mint calls these coins "uncirculated" but they have become universally known as "proof-like". Their quality has generally been good although in 1965 and again in 1968-69 difficulties in producing a good surface on the coins was encountered.

The packaging for the sets changed from cardboard in cellophane to a sealed pliofilm pouch beginning in 1961. Each pliofilm pouch has ROYAL CANADIAN MINT impressed into the dividing areas. Issue prices for "Proof-like" sets were as follows: 1953 - $2.20; 1954 to 1959 - $2.50; 1960 to 1964 - $3.00; 1965 to 1973 - $4.00; 1974 and 1975 $ 5.00; 1976 to 1978 - $5.25; 1979 - $6.25; 1980 - $8.00.

In most years it has been possible to order dollars separately, although they were not officially issued in the following years: 1953, 1965, 1966, and 1967. "Proof-like" dollars for these years can be found but these have been removed from the full mint sets by collectors. From 1970 to 1976 "proof-like" dollars were issued in special cases and in "proof-like" sets but beginning in 1977 this practice was discontinued and they are now available only in "proof-like" sets.

PROOF-LIKE SETS

Date	Qty. Minted	Value
1953 Shoulder Fold	*	$1,200
1954 No Shoulder Fold 1¢	7,426**	675.00
1954 Shoulder Fold 1¢	incl. above	500.00
1955	6,301**	425.00
1955 Arnprior	incl. above	550.00
1956	9,018**	175.00
1957	11,862**	100.00
1958	18,259	85.00
1959	31,577	40.00
1960	64,097	30.00
1961	98,373	30.00
1962	200,950	24.00
1963	673,006	24.00
1964	1,653,162	24.00
1965 Pointed 5 dollar	2,904,352	24.00
1965 Blunt 5 dollar	incl. above	24.00
1966	672,514	24.00
1967	963,714	26.00
1968	521,641	3.50
1969	326,203	3.50
1970	349,120	7.50
1971	253,311	6.00
1972	224,275	5.50
1973 Small bust 25¢	243,695	6.00
1973 Large bust 25¢	incl. above	250.00
1974	213,589	6.00
1975	197,372	5.50
1976	171,737	8.50
1977	225,307	8.00
1978	260,000	6.00
1979	187,624	10.00
1980	169,390	22.50

PROOF-LIKE DOLLARS

Date	Qty. Minted	Value
1949	*	$90.00
1950	*	250.00
1951	*	250.00
1952 No Water Lines	*	250.00
1953 Shoulder Fold	*	600.00
1954	1,268**	240.00
1955	5,501**	200.00
1955 Arnprior	incl. above	400.00
1956	6,154**	110.00
1957	4,379**	45.00
1958	14,978	45.00
1959	13,583	25.00
1960	18,631	20.00
1961	22,555	18.00
1962	47,591	18.00
1963	290,529	17.00
1964	1,209,279	17.00
1965 Pointed 5	—	17.00
1965 Blunt 5	—	17.00
1966	—	17.00
1967	—	22.00
1968	885,124	2.00
1969	211,112	2.00
1970	297,547	3.00
1971	181,091	3.00
1972	143,392	2.75
1973	174,810	2.75
1974	105,901	3.00
1975	88,102	2.75
1976	74,207	3.50
1977	—	3.50
1978	—	3.50
1979	—	3.50
1980	—	6.00

* Unknown
** Estimated
NOTE: Nickel dollars from 1970 to 1976 were cased individually and in "prooflike" sets. After 1976, all "prooflike" dollars have been only available in "prooflike" (uncirculated) sets.

UNCIRCULATED SETS 1981-

Beginning in 1981, the Royal Canadian Mint made the decision to offer collectors 3 coin sets of proof, specimen and uncirculated quality. The "uncirculated" coin sets would replace the pliofilm-packaged "proof-like" sets. Similarly sealed in pliofilm, the "uncirculated" sets would be made up of the finest quality circulating coins available.

UNCIRCULATED SETS

Date	Qty. Minted	Value
1981	186,250	12.00
1982	203,287	8.50
1983	191,000	8.50
1984		8.50

UNCIRCULATED DOLLARS

Date	Qty. Minted	Value
1981	—	5.00
1982	—	5.00
1983	—	5.00
1984	—	5.00

SPECIMEN & PROOF SETS

From the early days of the 19th century, mints around the world have struck small quantities of coins in superior quality for presentation to visiting dignitaries, etc. In some years these "specimen" sets were made available to the general public to add to their collections. These coins are from immaculately treated dies and planchets and are struck on slow-moving presses under higher than normal pressure. The coins so produced all have unusually sharp details and sharp edges. Although the device is usually frosted, the fields can be either frosted or mirror-like. Specimen coins from the 1858 Province of Canada and the 1870 Dominion of Canada issues were made available to collectors. Since its inception in 1908, the Royal Canadian Mint, Ottawa has produced in most years a small number of specimen sets, although sets were offered for sale to the public only in the years 1908, 1911 and 1937. The appearance of some specimen pieces of Canadian coins has rivalled that of coins produced as "proof" in the United States, however, the Royal Canadian Mint has never considered them to be of the superlative quality of Royal Mint (London) proofs. Thus Canada's strikings prior to 1980 have been officially designated *specimen coins*. Beginning in 1981, the Royal Canadian Mint began offering Proof quality coins as well as Specimen sets.

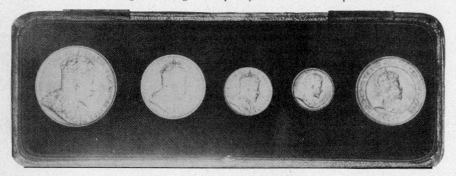

Specimen Sets, 1858-1965

Date	Description	Case	Value
1858	Victoria 1¢, 5¢ (small date), 10¢, 20¢	None	$7,000
1858	Victoria 1¢, 5¢ (large date), 10¢, 20¢	None	8,000
1858	Victoria Double Set - 2 each 1¢, 5¢ (small date), 10¢, 20¢	Leather	15,000
1870	Victoria 5¢, 10¢, 25¢, 50¢	None	15,000
1870	Victoria Double Set - 2 each 5¢, 10¢, 25¢, 50¢	Leather	32,500
1902	Edward VII 1¢, 5¢, 10¢, 25¢, 50¢	None	8,500
1908	Edward VII 1¢, 5¢, 10¢, 25¢, 50¢	Leather	2,800
1911	George V 1¢, 5¢, 10¢, 25¢, 50¢	Leather	8,000
1911-1912	George V 1¢, 5¢, 10¢, 25¢, 50¢, £1, $5, $10	Leather	35,000
1921	George V 1¢, 5¢, 10¢, 25¢, 50¢	None	110,000
1929	George V 1¢, 5¢, 10¢, 25¢, 50¢	None	18,000
1930	George V 1¢, 5¢, 10¢, 25¢	None	5,000
1934	George V 1¢, 5¢, 10¢, 25¢, 50¢	None	11,000
1936	George V 1¢, 5¢, 10¢, 25¢, 50¢	None	10,500
1937	George VI 1¢, 5¢, 10¢, 25¢, 50¢, $1.00 (mirror finish)	Leather	1,600
1937	George VI 1¢, 5¢, 10¢, 25¢, 50¢, $1.00 (mirror finish)	Cardboard	1,500
1937	George VI 1¢, 5¢, 10¢, 25¢, 50¢, $1.00 (matte finish)	Cardboard	1,000
1937	George VI 1¢, 5¢, 10¢, 25¢ (mirror finish)	Leather	750.00
1938	George VI 1¢, 5¢, 10¢, 25¢, 50¢, $1.00	Leather	20,000
1944	George VI 1¢, 5¢, 10¢, 25¢, 50¢	None	15,000
1945	George VI 1¢, 5¢, 10¢, 25¢, 50¢, $1.00	Leather	6,500
1946	George VI 1¢, 5¢, 10¢, 25¢, 50¢, $1.00	Leather	7,000
1947	George VI 1¢, 5¢, 10¢, 25¢, 50¢, $1.00	Leather	10,000
1947ML	George VI 1¢, 5¢, 10¢, 25¢, 50¢, $1.00 (50¢ curved right)	Leather	12,000

Date	Description	Case	Value
1947ML	George VI 1¢, 5¢, 10¢, 25¢, 50¢, $1.00 (50¢ curved left)	Leather	7,000
1948	George VI 1¢, 5¢, 10¢, 25¢, 50¢, $1.00	Leather	9,500
1949	George VI 1¢, 5¢, 10¢, 25¢, 50¢, $1.00	Leather	3,500
1950	George VI 1¢, 5¢, 10¢, 25¢, 50¢, $1.00	Leather	3,250
1951	George VI 1¢, 5¢ (both types), 10¢, 25¢, 50¢, $1.00	None	3,250
1952	George VI 1¢, 5¢, 10¢, 25¢, 50¢, $1.00 (no water lines)	Leather	3,500
1952	George VI 1¢, 5¢, 10¢, 25¢, 50¢, $1.00 (water lines)	Leather	3,500
1953	Elizabeth II 1¢, 5¢, 10¢, 25¢, 50¢, $1.00 (no shoulder fold)	Leather	1,600
1953	Elizabeth II 1¢, 5¢, 10¢, 25¢, 50¢, $1.00 (shoulder fold)	Leather	1,800
1964	Elizabeth II 1¢, 5¢, 10¢, 25¢, 50¢, $1.00	Leather	600.00
1965	Elizabeth II 1¢, 5¢, 10¢, 25¢, 50¢, $1.00	Leather	600.00

1967 Centennial Presentation Set

Two special cased coin sets were produced by the Mint to commemorate the 100th anniversary of Canada's Confederation. The Gold Presentation Set, containing 1¢ to $1 and a $10 gold coin, was sold to the public for $40.00. The coins were contained in a black leather box and were of specimen quality. In addition to the Gold Presentation set, a special Silver Medallion set was offered in a red presentation case containing the 1¢ to $1 plus a sterling silver medallion designed by Thomas Shingles. The coins were all of proof-like quality.

	Qty. Minted	Value
1967 1¢ to $1.00 plus $30.00 gold (Specimen quality)	337,688	$300.00
1967 1¢ to $1.00 plus silver medal (Proof-like quality)	Unknown	40.00

V.I.P. Specimen Presentation Sets, 1969-1976

A very limited number of cased Specimen sets were produced by the Mint beginning in 1969 for presentation to dignitaries visiting the Royal Canadian Mint or other parts of Canada. (A small quantity of 1970 cased Specimen sets were sold to the public for $13.00 each.) The coins, 1¢ to $1.00 were cased in long narrow leather cases (black and other colours).

Date	Qty. Issued	Value	Date	Qty. Issued	Value
1969	2 known	$2,250	1973	26	$575.00
1970	100	650.00	1974	72	500.00
1971	69	500.00	1975	94	500.00
1972	25	575.00	1976	Unknown	500.00

Note: Sets may have been issued in 1977, 1978, 1979 and 1980 (information unavailable).

Custom and Prestige Sets, 1971-1980

Beginning in 1971, the Mint began a program offering 3 coin sets to the public. In addition to the popular "Proof-like" sets which had been issued in a sealed pliofilm pack since 1961, the Mint now offered Custom and Prestige sets.

Custom sets were sold in a square, vinyl covered box containing one piece of each denomination 1¢ to $1, with an extra cent to show the obverse. From 1971 to 1976 quality was proof-like but since then it has been specimen.

Prestige sets were sold in rectangular black leather cases containing one piece of each denomination 1¢ to $1 (nickel) plus the silver dollar (1971-1972 extra dollar was nickel). Coin quality was always specimen. From 1974 to 1980 the coins were mounted in a plastic page frame.

DOUBLE CENT "CUSTOM" SET

Date	Issue Price	Qty. Minted	Value
1971	$6.50	33,517	$8.00
1972	6.50	38,198	8.00
1973 25¢ large bust	6.50	49,376	250.00
1973 25¢ small bust		incl. above	8.00
1974	8.00	44,296	8.00
1975	8.15	36,851	9.00
1976	8.15	28,162	13.00
1977	8.15	42,198	16.00
1978	8.75	41,000	10.00
1979	10.75	31,174	13.00
1980	12.50	41,447	17.50

DOUBLE DOLLAR "PRESTIGE" SET

Date	Issue Price	Qty. Minted	Value
1971	$12.00	66,860	$20.00
1972	12.00	36,349	80.00
1973 25¢ large bust	12.00	119,891	275.00
1973 25¢ small bust		incl. above	22.00
1974	15.00	85,230	22.00
1975	15.00	97,263	22.00
1976	16.00	87,744	28.00
1977	16.00	142,577	28.00
1978	16.50	147,000	20.00
1979	18.50	155,698	35.00
1980	36.00	162,875	55.00

Specimen and Proof Sets, 1981-

Beginning in 1981, the Royal Canadian Mint began to offer Specimen Sets and Proof Sets, replacing the Custom and Prestige Sets.

	SPECIMEN SET				PROOF SET		
Date	Issue Price	Qty. Minted	Value	Date	Issue Price	Qty. Minted	Value
1981	$10.00	71,300	$17.00	1981	$36.00	199,000	$60.00
1982	11.50	62,298	16.00	1982	36.00	180,908	50.00
1983		60,500	15.00	1983		168,000	45.00
1984		—	15.00	1984		—	45.00

OLYMPIC COINS 1973-1976

$5 Olympic: Diameter: 38 mm; weight: 24.30 grams; composition: .925 silver, .075 copper alloy; edge: reeded.
$10 Olympic: Diameter: 45 mm; weight: 48.60 grams; composition: .925 silver, .075 copper alloy; edge: reeded.

$5 Obverse $10 Obverse

Following the lead of other Olympic host nations which have honored such occasions with Olympic coinage in the past, Canada undertook without doubt one of the most ambitious single-event numismatic programs to date. The Olympic (1976) Act, passed by Parliament on July 27, 1973 authorizing issuance of collectors' Olympic coins, signaled the beginning, and by December of that year the first four coins were already on sale. Struck by the Royal Canadian Mint at its satellite mint in Hull, Quebec, these coins were intended to play a large part in financing the cost of the XXI Olympiad held in Montreal in 1976.

In total there were 28 different silver issues and two varieties of a $100 gold piece made from 1973 to 1976. Released in seven separate Series, struck in both uncirculated and proof, each silver set was comprised of four coins (two $5 and two $10) depicting distinctive Olympic themes. The 1976 $100 gold was made in uncirculated and proof (see page 83).

The Patrick Brindley modification of Arnold Machin's bust of Queen Elizabeth II was the design application used for all obverse motifs. Details of reverse designs are included with each individual Series listings (starting next page).

Insofar as possible, obverse dates reflected actual years of minting. However, a large number of Series I 1973 coins were produced in 1974 simultaneously with the striking of the 1974 Series II. Thus, an element for possible confusion in the Mint was present. The result was a 10 dollar piece dated 1974 with a 1973 (map) reverse.

A large array of protective and embellishing containers (ranging from clear styrene encapsulators for single coins to plush lined four-coin presentation cases made of Canadian white birch and tanned steerhide) was used as a merchandising vehicle for all the Series. A small fraction of the Series I coins, because of the need to monetize the issues, were also distributed at face value without encasement through banks and other financial institutions within Canada. Various quantities of other nonencapsulated Series have also been released; they are worth slightly less than encapsulated ones.

	Issue Price	Value		Issue Price	Value
$5.00 Uncirculated			**Custom Sets** (two $5.00 and two $10.00 coins)		
Encapsulated Series I	$6.00	$12.50	Series I	45.00	75.00
Encapsulated Series II	7.50	12.50	Series II-VII	55.00	75.00
Encapsulated Series III-VII	8.00	12.50	**Prestige Sets** (two $5.00 and two $10.00 coins)		
$10.00 Uncirculated			Series I	50.00	80.00
Encapsulated SeriesI	12.00	25.00	Series II-VII	60.00	80.00
Encapsulated Series II	15.00	25.00	**Deluxe Proof Sets** (two $5.00 and two $10.00 coins)		
Encapsulated Series III-VII	15.75	25.00	Series I	72.50	90.00
			Series II-VII	82.50	90.00

Series I: Geographic 1973

Release date: December 13, 1973.
Designer: (by invitation) Georges Huel.
Modelers:$5 and $10 Map issues — NONE (designs, photographically etched) Kingston — Terrence Smith; Montreal — Ago Aarand.
$5 Landmarks of Kingston: Host to the yachting events.
$5 Map of North America: Canada highlighted as host nation.
$10 Montreal Skyline: Host city.
$10 Map of World: Canada highlightedaation.

Series II: Olympic Motifs 1974

Release Date: September 16, 1974.
Designer (winner of invitational competition): Anthony Mann.
Modelers: Head of Zeus and Athlete with Torch — Patrick Brindley; Olympic Rings and Temple of Zeus — Walter Ott.
$5 Athlete with Torch: The flaming torch is the symbol of constant rebirth of the Olympics.
$5 Olympic Rings and Wreath: The laurel wreath was used to crown victors in the early games; the five rings now represent the five continents and the friendship of man.
$10 Head of Zeus: The early games were dedicated to Zeus, the mythical father of the ancient Greek gods.
$10 Temple of Zeus: Focal point of the early games.

Series III: Early Canadian Sports 1974

Release date: April 16, 1975.
Designer (winner of invitational competition): Ken Danby.
Modelers: Canoeing — Patrick Brindley; Lacrosse — Walter Ott; Others — combined work of Brindley, Ott, Smith and Aarand.
$5 Canoeing: Featured in early competitions between Indians and Voyageurs.
$5 Rowing: Shown is a man sculling, around the turn of the century.
$10 Cycling: Popular in Canada in the 1870's.
$10 Lacrosse: Developed by the North American Indians and became Canada's official sport in 1867.

Series IV: Olympic Track and Field Sports 1975

Release Date: August 12, 1975.
Designer (winner of invitational competition): Leo Yerxa. All designs include stylized Algonquin quill-work.
Modelers: $10 issues — Patrick Brindley; $5 issues — Walter Ott.
$5 Marathon Runner: Two stylized quill-work birds in migratory flight suggest the energy athletes require for the marathon.
$5 Women's Javelin: Quill-work type spear heads show the direction and flight of the javelin.
$10 Women's Shot Put: The flame of the sun and passage through the sky depict the flight of the shot.
$10 Men's Hurdles: The quill-work depicts deer jumping over fallen trees in the forest, symbolizing the fluid motion of the jumping athlete.

Series V: Olympic Water Sports 1975

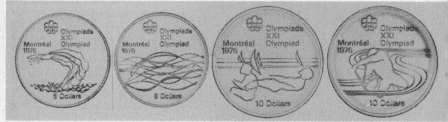

Release date: December 1, 1975.
Designer (winner of open national competition): Lynda Cooper.
Modelers: NONE. (designs photographically etched).
$5 Diver: The figure is shown as a time-lapse sequence.
$5 Swimmer: Shows refracted image of swimmer in water.
$10 Sailing: One sailor is at the tiller and the other is leaning to counter-balance the boat; distant sails are on the horizon.
$10 Paddler: The paddler is shown with the watercourse swirling around him; represents rowing, canoeing and kayaking.

Series VI: Olympic Team and Body Contact Sports 1976

Release date: March 1, 1976.
Designer (winner of open international competition): Shigeo Fukuda.
Modelers: NONE (designs photographically etched).
$5 Fencing: ⎫
$5 Boxing: ⎪   Designs consist of repeated silhouettes of athletes
$10 Field Hockey: ⎬   performing against a sunburst background.
$10 Soccer: ⎭

Series VII: Olympic Souvenir Issue 1976

Release date: June 1, 1976.
Designer (winner of invitational competition between several Canadian design houses): Elliot Morrison, using for the $10 pieces architectural drawings by Roger Taillibert. The converging sets of parallel lines in the designs symbolize the coming together of the athletes and an international audience in Montreal.
Modelers: Village — Sheldon Beverage; Flame — Walter Ott (principally) and Patrick Brindley; Stadium — Ago Aarand; Velodrome — Terrence Smith.
$5 Olympic Village: Housed the athletes.
$5 Olympic Flame: Lit at the opening and extinguished at the closing of the games.
$10 Stadium: Location of the track and field, swimming and other events.
$10 Velodrome. Scene of most cycling and judo events.

4
PRE-CONFEDERATION
PROVINCIAL DECIMAL ISSUES

NEW BRUNSWICK DECIMAL COINAGE
½ CENT
Victoria, Half Cent, 1861

Diameter: 20.65 mm; weight: 2.835 grams; composition: .950 copper, .040 tin, .010 zinc; edge: plain.

G: Hair over ear worn through.
VG: Little detail to hair over ear or braid.
Fine: Strands of hair over ear begin to merge; braid is worn.
VF: Hair over ear is worn; braid is clear but no longer sharp.
EF: Slight wear on hair over ear; braid that holds knot in place is sharp and clear.

In 1860 New Brunswick adopted a monetary system consisting of dollars and cents, with the dollar equal to the United States gold dollar. This made the British shilling worth slightly more than 24 cents and the 6d slightly more than 12 cents. Consequently, it was not necessary for the province to issue half cents to make change for the 6d. The Royal Mint nevertheless struck over 200,000 New Brunswick half cents. The mistake was soon discovered and most of the coins melted. The only ones to escape were a few proofs and an unknown number of business strikes (perhaps in the hundreds) that were mixed with the Nova Scotia half cents and sent to Halifax.

The obverse design is identical to that used for the Nova Scotia coins of the same denomination and is one of those (Peck's obv. 3) for the British bronze farthing.

The reverse is similar to that for the Nova Scotia half cent.

Date	Qty. Minted	G-4	VG-8	F-12	VF-20	EF-40	AU-50	Unc-60	BU-60
1861	(originally 222,800)	$40.00	$65.00	$85.00	$120.00	$160.00	$260.00	$465.00	$1,100

1 CENT
Victoria Cents, 1861-1864

Diameter: 25.53 mm; weight: 5.670 grams; composition: .950 copper, .040 tin, .010 zinc; edge: plain.

Short tip 6   Long tip 6

The obverse is identical to that for the Nova Scotia coins of the same denomination and is one of those (Peck's obv. 6) used for the British halfpenny. The designer and engraver was L.C. Wyon.

The reverse design is very similar to that used for the Nova Scotia issue; the wreath differs only in minor respects. The design was adapted from a model by C. Hill.

ate	Qty. Minted	G-4	VG-8	F-12	VF-20	EF-40	AU-50	Unc-60	BU-60
861	1,000,000	1.50	2.50	3.75	7.50	15.00	37.50	85.00	225.00
864 short tip 6	1,000,000	1.50	2.50	3.75	7.50	15.00	37.50	85.00	225.00
long tip 6	incl. above	1.50	2.50	3.75	7.50	15.00	37.50	85.00	225.00

5 CENTS
Victoria, 5 Cents Silver, 1862-1864

Diameter: 15.49 mm; weight: 1.162 grams; composition: .925 silver, .075 copper; edge: reeded.

G: *Braid around ear worn through.*
VG: *No details in braid around the ear.*
Fine: *Segments of braid begin to merge into one another.*
VF: *Braid is clear but not sharp.*
EF: *Braid is slightly worn but generally sharp and clear.*

The obverse, designed and engraved by L.C. Wyon, has a portrait of Victoria that would later be used on the Dominion of Canada issues (Portrait 2, page 25).

The reverse wreath is of maple; the design is identical to that used for the Province of Canada five cents of 1858.

Small 6 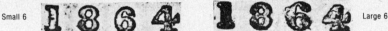 Large 6

962	100,000	$25.00	$40.00	$60.00	$110.00	$225.00	$800.00	$1,850	$2,750
864 small 6	100,000	25.00	40.00	60.00	110.00	225.00	800.00	1,850	2,750
large 6	incl. above	25.00	40.00	60.00	110.00	225.00	800.00	1,850	2,750

10 CENTS
Victoria, 10 Cents Silver, 1862-1864

Diameter: 17.91 mm; weight: 2.324 grams; composition: .925 silver, .075 copper; edge: reeded.

The obverse is virtually identical to and was derived from Canadian Portrait 6, page 37 (that particular Canadian obverse existed long before it appeared on the issues of 1892). The designer and engraver was L.C. Wyon.

The reverse design, the device of which is a wreath of maple surmounted by the St. Edward's crown, is identical to that used for the Province of Canada ten cents of 1858.

Normal 2   Double-punched 2

862 normal date	150,000	25.00	37.50	55.00	100.00	220.00	700.00	1,750	2,400
double-punch 2 ...	incl. above	25.00	37.50	55.00	100.00	220.00	700.00	1,750	2,400
864	150,000	25.00	37.50	55.00	100.00	220.00	700.00	1,750	2,400

20 CENTS
Victoria, 20 Cents silver, 1862-1864
Diameter: 22.99 mm; weight: 4.648 grams; composition: .925 silver, .075 copper; edge: reeded.

The obverse, designed and engraved by L.C. Wyon, has a portrait that is similar to that on the Province of Canada issue of the same denomination.

The reverse is also similar to that used for the Province of Canada issue and, indeed, was probably initially intended for that coin. The designer and engraver may have been L.C. Wyon, but this is not known with certainty.

Date	Qty. Minted	G-4	VG-8	F-12	VF-20	EF-40	AU-50	Unc-60	BU-60
1862	150,000	$15.00	$20.00	$30.00	$55.00	$130.00	$500.00	$1,500	$2,100
1864	150,000	15.00	20.00	30.00	55.00	130.00	500.00	1,500	2,100

NEWFOUNDLAND DECIMALS 1865-1947
In an act of 1863 Newfoundland turned to decimal currency, adopting the Spanish dollar as the unit. This made the British shilling equivalent to 24 cents and the sixpence to 12 cents.

1 CENT
Victoria Large Cents, 1865-1896
Diameter: 25.53 mm; weight: 5.670 grams; composition: .950 copper, .040 tin, .010 zinc; edge: plain.

G: Hair over ear worn through.
VG: Little detail to hair over ear or braid.
Fine: Strands of hair over ear begin to merge, braid is worn.
VF: Hair over ear is worn, braid is clear but no longer sharp.
EF: Slight wear on hair over ear, braid that holds knot in place is sharp and clear.

The obverse, designed and engraved by L.C. Wyon, is unusual in two respects. First, the portrait was one of those used for the British halfpence (from Peck's obv. 6) and second, the lettering is in simple, very bold type.

The reverse was engraved by Wyon's assistant, T.J. Minton, from a design by Horace Morehen. The wreath consists of pitcher plant (see page 100) and oak.

1880 date varieties. Two styles of the 0, narrow and wide, are known. The position of the wide 0 also varies; however, these positional differences are considered trivial and will not be perpetuated here.

Die axis varieties. With the exception of the 1872H, all of the Victorian Newfoundland cents have the die axes arranged ↑↑. The opposite alignment ↑↓ (reverse die rotated 180°) on the 1872H is probably due to its not being specified and Heaton's assuming it was the same as on the silver coins.

Date	Approx. Minted	G-4	VG-8	F-12	VF-20	EF-40	AU-50	Unc-60	BU-60
1865	240,000	$1.50	$2.75	$4.00	$7.50	$15.00	$75.00	$190.00	$450.00
1872H	200,000	1.50	2.75	4.00	7.50	15.00	60.00	145.00	350.00
1873	200,025	1.50	2.75	4.00	7.50	15.00	90.00	220.00	550.00
1876H	200,000	1.50	2.75	4.00	7.50	15.00	90.00	225.00	575.00

Narrow 0   Wide 0

Date	Approx. Minted	G-4	VG-8	F-12	VF-20	EF-40	AU-50	Unc-60	BU-60
1880 narrow 0	400,000	50.00	80.00	90.00	125.00	200.00	450.00	900.00	2,000
wide 0	incl. above	1.50	2.75	4.00	8.00	15.00	70.00	175.00	450.00
1885	40,000	15.00	22.00	26.00	35.00	75.00	150.00	375.00	900.00
1888	50,000	15.00	20.00	24.00	30.00	50.00	120.00	275.00	750.00
1890	200,000	1.25	2.00	3.50	6.00	10.00	75.00	185.00	450.00
1894	200,000	1.25	2.00	3.50	6.00	10.00	75.00	185.00	450.00
1896	200,000	1.25	2.00	3.50	6.00	10.00	75.00	185.00	450.00

Edward VII, Large Cents, 1904-1909

Diameter: 25.53 mm; weight: 5.670 grams; composition: .950 copper, .040 tin, .010 zinc; edge: plain.

G: *Band of crown worn through.*
VG: *Band of crown is worn through at highest point.*
Fine: *Jewels in band of crown will be blurred.*
VF: *Band of crown is still clear but no longer sharp.*
EF: *Band of crown slightly worn but generally sharp and clear.*

The obverse was derived from a portrait model by G.W. De Saulles; the portrait is unusually large for the size of the coin.

The reverse design is the same as that for the Victoria series, except for the substitution of the Imperial State crown for the St. Edward's crown. The modification was made by W.H.J. Blakemore.

Date	Approx. Minted	G-4	VG-8	F-12	VF-20	EF-40	AU-50	Unc-60	BU-60
1904H	100,000	$5.00	$7.50	$11.00	$20.00	$35.00	$110.00	$275.00	$800.00
1907	200,000	1.25	2.25	3.50	6.00	15.00	75.00	165.00	450.00
1909	200,000	1.25	2.25	3.50	6.00	15.00	75.00	165.00	450.00

George V, Large Cents, 1913-1936

Diameter 1913,1929, 1936: 25.53 mm; 1917-1920: 25.40 mm; weight: 5.670 grams; composition 1913-1920: .950 copper, .040 tin, .010 zinc; 1929-1936: .955 copper, .030 tin, .015 zinc; edge: plain.

G: *Band of crown worn through.*
VG: *Band of crown worn through at highest point.*
Fine: *Jewels in band of crown will be blurred.*
VF: *Band of crown still clear but no longer sharp.*
EF: *Band of crown slightly worn but generally sharp and clear.*

The obverse, from a portrait model by Sir E.B. MacKennal (B.M. on truncation), is identical to that for the Canadian issues of the same denomination.

The reverse is a continuation of the design introduced in the Edward VII series.

Date	Qty. Minted	G-4	VG-8	F-12	VF-20	EF-40	AU-50	Unc-60	BU-60
1913	400,000	$ .75	$1.25	$2.25	$3.75	$6.50	$27.50	$60.00	$175.00
1917C	702,350	.75	1.25	2.25	3.75	6.50	27.50	65.00	185.00
1919C	300,000	.75	1.25	2.25	3.75	6.50	40.00	90.00	275.00
1920C	302,184	.75	1.25	2.25	3.75	6.50	40.00	90.00	275.00
1929	300,000	.75	1.25	2.25	3.75	6.50	40.00	85.00	250.00
1936	300,000	.75	1.25	2.00	3.50	6.00	22.00	50.00	155.00

George VI, Small Cents, 1938-1947

Diameter: 19.05 mm; weight: 3.240 grams; composition: .955 copper, .030 tin, .015 zinc; edge: plain.

VG: Band of crown almost worn through; little detail in hair.

Fine: Band of crown considerably worn; strands of hair begin to merge together.

VF: Wear extends along band of crown; hair is clear but no longer sharp.

EF: Band of crown shows slight wear; hair is sharp and clear.

Because of the need to have new obverses for the George VI coinage, the Newfoundland government considered the question of changing to a smaller cent and larger five cents similar to those already in circulation in Canada and the U..S. Despite the economic advantages of such a change, there was a strong conservative element in favor of retaining the old sizes. The final decision was to alter only the one cent.

The obverse for the new small cent was derived from a portrait model for the British colonial coinages by Percy Metcalfe (P.M. below neck). The reverse device is the insectivorous pitcher plant, *Sarracenia purpurea*, which is native to the island. The die was engraved by W.J. Newman, a senior engraver at the Royal Mint, from designs submitted from Newfoundland.

The 1938 issue was produced in London. However, due to the danger of loss of trans-Atlantic shipments during World War II, all later coinages were struck at the Royal Canadian Mint in Ottawa. The C mint mark was inadvertently omitted in 1940 and 1942.

1938	500,000	$ .50	$ .75	$1.00	$2.00	$4.00	$10.00	$25.00	$55.00
1940(C)	300,000	1.25	2.75	3.75	6.00	12.50	27.50	60.00	175.00
1941C	827,662	.25	.50	.75	1.25	3.00	9.50	20.00	50.00
1942 (C)	1,996,889	.25	.50	.75	1.25	3.00	9.50	20.00	50.00
1943C	1,239,732	.25	.50	.75	1.25	3.00	9.50	20.00	50.00
1944C	1,328,776	1.00	2.00	3.00	4.00	6.00	22.00	45.00	125.00
1947C	313,772	.50	1.00	1.50	2.50	4.50	20.00	40.00	100.00

5 CENTS
Victoria, Five Cents Silver, 1865-1896

Diameter: 15.49 mm; weight: 1.178 grams; composition: .925 silver, .075 copper; edge: reeded.

G: Braid around ear worn through.

VG: No details in braid around ear.

Fine: Segments of braid begin to merge into one another.

VF: Braid is clear but not sharp.

EF: Braid slightly worn but generally sharp and clear.

The initial obverse was derived from that for New Brunswick by the appropriate modification of the legend. Periods are present on both sides of NEWFOUNDLAND. A second variety lacks the periods. On the final obverse the Queen has more aged facial features with epressed upper lip and recessed forehead, and the period after NEWFOUNDLAND was estored (closer to the D however).

Two noteworthy reverses are known for this series. The first has a Roman I in the date, while the second has the more conventional Arabic 1.

The first and probably all later obverse and reverse varieties were designed and engraved y L.C. Wyon.

The weights of the silver denominations were made proportional to those of the quivalent values in English silver coin; that is, 5.6552 grams per shilling (12 pence). The value of the 5 cents was 2½d.

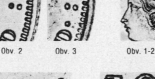

Obv. 1   Obv. 2   Obv. 3   Obv. 1-2   Obv. 3

Roman I   Arabic 1

Date	Qty. Minted	G-4	VG-8	F-12	VF-20	EF-40	AU-50	BU-60	CH-63
Roman I Reverse (1865)									
1865 ....obv. 1,2	80,000	$22.50	$45.00	$70.00	$120.00	$235.00	$500.00	$2,000	$3,200
Arabic 1 Reverse (1870-1896)									
1870 ....obv. 1,2	40,000	35.00	65.00	90.00	135.00	275.00	725.00	2,500	4,000
1872H ....obv. 2	40,000	22.50	45.00	70.00	120.00	230.00	500.00	1,800	2,750
1873 ....obv. 2	44,260	37.50	65.00	90.00	145.00	300.00	725.00	2,400	3,800
1873H ....obv. 2 ..... incl. above		450.00	950.00	1,400	2,000	3,250	5,250	12,000	20,000
1876H ....obv. 2	20,000	55.00	110.00	160.00	275.00	525.00	1,300	4,000	6,250
1880 ....obv. 2	40,000	20.00	35.00	55.00	100.00	210.00	600.00	2,000	3,000
1881 ....obv. 2	40,000	20.00	35.00	55.00	100.00	210.00	600.00	2,000	3,000
1882H ....obv. 3	60,000	15.00	30.00	45.00	75.00	165.00	475.00	1,750	2,500
1885 ....obv. 2	16,000	80.00	150.00	225.00	350.00	725.00	1,600	5,000	7,500
1888 ....obv. 2,3	40,000	20.00	35.00	55.00	85.00	185.00	500.00	1,750	2,500
1890 ....obv. 3	160,000	9.00	16.00	30.00	62.50	120.00	425.00	1,500	2,200
1894 ....obv. 3	160,000	9.00	16.00	30.00	62.50	120.00	425.00	1,500	2,200
1896 ....obv. 3	400,000	6.50	11.00	21.00	42.00	85.00	300.00	1,200	1,850

Edward VII, Five Cents Silver, 1903-1908

Diameter: 15.49 mm; weight: 1.178 grams; composition: .925 silver, .075 copper; edge: reeded.

G: Band of crown worn through.
VG: Band of crown worn through at highest point.
Fine: Jewels in band of crown will be blurred.
VF: Band of crown still clear but no longer sharp.
EF: Band of crown slightly worn but generally sharp and clear.

The obverse, designed and engraved by G.W. De Saulles (DES. below bust), is identical to that for the Canadian issues.

The reverse was also the work of De Saulles.

	Qty. Minted	G-4	VG-8	F-12	VF-20	EF-40	AU-50	BU-60	CH-63
1903	100,000	$3.50	$7.00	$13.50	$40.00	$110.00	$425.00	$1,100	$1,800
1904H	100,000	3.00	6.25	12.00	35.00	85.00	300.00	1,000	1,500
1908	400,000	2.50	5.25	10.00	26.50	65.00	235.00	725.00	1,150

George V, 5 Cents Silver, 1912-1929

Diameter 1912-1919: 15.49 mm; 1929: 15.69 mm; weight 1912: 1.178 grams; 1917-1929: 1,166 grams; composition: .925 silver, .075 copper; edge: reeded.

G: *Band of crown worn through.*
VG: *Band of crown worn through at highest point.*
Fine: *Jewels in band of crown will be blurred.*
VF: *Band of crown still clear but no longer sharp.*
EF: *Band of crown slightly worn but generally sharp and clear.*

The obverse bears a portrait derived from a model by Sir E.B. MacKennal (B.M. on truncation) and is identical to that for the Canadian issues.
     The reverse is as for the Edward VII series.

Date	Qty. Minted	G-4	VG-8	F-12	VF-20	EF-40	AU-50	BU-60	CH-63
1912	300,000	1.50	3.00	5.25	10.00	35.00	195.00	575.00	1,000
1917C	300,319	1.50	3.00	5.25	10.00	35.00	195.00	575.00	1,000
1919C	100,844	2.75	4.50	9.00	17.50	52.00	235.00	825.00	1,250
1929	300,000	1.50	2.50	5.00	8.50	32.00	160.00	475.00	775.00

George VI, 5 Cents Silver, 1938-1947

Diameter 1938: 15.69 mm; 1940-1947: 15.49 mm; weight: 1,166 grams; composition 1938-1944: .925 silver, .075 copper 1945-1947: .800 silver, .200 copper; edge: reeded.

VG: *Band of crown almost worn through.*
Fine: *Band of crown considerably worn; strands of hair begin to merge together.*
VF: *Wear extends along band of crown; hair is clear but no longer sharp.*
EF: *Band of crown shows slight wear; hair is sharp and clear.*

The obverse is derived from a portrait model by Percy Metcalfe (P.M. below neck) intended for English colonial coinages.
     The reverse is as for the Edward VII and George V issues.

1938	100,000	.75	1.00	1.65	3.25	6.00	45.00	200.00	350.00
1940C	200,000	.75	1.00	1.65	2.75	5.75	27.50	100.00	185.00
1941C	612,641	.65	.75	1.35	2.00	4.25	15.00	52.50	85.00
1942C	298,348	1.00	1.50	2.25	4.25	7.50	35.00	90.00	145.00
1943C	351,666	.75	1.00	1.25	2.25	4.50	18.00	55.00	85.00
1944C	286,504	.75	1.25	2.00	3.50	6.00	27.50	100.00	195.00
1945C	203,828	.75	1.00	1.25	2.50	5.00	20.00	60.00	90.00
1946C	2,041	150.00	265.00	350.00	475.00	700.00	1,100	3,500	5,000
1947C	38,400	3.00	5.50	8.25	12.00	25.00	65.00	225.00	350.00

10 CENTS

Victoria, 10 Cents Silver, 1865-1896

Diameter: 17.98 mm; weight: 2.356 grams; composition: .925 silver, .025 copper; edge: reeded.

G: *Braid around ear worn through.*
VG: *No details in braid around ear.*
Fine: *Segments of braid begin to merge together.*
VF: *Braid is clear but not sharp.*
EF: *Braid slightly worn but generally sharp and clear.*

The initial obverse was derived from that for the New Brunswick 10 cents by the appropriate modification of the legend. A second variety lacks the period after NEWFOUNDLAND and a third variety has the period restored (but closer to the D) and has a Queen with more aged facial features. Two noteworthy reverses are known for this series. The first has Roman I's in the I0 and date, while the second has the more conventional Arabic 1's. There are also slight differences in the devices and rim denticles.

1871H Newfoundland/Canada mule. Quite possibly the result of an inadvertent muling combining the 10 cent dies of a Canadian 1871H reverse with a Newfoundland obverse, also with an H. The two known examples of this interesting and extremely rare variety are in well circulated condition, adding credence to the proposition that it is not a pattern.

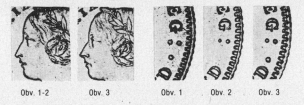

Obv. 1-2   Obv. 3   Obv. 1   Obv. 2   Obv. 3

1880 2nd 8 over 7. All of the 10 and 50 cents of 1880 examined have the second 8 in the date punched over a 7. By the latter part of the 1870's, the dies for these denominations were sunk from reverse punches bearing the partial date 187-; the final digit was hand punched into each die. In 1880, then, the Mint was faced with either making new punches or using the old ones and correcting the 7 in each die, in addition to adding the final digit. The latter course of action was chosen in 1880, probably because of a lack of time and the small number of dies which had to be made for Newfoundland in that year. The reverse punches for the other denominations lacked both the third and the fourth digits, so this problem did not arise for them.

Roman I   Arabic 1 (note 2nd 8 over 7)

Date	Qty. Minted	G-4	VG-8	F-12	VF-20	EF-40	AU-50	BU-60	CH-63
Roman I's Reverse (1865-1870)									
1865 ....obv. 1	80,000	$12.50	$25.00	$42.00	$85.00	$235.00	$750.00	$2,750	$4,800
1870 ....obv. 1,2	30,000	120.00	185.00	285.00	525.00	1,100	2,150	6,750	12,000
Arabic 1's Reverse (1872-1896)									
1871H mule	40,000				Very Rare				
1872H ....obv. 2	40,000	12.50	25.00	50.00	90.00	265.00	1,150	2,850	4,100
1873 ....obv. 1,2	23,614	18.00	37.50	57.50	115.00	360.00	1,200	4,200	5,800
1876H ....obv. 2	10,000	22.50	45.00	80.00	175.00	475.00	1,350	5,250	7,750
1880 2nd 8 over 7									
..........obv. 2.........	10,000	22.50	45.00	80.00	175.00	475.00	1,350	5,250	7,750
1882H ....obv. 3	20,000	13.50	27.50	45.00	90.00	250.00	850.00	2,400	4,200
1885 ....obv. 2	8,000	50.00	95.00	190.00	425.00	900.00	2,000	6,500	10,000
1888 ....obv. 3	30,000	15.00	28.00	50.00	95.00	275.00	900.00	2,700	5,200
1890 ....obv. 3	100,000	$5.50	$12.50	$22.00	$55.00	$165.00	$550.00	$1,750	$3,500
1894 ....obv. 2,3	100,000	5.50	12.50	22.00	55.00	165.00	550.00	1,700	3,000
1896 ....obv. 3	230,000	5.00	9.00	19.00	50.00	150.00	500.00	1,450	2,650

Edward VII, 10 Cents Silver, 1903-1904

Diameter: 17.96 mm; weight: 2.356 grams; composition: .925 silver, .025 copper; edge: reeded

G: Band of crown worn through.
VG: Band of crown worn through at highest point.
Fine: Jewels in band of crown will be blurred.
VF: Band of crown still clear but generally no longer sharp.
EF: Band of crown slightly worn but generally sharp and clear.

The obverse, designed and engraved by G.W. De Saulles (DES. below bust), is identical to that for the Canadian issues.
    The reverse was also done by De Saulles.

Date	Qty. Minted	G-4	VG-8	F-12	VF-20	EF-40	AU-50	BU-60	CH-63
1903	100,000	5.00	10.00	20.00	50.00	155.00	425.00	1,750	3,000
1904H	100,000	4.00	7.50	15.00	40.00	135.00	385.00	1,325	2,150

George V, 10 Cents Silver, 1912-1919

Diameter 1912: 17.96 mm; 1917, 1919: 18.03 mm; weight 1912: 2.356 grams; 1917, 1919: 2.333 grams; composition: .925 silver, .075 copper; edge: reeded.

G: Band of crown worn through.
VG: Band of crown worn through at highest point.
Fine: Jewels in band of crown will be blurred.
VF: Band of crown still clear but no longer sharp.
EF: Band of crown slightly worn but generally sharp and clear.

The obverse bears a portrait derived from a model by Sir E.B. MacKennal (B.M. on truncation) and is identical to that for the Canadian issues.
    The reverse is identical to that of the Edward VII series.

1912	150,000	2.50	4.50	9.50	24.00	80.00	300.00	1,150	1,750
1917C	250,805	2.00	3.50	6.50	16.50	50.00	200.00	875.00	1,450
1919C	54,342	3.00	5.50	11.00	27.50	100.00	325.00	950.00	1,650

George VI, 10 Cents Silver, 1938-1947

Diameter: 18.03 mm; weight: 2.333 grams; composition 1938-1944: .925 silver, .075 copper; 1945-1947: .800 silver, .200 copper; edge: reeded.

VG: Band of crown almost worn through; little detail in the hair.
Fine: Band of crown considerably worn; strands of hair begin to merge together.
VF: Wear extends along band of crown; hair is clear but no longer sharp.
EF: Band of crown shows slight wear; hair is sharp and clear.

The obverse is derived from a portrait model by Percy Metcalfe (P.M. below neck) intended for English colonial coinages.
    The reverse is as for the Edward VII and George V issues.

Date	Qty. Minted	VG-8	F-12	VF-20	EF-40	AU-50	BU-60	CH-63
1938	100,000	$2.50	$4.25	$8.50	$20.00	$50.00	$260.00	$375.00
1940(C)	100,000	2.25	3.75	7.50	16.50	45.00	200.00	285.00
1941C	483,630	2.25	3.00	5.50	11.00	25.00	95.00	155.00
1942C	292,736	2.25	3.00	5.75	12.00	27.50	105.00	165.00
1943C	104,706	2.50	3.25	5.75	13.00	30.00	110.00	170.00

Date	Qty. Minted	VG-8	F-12	VF-20	EF-40	AU-50	BU-60	CH-63
944C	151,471	$2.25	$3.00	$5.50	$11.50	$35.00	$125.00	$275.00
945C	175,833	2.25	3.00	5.25	11.00	28.50	90.00	130.00
946C	38,400	8.00	11.00	21.50	45.00	100.00	375.00	525.00
947C	61,988	4.00	7.50	14.00	30.00	57.50	210.00	300.00

20 CENTS
Victoria, 20 Cents Silver, 1865-1900

Diameter: 23.19 mm; weight: 4.713 grams; composition: .925 silver, .075 copper; edge: reeded.

G: Braid around ear worn through.
VG: No details in braid around ear.
Fine: Segments of braid begin to merge together.
VF: Braid is clear but not sharp.
EF: Braid is slightly worn but generally sharp and clear.

The first obverse was derived from the New Brunswick 20 cent obverse by the necessary legend modification. A second design which was derived from the first, has the Queen with more aged facial features: slightly double chin, repressed upper lip and recessed forehead.

The reverses for the 1865 and 1880 issues have a Roman I in the date; later issues have the more conventional Arabic 1 in the date.

The weights of the silver denominations were made proportional to those of the equivalent values in English silver coin; that is, 5.6552 grams per shilling (12 pence). The value of the 20 cents was 10d.

Obv. 1   Obv. 2   Roman I   Arabic 1

Date	Qty. Minted	G-4	VG-8	F-12	VF-20	EF-40	AU-50	BU-60	CH-63
Roman I Reverse (1865-1880)									
865 ....obv. 1	100,000	$7.50	$15.00	$30.00	$85.00	$255.00	$750.00	$3,000	$4,500
870 ....obv. 1	50,000	11.50	22.50	45.00	115.00	350.00	925.00	3,750	5,300
872H ..obv. 1	90,000	7.50	14.00	26.50	75.00	225.00	715.00	2,750	3,750
873 ....obv. 1	45,799	8.50	16.50	32.50	85.00	275.00	800.00	3,200	4,500
876H ..obv. 1	50,000	10.00	20.00	40.00	100.00	315.00	875.00	3,400	4,900
880 ....obv. 1	30,000	11.25	24.00	45.00	120.00	375.00	965.00	3,450	5,000
Arabic 1 Reverse (1881-1900)									
881 ....obv. 1	60,000	5.50	9.50	21.50	62.00	195.00	650.00	2,300	3,200
882H ..obv. 2	100,000	5.00	9.50	21.50	60.00	185.00	600.00	2,250	3,100
885 ....obv. 1	40,000	7.00	13.50	25.00	65.00	225.00	750.00	2,900	4,250
888 ....obv. 2	75,000	5.50	9.50	20.00	55.00	175.00	625.00	2,300	3,500
890 ....obv. 2	100,000	5.00	8.00	15.00	40.00	110.00	500.00	1,800	2,700
894 ....obv. 1,2	100,000	5.00	8.00	15.00	40.00	110.00	500.00	1,800	2,700
896 sm. 96 ....obv. 2	125,000	4.50	8.00	15.00	40.00	110.00	500.00	1,800	2,700
lg. 96 .... obv. 1	incl. above	5.50	9.50	20.00	57.50	150.00	625.00	2,125	3,000
899 sm. 99 ....obv. 2	125,000	5.50	8.50	18.00	55.00	150.00	625.00	2,000	2,900
lg. 99 .... obv. 2	incl. above	4.50	7.50	14.50	40.00	105.00	465.00	1,800	2,700
900 ....obv. 2	125,000	4.00	7.00	12.50	30.00	85.00	450.00	1,800	2,700

Edward VII, 20 Cents Silver, 1904

Diameter: 23.19 mm; weight: 4.713 grams; composition: .925 silver, .075 copper; edge: reeded.

G: *Band of crown worn through.*
VG: *Band of crown worn through at highest point.*
Fine: *Jewels in band of crown will be blurred.*
VF: *Band of crown still clear but no longer sharp.*
EF: *Band of crown slightly worn but generally sharp and clear.*

The obverse was derived from a portrait model by G.W. De Saulles (DES. below bust).
The reverse was designed and engraved by W.H.J. Blakemore.

Date	Qty. Minted	G-4	VG-8	F-12	VF-20	EF-40	AU-50	BU-60	CH-63
1904H	75,000	$8.50	$15.00	$35.00	$100.00	$350.00	$775.00	$2,250	$3,400

George V, 20 Cents Silver, 1912

Diameter: 23.19; weight: 4.713 grams; composition: .925 silver, .075 copper; edge: reeded.

G: *Band of crown worn through.*
VG: *Band of crown worn through at highest point.*
Fine: *Jewels in band of crown will be blurred.*
VF: *Band of crown still clear but no longer sharp.*
EF: *Band of crown slightly worn but generally sharp and clear.*

The obverse was derived from a portrait model of the King by Sir E.B. MacKennal (B.M. on truncation).
The reverse was a continuation of the design introduced in the Edward VII series.

| 1912 .... | 350,000 | 5.50 | 6.00 | 9.00 | 27.50 | 80.00 | 385.00 | 1,250 | 2,000 |

25 CENTS

George V, 25 Cents Silver, 1917-1919

Diameter: 23.62 mm; weight: 5.832 grams; composition: .925 silver, .075 copper; edge: reeded.

G: *Band of crown worn through.*
VG: *Band of crown worn through at highest point.*
Fine: *Jewels in Band of crown will be blurred.*
VF: *Band of crown still clear but no longer sharp.*
EF: *Band of crown slightly worn but generally sharp and clear.*

Because of continuing difficulties arising from confusion of Canadian 25 and Newfoundland 20 cent pieces, the latter denomination was discontinued and a 25 cent coin struck instead.
The obverse, from a portrait model by Sir E.B. Mackennal (B.M. on truncation), is identical to that for the Canadian issues of the same denomination.
W.H.J. Blakemore designed and engraved the reverse.

| 1917C .... | 464,779 | 3.50 | 4.50 | 7.50 | 12.00 | 25.00 | 90.00 | 300.00 | 450.00 |
| 1919C .... | 163,939 | 3.50 | 4.50 | 8.00 | 13.00 | 30.00 | 125.00 | 400.00 | 600.00 |

50 CENTS
Victoria, 50 Cents Silver, 1870-1900

Diameter: 29.85 mm; weight: 11.782 grams; composition: .925 silver, .075 copper; edge: reeded.

G: *Braid around ear worn through.*
VG: *No detail in braid around ear.*
Fine: *Braid segments begin to merge together.*
VF: *Braid is clear but not sharp.*
EF: *Braid slightly worn but generally sharp and clear.*

This denomination has a laureate bust which thereby distinctly differs from that on the Canadian 50 cents. There are two portrait varieties; the first has a "youthful" prominent upper lip, while the second, derived from the first, has an "aged" repressed upper lip, a "droopy" mouth and a longer depression over the eye.

The initial reverse is characterized by the presence of thick loops near the rim denticles. A second design has thin loops.

L.C. Wyon was the designer and engraver of the first and probably the later designs as well.

The weights of the silver denominations were made proportional to those of the equivalent values in English silver coin; that is, 5.6552 grams per shilling (12 pence). The value of the 50 cents was 2s. 1d.

1880 2nd 8 over 7. See page 103 for details.

1870

Obv. 1   Obv. 2

Thick Loops

Date	Approx. Minted	G-4	VG-8	F-12	VF-20	EF-40	AU-50	BU-60	CH-63
Thick Loops Reverse (1870-1880)									
870 . . . .obv. 1	50,000	$10.00	$20.00	$30.00	$70.00	$315.00	$1,200	$4,000	$6,500
872H . . .obv. 1	48,000	10.00	20.00	30.00	70.00	315.00	1,200	4,000	6,500
873 . . . .obv. 1	37,675	10.00	20.00	30.00	70.00	315.00	1,200	4,000	6,500
874 . . . .obv. 1	80,000	10.00	20.00	30.00	70.00	315.00	1,200	4,000	6,500
876H . . .obv. 1	28,000	17.50	35.00	60.00	135.00	635.00	1,700	6,500	9,250
880 2nd 8 over 7 .obv. 1 . .	24,000	17.50	35.00	60.00	135.00	635.00	1,700	6,500	9,250

1899

Thin Loops

Thin Loops Reverse (1881-1900)									
881 . . . .obv. 1	50,000	10.00	24.00	40.00	85.00	400.00	1,300	5,000	7,500
882H . . .obv. 2	100,000	10.00	18.50	32.00	60.00	290.00	1,000	3,800	5,500
885 . . . .obv. 1	40,000	10.00	21.50	35.00	80.00	350.00	1,200	4,500	7,000
888 . . . .obv. 1	20,000	10.00	24.00	45.00	100.00	450.00	1,500	5,250	8,200
894 . . . .obv. 1	40,000	9.00	16.50	27.50	60.00	285.00	1,000	4,100	6,250

Date	Qty. Minted	G-4	VG-8	F-12	VF-20	EF-40	AU-50	BU-60	CH-63
1896 . . . . obv. 1,2	60,000	$7.50	$13.00	$22.00	$50.00	$250.00	$950.00	$3,600	$5,200
1898 . . . . obv. 1,2	76,607	7.50	13.00	22.00	50.00	250.00	950.00	3,600	5,200

Narrow, bold 9's  Wide, delicate 9's

1899 . . . . obv. 2									
narrow 9's	150,000	7.00	12.00	21.00	45.00	235.00	950.00	3,600	5,200
wide 9's	incl. above	7.00	12.00	21.00	45.00	235.00	950.00	3,600	5,200
1900 . . . . obv. 2	150,000	6.50	11.50	20.00	40.00	200.00	800.00	3,000	4,200

Edward VII, 50 Cents Silver, 1904-1909

Diameter: 29.85 mm; weight: 11.782 grams; composition: .925 silver, .075 copper; edge: reeded.

G: *Band of crown worn through.*
VG: *Band of crown worn through at highest point.*
Fine: *Jewels in band of crown will be blurred.*
VF: *Band of crown still clear but no longer sharp.*
EF: *Band of crown slightly worn but generally sharp and clear.*

The obverse, designed and engraved by G.W. De Saulles (DES. below bust), is identical to that for the Canadian issues.

The reverse was designed by W.H.J. Blakemore.

Date	Qty. Minted	G-4	VG-8	F-12	VF-20	EF-40	AU-50	BU-60	CH-63
1904H	140,000	$6.00	$11.00	$16.00	$32.50	$95.00	$340.00	$1,050	$1,550
1907	100,000	6.00	12.50	18.50	40.00	115.00	425.00	1,200	1,850
1908	160,000	5.00	9.50	14.00	28.00	90.00	275.00	900.00	1,250
1909	200,000	5.00	9.50	14.00	28.00	90.00	275.00	900.00	1,250

George V, 50 Cents Silver, 1911-1919

Diameter 1911: 29.85 mm; 1917-1919: 29.72 mm; weight 1911: 11.782 grams; 1917-1919: 11.664 grams; composition: .925 silver, .075 copper; edge: reeded.

G: *Band of crown worn through.*
VG: *Band of crown worn through at highest point.*
Fine: *Jewels in band of crown will be blurred.*
VF: *Band of crown still clear but no longer sharp.*
EF: *Band of crown slightly worn but generally sharp and clear.*

The obverse was derived from a portrait model by Sir E.B. MacKennal (B.M. on truncation) and is identical to that used for the 1912-36 Canadian issues. It should be noted that the legend contains DEI GRA: ("by the Grace of God"), a feature which was absent on the 1911 Canadian issue of the same denomination.

The reverse is as for the Edward VII series.

1911	200,000	5.00	9.00	13.00	26.50	100.00	285.00	925.00	1,400
1917C	375,560	5.00	9.00	12.00	24.00	70.00	215.00	565.00	825.00
1918C	294,824	5.00	9.00	12.00	24.00	70.00	215.00	565.00	825.00
1919C	306,267	5.00	9.00	12.00	24.00	70.00	220.00	600.00	850.00

GOLD 2 DOLLARS
Victoria, 2 Dollars Gold, 1865-1888

Diameter: 17.983 mm; weight: 3.328 grams; composition: .917 gold, .083 copper; edge: reeded.

Fine: *Segments of braid begin to merge together.*
VF: *Braid is clear but not sharp.*
EF: *Braid slightly worn but generally sharp and clear.*

This interesting series of "double dollars," as they were sometimes called, gives Newfoundland the distinction of being the only English colony with its own issue of gold.

This denomination is the same diameter as the 10 cents, and the obverses in both cases were derived from the same matrices and punches (and perhaps dies). See page 103 for details on the three obverse varieties.

The reverse was designed and engraved by L.C. Wyon.

Date	Qty. Minted	VF-20	EF-40	AU-50	BU-60	CH-63
1865 . . . .obv. 1	10,000	$350.00	$475.00	$650.00	$1,250	$2,100
1870 . . . .obv. 1,2	10,000	350.00	475.00	650.00	1,250	2,100
1872 . . . .obv. 2	6,050	475.00	650.00	925.00	1,750	3,200
1880 . . . .obv. 2	2,500	2,100	2,900	3,750	5,500	9,500
1881 . . . .obv. 2	10,000	300.00	375.00	475.00	900.00	1,450
1882H . . .obv. 3	25,000	275.00	360.00	460.00	825.00	1,375
1885 . . . .obv. 2	10,000	300.00	375.00	475.00	900.00	1,450
1888 . . . .obv. 2,3	25,000	275.00	360.00	460.00	825.00	1,375

NOVA SCOTIA DECIMALS 1861-1864

In 1859 Nova Scotia adopted a monetary system consisting of dollars and cents, but set its dollar at the rate of $5 per £ sterling. This enabled the province to utilize British silver (the shilling was equal to 25 cents and the 6d to 12½¢); however, it necessitated the issue of a half cent piece to make change for the 6d. Only cents and half cents were issued prior to Confederation in 1867.

½ CENT
Victoria, Half Cent, 1861-1864

Diameter: 20.65 mm; weight: 2.835 grams; composition: .950 copper, .040 tin, .010 zinc; edge: plain.

G: Hair over ear worn through.
CG: Little detail in hair over ear or braid.
Fine: Strands of hair over ear begin to merge; braid is worn.
VF: Hair over ear is worn; braid clear but no longer sharp.
EF: Slight wear on hair over ear; braid that holds knot in place is sharp and clear.

The obverse, bearing a laureated bust of Victoria, is identical to that used for the New Brunswick coins of the same denomination and is one of those (Peck's obv. 3) for the British bronze farthing. The designer and engraver was L.C. Wyon.

The original pattern for the issue had a reverse device consisting of the Imperial crown and a wreath of roses and rose leaves; however, as an outgrowth of a propaganda campaign led by J.S. Thompson (father of Sir John Thompson), the wreath of the adopted issue consisted of both roses and mayflowers. The mayflower, *Epigea repens*, is the provincial flower.

Date	Qty. Minted	G-4	VG-8	F-12	VF-20	EF-40	AU-50	Unc-60	BU-60
1861	400,000	$3.50	$8.00	$12.00	$15.00	$20.00	$35.00	$85.00	$200.00
1864	400,000	3.50	8.00	12.00	15.00	20.00	35.00	85.00	200.00

1 CENT
Victoria, Large Cent, 1861-1864

Diameter: 25.53 mm; weight: 5.670 grams; composition: .950 copper, .040 tin, .010 zinc; edge: plain.

The obverse is identical to that used for the New Brunswick coins of the same denomination and is one of those (Peck's obv. 6) used for the British bronze halfpence. Two reverses, stemming from different matrices, are known. The first was used only for some of the 1861 issue. The crown is very detailed and a rosebud at the lower right is large. The second reverse saw use in 1861-64 and has a somewhat plainer crown with a thinner headband, a smaller rosebud at the lower right and a repositioned inner circle and NOVA SCOTIA. All designs were by L.C. Wyon, the reverses being adapted from a model by C. Hill.

1862 issue. Although the reported mintages for the 1861 and 1862 cents were 800,000 and 1,000,000, respectively, the latter date is very scarce. Some, probably most, of the 1862 strikings are believed to have been made with dies dated 1861. Consequently, the figures have been combined for these two years.

Large bud   Small bud

Note position of I relative to ribbon tip.

Date	Qty. Minted	G-4	VG-8	F-12	VF-20	EF-40	AU-50	Unc-60	BU-60
Large Rosebud Reverse (1861)									
1861 lg. rosebud	1,800,000	1.75	2.75	5.00	9.50	16.50	35.00	100.00	220.00
Small Rosebud Reverse (1861-1864)									
1861 sm. rosebud	incl. above	1.50	2.50	4.00	8.00	12.50	32.00	85.00	200.00
1862	incl. above	15.00	25.00	35.00	70.00	125.00	190.00	385.00	950.00
1864	800,000	1.50	2.50	4.00	8.50	13.50	35.00	95.00	210.00

P.E.I. DECIMAL ISSUE 1871
1 CENT
Victoria, Large Cent, 1871

Diameter: 25.40 mm; weight: 5,670 grams; composition: .950 copper, .040 tin, .010 zinc; edge: plain.

G: Hair over ear worn through.
VG: No details in hair over ear.
Fine: Strands of hair over ear begin to merge.
VF: Hair and jewels no longer sharp, but clear.
EF: Hair over ear sharp and clear; jewels in diadem must show sharply and clearly.

In 1871 the island adopted a decimal system with a dollar equal to the U.S. gold dollar just as in Canada. Only the 1 cent denomination was issued prior to its entry into the Confederation in 1873.

The obverse was designed and engraved by L.C. Wyon, based on a portrait model by William Theed, and is identical to that for the Jamaica halfpenny of the same year.

The reverse was adapted by L.C. Wyon from the Government seal of the island. The device is composed of a large oak tree (representing England) sheltering three oak saplings. (representing the three countries of the island); beneath these is the Latin phrase *Parva Sub Ingenti*, meaning "The small beneath the great."

The issue is distinctive in that it was struck at the Heaton Mint in Birmingham, but lacks the familiar H mint mark and has English titles rather than Latin on the obverse.

Date	Qty. Minted	G-4	VG-8	F-12	VF-20	EF-40	AU-50	Unc-60	BU-60
1871	2,000,000		$2.00	$3.50	$7.50	$15.00		$125.00	$325.00

5
THE FRENCH REGIME

None of the coins of the French regime is strictly Canadian. They were all general issues for the French colonies of the New World. The coinage of 1670 was authorized by an edict of Louis XIV dated February 19, 1670, for use in New France, Acadia, the French settlements in Newfoundland, and the French West Indies. The copper of 1717 to 1722 was authorized by edicts of 1716 and 1721 for use in New France, Louisiana, and the French West Indies.

ISSUE OF 1670

The coinage of 1670 consisted of silver 5 and 15 sols. A copper 2 deniers was also authorized but never struck. A total of 200,000 of the 5 sols was struck, and 40,000 of the 15 sols, at Paris. Old copper coin was to have been melted down at Nantes, but this was not done; the reasons for this may never be known, since the archives of the Nantes mint before 1700 were destroyed. The only known specimen is a pattern struck at Paris. These coins were not popular in New France. The silver coins were raised in value by a third in 1672 to keep them circulating, but in vain. They rapidly disappeared, and by 1680 none was to be seen. Later they were restored to their original value.

Note: Silver pieces similar to the 5 and 15 sols, with other dates and inscribed SIT NOMEN DOMINI BENEDICTUM were struck for use in France. Their use in the colonies was not intended at first. Most of these pieces are much more common than the colonial issue of 1670.

Copper

	VG-8	F-12	VF-20	EF-40
Double or 2 Deniers 1670		Unique		

Silver

	VG-8	F-12	VF-20	EF-40
5 sols 1670	$600.00	$900.00	$1,200	$1,750
15 sols 1670	7,000	9,000	13,500	23,500

COINAGE OF 1717-1720

The copper 6 and 12 deniers of 1717 were authorized by an edict of Louis XV dated December 1716, to be struck at Perpignan. The order could not be carried out, for the supply of copper was too brassy. A second attempt in 1720 also failed, probably for the same reason. All these coins are extremely rare, the 6 deniers of 1720 probably being unique.

Copper

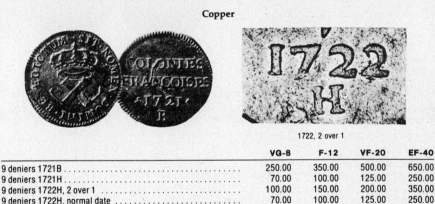

	VG-8	F-12	VF-20	EF-40
6 deniers 1717	$2,000	$3,000	$5,000	
6 deniers 1720		Unique		
12 deniers 1717	2,000	3,000	5,000	

COINAGE OF 1721-1722

The copper coinage of 1721-1722 was authorized by an edict of Louis XV dated June 1721. The coins were struck on copper blanks imported from Sweden. Rouen and La Rochelle struck pieces of 9 deniers in 1721 and 1722. New France received 534,000 pieces, mostly from the mint of La Rochelle, but only 8,180 were successfully put into circulation as the colonists disliked copper. In 1726 the rest of the issue was sent back to France.

Copper

1722, 2 over 1

	VG-8	F-12	VF-20	EF-40
9 deniers 1721B	250.00	350.00	500.00	650.00
9 deniers 1721H	70.00	100.00	125.00	250.00
9 deniers 1722H, 2 over 1	100.00	150.00	200.00	350.00
9 deniers 1722H, normal date	70.00	100.00	125.00	250.00

FRENCH BILLON COINS USED IN CANADA

Almost every type of French coin minted between 1600 and 1759 sooner or later found its way into Canada. To enumerate all these would be unwise, and therefore we have confined the listings to the billon coinages, large shipments of which were known to have been sent to Canada. There are several types which were brought to New France. They are:

(a) The countermarked douzains of 1640. In 1640 all old douzains in France were stamped with a fleur de lys in an oval and re-issued at 15 deniers.

(b) The douzain of 1658. This was issued at 12 deniers, but raised to 15 deniers four months later.

(c) The 15 deniers of 1692-1707

(d) The mousquetaire of 30 deniers 1709-1713, with its half, already listed.

(e) The 23 deniers of 1738-1760 and its half, already listed.

The John Law Coinage. At the instigation of John Law many changes were made in the French coinage. Copper pieces of 3, 6, and 12 deniers were introduced in 1719 and 1720 and coined till 1724. A coinage of silver ecus, halves, thirds, sixths, and twelfths was introduced in 1720 and coined till 1724. The petit louis d'argent of 3 livres was coined in 1720, and a pure silver livre was also coined. Gold louis and halves were coined from 1720 to 1723.

	VG-8	F-12	VF-20	EF-40
15 deniers 1710-1713AA	$125.00	$200.00	$300.00	$500.00
30 deniers 1709-1713AA	100.00	150.00	200.00	325.00
30 deniers 1709-1713D	100.00	150.00	200.00	325.00

Half sol marque 1738-54	90.00	120.00	175.00	250.00
Sol marque 1738-1760*	25.00	40.00	75.00	120.00

The piece of 30 deniers was called a *mousquetaire*, and was coined at Metz and Lyons. The 15 deniers was coined only at Metz. The sol marque and half were coined at almost every French mint, those of Paris being most common.

*Specimens of the sol marque dated after 1760 were not used in Canada, which by then was firmly in British hands.

Mint marks on French Regime coins:
Paris - A; Metz - AA; Roven - B; Lyons - D; La Roche - H; Perpignan - Q.

PLAYING CARD MONEY

In the early days of New France the first ship arriving from France in the spring of each year carried a supply of coins to be used for paying the troops and purchasing furs and other raw products. Everything that New France could not produce for itself had to be imported from France, with payment in cash. Taxes were also paid in cash. In spite of a rich trade in furs New France imported more than it exported with the result that most of the coinage received from France was shipped back (sometimes on the next ship) in payment to France. The resultant shortage of coins (particularly in winter when no ships would arrive from France) caused considerable inconvenience.

In 1685 the Intendant, Jacques de Meulles, decided to introduce an emergency issue of paper money for paying the troops. There were no printing presses in New France and the only available paper was writing paper which was not durable enough to be used as currency. Playing cards were plentiful in New France and made to be handled repeatedly, and de Meulles issued the first such notes on the backs of playing cards.

The first series of playing card money was issued in three denominations; four livres (equivalent to four English pounds) written on an entire card; two livres written on half a card; and 15 sols (the sol or sou being considered equivalent to the English shilling) written on a quarter card.

The measure adopted by de Meulles brought only temporary relief and the need for card money was met in the same manner by successive Governors and Intendants. Each new issue replaced the previous issue and stiff penalties were imposed on anyone keeping old cards after new ones were issed. It is for this reason that not a single specimen of the first eight issues of card money is known to exist today. After the first five issues, plain card was used rather than the backs of playing cards and a few of these can be found today in museum collections.

From 1685 to 1760 there were no fewer than 22 issues of card money used in New France. In the latter part of this period the supply of card money was supplemented by the issue of ordonnances (notes drawn on the Treasury at Quebec) which were printed and written on ordinary paper. Although the issuance of card money was originally intended as a temporary expedient, the economy of New France was run almost entirely on locally produced paper money of this nature for a period of seventy-five years (two and a half generations).

All playing card money is very rare.

6
PRE-CONFEDERATION COLONIAL ISSUES

MAGDALEN ISLANDS

The penny token was issued by Isaac Coffin, who planned to rule the islands like a feudal baron. At this time the islands belonged to the colony of Lower Canada. Coffin soon learned that he did not have the powers of a colonial governor, but his pennies must have circulated for a long time, since they are rather rare in very fine or better condition. The islands had been granted to Coffin, but were taken from him and put under the direct administration of Lower Canada, now the province of Quebec. There is evidence that this token was used in Halifax, Nova Scotia after being rejected by the Magdalen Islanders, and that it circulated in Halifax to a considerable extent at one time.

	Breton No.		G-4	VG-8	F-12	VF-20	EF-40
1	520	Penny token 1815	$14.00	$30.00	$75.00	$175.00	$375.00

NEWFOUNDLAND

Newfoundland was discovered by John Cabot in 1497 and claimed for England. The city of St. John's dates from about 1500. English authority was firmly established by Sir Humphrey Gilbert in 1583. Further settlements took place after 1600, but the French planted some colonies along the south coast at and near Placentia. These were ceded to the British in 1710.

Rutherford Tokens

There was no coinage specifically for Newfoundland until 1841, when the first copper tokens appeared. These were issued by R. & I.S. Rutherford of St. John's. The Rutherford family arms on the reverse contains the Latin phrase PER MARE PER TERRAS, meaning, "by land, by sea."

2-3 obv.   2 rev.   3 rev.

Breton No.			G-4	VG-8	F-12	VF-20	EF-40
2	952	RUTHERFORD etc., reverse no date	$2.00	$3.50	$7.00	$15.00	40.00
3		Same, 1841	2.00	3.50	7.00	15.00	40.00

The second issue of Rutherford tokens was issued by Rutherford Bros. of Harbour Grace. These latter pieces were struck by Ralph Heaton & Sons, whose initials RH appear above the date. Eventually the Rutherford tokens became too plentiful and fell into discredit.

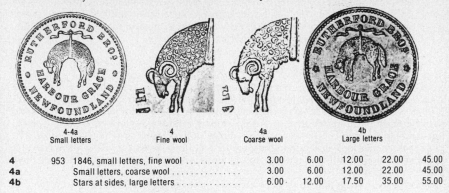

4-4a Small letters	4 Fine wool	4a Coarse wool	4b Large letters

4	953	1846, small letters, fine wool	3.00	6.00	12.00	22.00	45.00
4a		Small letters, coarse wool	3.00	6.00	12.00	22.00	45.00
4b		Stars at sides, large letters	6.00	12.00	17.50	35.00	55.00

M'Auslane Token

Number 5, of farthing size, appeared about 1845. It was not a farthing but an advertising piece issued by Peter M'Auslane, a general merchant whose business at St. John's was destroyed by fire shortly afterward. He then quit the island and settled in Ontario.

5	956	PETER M'AUSLANE etc., brass				**Extremely Rare**

Anonymous Issues

At this time lightweight halfpennies were being brought over by the barrel from Prince Edward Island, and in 1851 and again in 1860 the government had to forbid their further importation and use. The rare ship token of 1858 was struck by Heaton and issued at St. John's anonymously. It has been faked, but according to Breton, the fakes were easily exposed.

The "Fishery Rights" token of 1860 commemorates the signing of a treaty by the major fishing nations to regulate the fisheries. Shore limits were fixed, the rights of local fishermen were recognized, and steps were taken to control the behavior of foreign seamen whose vessels had to use local harbours for shelter or repairs.

	Breton No.		VG-8	F-12	VF-20	EF-40
6	954	Ship, 1858	$275.00	$350.00	$450.00	$650.00
7	955	FISHERY RIGHTS etc., 1860	30.00	40.00	50.00	125.00

PRINCE EDWARD ISLAND

Prince Edward Island was colonized by France and originally named Isle St. Jean. It was acquired by Great Britain in 1758 and governed from Nova Scotia until 1770, when it was given the status of separate colony. In 1794 it was given its present name in honour of Edward, Duke of Kent, the father of Queen Victoria.

The "Holey Dollar" and "Plug" of 1813

In 1813 the newly-arrived governor found a serious commercial crisis resulting from a lack of coined money on the island. His solution was to issue mutilated Spanish-American "dollars" (8 reales pieces), just as was being done in some of the colonies in the West Indies and elsewhere. He thus directed that up to 1,000 dollars would be perforated, forming "plugs" (the discs punched out of the center) and "holey dollars" (the rings that remained). The plugs were to pass for 1 shilling and the rings for 5 shillings; this over-rating (the whole dollars went for only 5 shillings), plus the mutilation was believed to be sufficient to keep these pieces in circulation.

Unfortunately, some individuals saw a chance to make a quick profit, and soon the colony was plagued with additional "holey" dollars (and "plugs"?) privately issued in imitation of those officially issued by the government treasury. This forced the recall of the official issue in 1814. Interestingly, the merchants then agreed to continue to accept the imitations in trade, thus raising them to the status of tokens.

Although we know of no documentary evidence regarding how the official issues were marked, purely circumstantial evidence points to a counterstamp, consisting of 10 triangles arranged in a circle, resembling a rayed sun. Furthermore, it is quite possible that the countermark was applied such that it overlapped the King's forehead on the dollars and his throat on the plugs..

There is presently no way of positively authenticating the supposed government counterstamp punch (or punches). The official and imitation issues are listed together for that reason.

Unfortunately, the situation is further complicated by the fact that later forgeries have been produced to deceive collectors. Some are complete fabrications and hence easily detected; however, others are made from genuine Spanish-American dollars and can be very difficult to differentiate from the pieces that circulated in P.E.I. Needless to say, great caution should be exercised in purchasing a purported P.E.I. "holey" dollar or "plug."

	VG-8	F-12	VF-20	EF-40	BU-60
"Holey" dollar, original or contemporary imitation	$2,000	$2,500	$4,000	$6,000	—
"Plug," original or contemporary imitation	3,500	4,500	6,500	—	—

Ships, Colonies & Commerce Tokens

The inscription on these pieces is an allusion to a remark made by Napoleon at the battle of Ulm. Ships, colonies, and commerce, he said, were the three British advantages that would defeat him in the end. The first tokens came out about 1829. These were struck in New York by Wright & Bale, and bear a striped flag superficially resembling the United States flag. These pieces were popular, and later issues were imported from England. Most were designed by Thomas Halliday. The two brass pieces dated 1815 were struck after 1830, being antedated to evade laws against anonymous tokens. The reverse of No. 9 is that of a private token of the Isle of Man.

	Breton No.		VG-8	F-12	VF-20	EF-40	BU-60
8	995	ONE HALFPENNY TOKEN, 1815	$6.00	$10.00	$20.00	$37.50	—
9	996	FOR PUBLICK ACCOMMODATION, 1815	6.00	10.00	20.00	37.50	—

	Lees No.		VG-8	F-12	VF-20	EF-40	BU-60
10	1	Ship with U.S. flag	$8.00	$14.00	$22.50	$35.00	$150.00
10a	2	Same with W & B N.Y.	12.00	20.00	30.00	60.00	225.00

It is doubtful if No. 11 (Breton's No. 999) will ever be positively identified. Its obverse, as drawn by Breton, shows a small ship very much like that of such Nova Scotia tokens as the Starr & Shannon pieces. Its reverse die has yet to be identified. The high poopdeck variety (12) has been said to be Breton 999, but this is not so. Judge Lees, who published these pieces in *The Numismatist* in 1926, made this point very clear.

11		Small ship	Existance doubted
12	5a	High poopdeck, blank flag	Extremely Rare

NOTE: Tokens #10-12 are also known to have been used in Lower Canada.

The next three varieties bear the same reverse, characterized by very large, bold lettering. The first, Lees 5b, is very rare. It has been called fraudulent, and its status is still in question.

13   13a   13b

Lees No.			VG-8	F-12	VF-20	EF-40	BU-60
13	5b	Long, low hull, no poopdeck		Extremely Rare			
13a	6	Short, choppy waves	10.00	15.00	30.00	65.00	—
13b	7	Long, running waves	7.50	12.00	20.00	45.00	—

NOTE: Tokens #13-13b are also known to have been used in Lower Canada.

The next tokens, numbered 997 by Breton, have over forty minor die varieties, some of which are very rare. They were struck in Birmingham and designed by Thomas Halliday. Most of the varieties are in the reverse inscription. For example, four styles of "&" are found on varieties of 14, 14b and 14c. The varieties of 14a all have the "&" ending in a short horizontal bar.

14a

14	23-33	Raised H on exergue line	2.50	4.00	6.00	12.00	75.00
14a	9-13	No H on exergue line	6.00	10.00	15.00	32.50	100.00

14b   14c

14b	14-22	Two guys at top of spritsail	12.00	20.00	30.00	45.00	120.00
14c	34-36	H on exergue line and in water	5.00	10.00	15.00	30.00	95.00

The next three pieces are all characterized by ships having a drooping flag at the stern. Numbers 15 and 15a, which correspond to Lees 3, are from "complete" dies in which all of the design (including rim beads) is present. There are thick (presumably struck first) and thin varieties. Lees 4, a lightweight piece of "blacksmith-like" character (see 257 and 258), was produced from the obv. die of 15, 15a and a reverse die lacking rim beads. Care should be taken not to confuse worn lightweight specimens of Lees 3 (15a) for Lees 4 (15b).

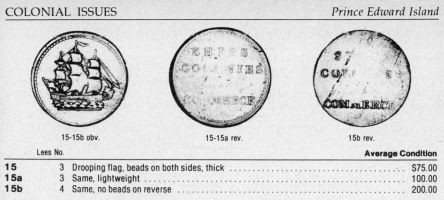

| 15-15b obv. | 15-15a rev. | 15b rev. |

Lees No.			Average Condition
15	3	Drooping flag, beads on both sides, thick	$75.00
15a	3	Same, lightweight	100.00
15b	4	Same, no beads on reverse	200.00

NOTE: Tokens #15, 15a and 15b are known to have also been used in Lower Canada.

Local Tokens 1840-1858

Local tokens appeared first in 1840, the rarest being the sheaf of wheat halfpenny. It was struck by James Milner of Charlottetown with dies and machinery imported from the United States. The "Success to the Fisheries" tokens (17-17c) were issued by E. Lydiard and F. Longworth of Charlottetown. Those with a clevis to the plow were issued in 1840, and those with a hook in 1857. The large tail to the fish fillet is well struck up, while the small tail is weak. These and all later tokens were struck by Ralph Heaton & Sons.

16

Breton No.			VG-8	F-12	VF-20	EF-40	BU-60
16	916	Sheaf of wheat 1840	$250.00	$350.00	$475.00	$700.00	—

Clevis   Hook

Weak Tail   Bold Tail

			VG-8	F-12	VF-20	EF-40	BU-60
17	917	Clevis, weak tail	2.50	5.50	11.50	22.50	65.00
17a		Clevis, bold tail	5.00	10.00	20.00	32.00	100.00
17b		Hook, weak tail	5.00	10.00	18.00	30.00	80.00
17c		Hook, bold tail	2.50	5.00	10.00	20.00	40.00

The "Cent" of 1855 was issued by James Duncan, a hardware merchant who moved to Charlottetown from Montreal. This is the first Canadian decimal piece. It is doubtful if it was accepted as a hundredth of a dollar, for it weighed the same as the other tokens which were halfpennies and which went at 150 to the Spanish dollar. Specimens on thicker flans may have been an attempt to pass them as cents by increasing the weight.

The token showing the paddle steamer was issued in 1858, probably by James Duncan, though this has not been established. Early writers attributed it to Newfoundland.

18   19

	Breton No.		VG-8	F-12	VF-20	EF-40	BU-60
18	920	ONE CENT 1855	$3.00	$6.00	$10.00	$18.00	$65.00
19	921	Paddle steamer	7.00	9.00	14.00	30.00	125.00

The tokens inscribed SELF GOVERNMENT AND FREE TRADE were issued by Henry Haszard and George and Simeon Davies. Numerous minor varieties are known. The most noticeable differences are in the island name and the style of 5 in the date. The first issues have the name rendered as PRINCE EDWARD'S ISLAND, and have 5's with short, thick tops. Later issues show first a change to 5's with longer, thinner tops, followed by a change to PRINCE EDWARD ISLAND.

20 obv.
Thick-topped 5's

21 obv.
Thin-topped 5's

20-22 rev.

20	918	PRINCE EDWARD'S 1855, thick topped 5's	2.50	5.00	8.00	12.50	50.00
20a		Same, thin-topped 5's	3.50	7.00	12.00	20.00	85.00
21	919	PRINCE EDWARD 1855	2.50	5.00	9.00	20.00	85.00
22		Same, 1857	2.00	4.00	6.00	12.00	50.00

NOVA SCOTIA

Nova Scotia was colonized for the first time in 1604 by Sieur de Monts, who claimed the land for France under the name of Acadia. Captured several times by the British, it was always returned to France, but in 1713 it passed permanently into British hands and was renamed Nova Scotia.

Very little coined money was available in the early days under the British. Some Spanish dollars and occasional shipments of British halfpennies and farthings were almost the only coins to be had. The Spanish dollar was accepted in Halifax at five shillings, which rating became legal by 1758. Halifax Currency, as this rating was called, was destined to become the standard of all the Canadian colonies.

Trade & Navigation Tokens 1812-1814

After 1800 the shortage of copper began to become serious, and about 1812 local merchants started to import tokens from England and Ireland. The first were the "Trade & Navigation" tokens, struck over the tokens of Samuel Guppy of Bristol. The farthing is known to have been imported by a Halifax merchant named Haliburton.

For many years there have been reports of a penny bearing the date 1812, but in recent years none has been found. Early auction sales record specimens dated 1812, but none has been traced.

23

24-25

1814, 1 over 0
(blundered die)

27a

26-27

	Breton No.		VG-8	F-12	VF-20	EF-40	BU-60
23	964	Farthing 1813	$32.50	$45.00	$75.00	$110.00	$285.00
24	963	Halfpenny 1812	3.50	5.50	7.50	17.00	100.00
25		Halfpenny 1813	3.50	5.50	8.50	20.00	125.00
—	(962)	Penny 1812		Existance Doubtful			
26	962	Penny 1813	6.00	9.00	16.00	36.00	135.00
27		Penny 1814, normal date	7.00	12.00	18.00	45.00	175.00
27a		Penny 1814, 2nd 1 over 0	12.00	20.00	30.00	70.00	225.00

28

28	965	Ship under topsails, 1813	3.50	5.50	11.00	24.00	100.00

Broke Token of 1814

The Broke tokens were struck in honor of Captain P.B. Vere Broke, who commanded H.M.S. *Shannon* and captured U.S.S. *Chesapeake* in 1813. This was the first British naval victory in the War of 1812.

Breton No.			VG-8	F-12	VF-20	EF-40	BU-60
29	879	Broke, 1814	$8.00	$15.00	$25.00	$50.00	$135.00

Local Merchants' Tokens 1814-1820

In 1814 merchants began to issue tokens of their own design, a few being issued anonymously. There was a great variety of these pieces issued from 1814 to 1816, and in 1817 the government ordered their removal from circulation within three years because they had become too plentiful. Most were struck in England.

31	880	FOR . . . TRADE, 1814	15.00	24.00	40.00	70.00	175.00
32	881	CARRITT & ALPORT, 1814	10.00	17.50	28.00	45.00	125.00

The tokens 33 to 38 were engraved and struck by Thomas Halliday of Birmingham. The smaller pieces (34-37) show a close relationship through the use of common obverse dies.

33	882	HOSTERMAN & ETTER, 1814	8.00	12.00	25.00	45.00	130.00

34-37
Typical obv.

Hostermann rev.   Barry rev.   British Copper rev.   Halifax rev.

Breton No.			VG-8	F-12	VF-20	EF-40	BU-60
34	883	HOSTERMAN & ETTER, 1815	$8.00	$12.00	$25.00	$45.00	$130.00
35	891	JOHN A. BARRY, 1815	5.00	10.00	20.00	38.00	125.00
36	886	GENUINE BRITISH COPPER, 1815	5.00	10.00	20.00	38.00	125.00
37	889	HALIFAX, 1815	5.00	10.00	20.00	38.00	125.00

| **38** | 888 | SUCCESS TO NAVIGATION & TRADE, 1815 ..... | 5.00 | 8.00 | 16.00 | 36.00 | 105.00 |
| **39** | 887 | GENUINE BRITISH COPPER, 1815 .... | 15.00 | 25.00 | 40.00 | 70.00 | 175.00 |

The crude pieces 41 and 42 were made, probably locally, for merchant J. Brown, and the bust and harp piece (40) may also have been made for him. All are of a "blacksmith-like" character (see page 164).

Bust obv.   Harp in wreath rev.

Warehouse obv.   JB rev.

Breton No.			Average Condition
40	—	Bust, 1815, harp in wreath	Extremely Rare
41	—	Warehouse, harp in wreath	Extremely Rare
42	—	Warehouse, script JB	$200.00

The halfpenny of J. Brown (43) was once attributed to Scotland because of its design. It has an obverse with a thistle and the Latin legend NEMO ME IMPUNE LACESSIT. The translation is "No one may hurt me with impunity."

Breton No.			VG-8	F-12	VF-20	EF-40	BU-60
43	—	PAYABLE....J. BROWN	$4.50	$7.50	$18.00	$35.00	$125.00
44	895	SUCCESS	30.00	42.50	70.00	90.00	175.00

45 obv.   46 obv.   45-46 rev.

45	885	COMMERCIAL CHANGE 1815	5.00	10.00	20.00	45.00	125.00
46	884	STARR & SHANNON 1815	4.00	8.00	16.00	32.50	100.00

47

47	890	MILES W. WHITE etc., 1815	7.00	14.00	22.50	45.00	130.00

48   49

48	892	HARDWARE 1816	4.00	7.00	12.50	24.00	85.00
49	893	W.A. & S. BLACK, 1816	5.00	8.00	15.00	30.00	85.00

The Trade & Navigation tokens of 1820 are attributed to Nova Scotia on account of this inscription. Since they are dated 1820, they would have been issued in violation of the law, for by 1820 all private tokens were to be out of circulation as required by a law passed in 1817. A variety with two shamrocks growing under the harp has been reported, but none has been seen in Canada.

50

	Breton No.		VG-8	F-12	VF-20	EF-40	BU-60
50	894	TRADE & NAVIGATION, 1820, copper	$6.50	$9.50	$18.50	$32.00	$85.00

SEMI-REGAL TOKENS 1823-1843

The withdrawal of private tokens after 1817 created a fresh shortage of small change which by the early 1820's became quite serious. Because British regal coppers could not be obtained, the provincial government made arrangements with a private coiner in England to provide coppers that were slightly lighter in weight than the corresponding official coins. This was done without the knowledge of the British government, who would surely not have allowed such a local issue at that time. These coppers are therefore best described as semi-regal tokens, as they lacked the authority of the home government.

George IV Thistle Tokens 1823-1832

The first government or semi-regal tokens were issued in 1823. These and the later issues through 1843 are known as the Thistle Tokens because of their reverse design. All issues were struck in Birmingham. There was an issue of 400,000 halfpennies in 1823 and in 1824 there was an issue of 217,776 pennies and 118,636 halfpennies.

In 1832 there was an issue of 200,000 pennies and 800,000 halfpennies. They bear the bust of George IV although coined two years after his death. Presumably the order for coins "similar in design" to those of 1824 was taken too literally.

51 obv.   51a obv.   Typical rev.

51	867	Halfpenny 1823	5.00	7.50	11.00	27.50	130.00
51a	—	Same, no hyphen in NOVA SCOTIA	10.00	15.00	20.00	40.00	200.00
52	869	Halfpenny 1824	6.50	10.00	18.50	35.00	185.00
53	871	Halfpenny 1832	3.75	7.00	12.00	32.00	100.00

54-55

Breton No.			VG-8	F-12	VF-20	EF-40	BU-60
54	868	Penny 1824	$7.00	$10.00	$24.00	$50.00	$160.00
55	870	Penny 1832	5.00	8.00	15.00	40.00	135.00

Imitations of George IV Thistle Tokens

Among the products of the clandestine "mints" of Lower Canada in the 1830's were struck imitations of the 1832 thistle tokens. They were shipped to Nova Scotia and for a time circulated along with the government issue. One much prized variety of the imitation halfpenny has the date 1382, resulting from a blundered die. This was apparently soon discovered, for a second variety with the date altered to 1832 exists. Pieces from this altered die at first glance appear to be dated 1882. Fakes have been made of the 1382 variety in order to deceive collectors; these, however, have a round topped 3 in the date as opposed to a flat topped 3 on the true 1382's.

56

Error date   Corrected date

Imitation Halfpennies

56	871	Imitation, normal date 1832	5.00	10.00	15.00	20.00	—
56a	872	Imitation, error date 1382	185.00	400.00	800.00	—	—
56b	873	Imitation, corrected date 1832	6.00	12.00	20.00	40.00	—

57

Imitation Pennies

Breton No.			VG-8	F-12	VF-20	EF-40	BU-60
57	870	Imitation penny 1832	$10.00	$16.00	$25.00	$40.00	—

Victoria Thistle Tokens 1840-1843

On the 1840 and 1843 issues of thistle tokens the portrait was that of the current British monarch, Victoria. The coiners attempted to copy William Wyon's beautiful bust used on the British regal coinage, but were not very successful. The weight and size of the Victorian thistles, particularly the 1840 halfpennies, is somewhat variable. The amount of the issue was 300,000 halfpennies and 150,000 pennies of each date. Very rare cast imitations of the 1840 halfpenny are known.

1840 0 varieties

Large   Medium   Small

58	874	Halfpenny 1840, large 0	6.00	10.00	20.00	40.00	150.00
58a		Same, medium 0	3.25	5.00	12.00	20.00	100.00
58b		Same, small 0	4.00	6.00	16.00	30.00	125.00
59		Halfpenny 1843	3.25	5.00	12.00	25.00	110.00

60	873	Penny 1840	4.00	6.50	12.00	20.00	100.00
61		Penny 1843, 3 over 0	12.00	20.00	30.00	45.00	175.00
61a		Penny 1843, normal date	5.00	8.00	16.00	32.00	105.00

Imitations of Victoria Thistle Tokens

62

| 62 | 874 | Imitation halfpenny 1840 .... | Very Rare |

PRE-DECIMAL COINAGE
Mayflower Coinage 1856

By the 1850's the attitude in Great Britain was more favorable toward the issue of local coppers in British North America and the Nova Scotia government applied for a coinage of halfpennies and pennies. Their application was accepted and the first true coins were struck for this province. They are popularly known as the Mayflower coppers because of their reverse designs and are among the most beautiful of all the Canadian colonial coppers. The master tools were engraved by Leonard C. Wyon, using his own design for the obverse and that of Halifax botanist John S. Thompson for the reverse. The halfpennies with L.C.W. under the bust exist only in proof and are most likely patterns; hence, they are not listed here (see comments in the Introduction). The coinage was executed by Heaton's Mint in Birmingham because the Royal Mint in London was too busy with the Imperial coinage at the time. Most of the pieces were struck in bronze, although the halfpenny is also known in brass.

63

64

Breton No.			VG-8	F-12	VF-20	EF-40	BU-60
63	876	Halfpenny 1856, bronze	$4.00	$6.00	$10.00	$22.50	$100.00
63a		Same, brass	25.00	40.00	60.00	—	—
64	875	Penny 1856, L.C.W. under bust	6.50	10.00	15.00	27.50	120.00
64a		Same, no L.C.W.	8.00	12.00	20.00	35.00	200.00

NEW BRUNSWICK

New Brunswick was claimed by France as part of Acadia. It was not settled until 1631, when a fort was built at the mouth of the St. John River. When Acadia was ceded to Great Britain in 1713, the French continued to dispute the British claim to New Brunswick, but gave up all claims in 1763.

Under British rule it was governed from Nova Scotia until 1784, when it was detached from Nova Scotia at the request of the inhabitants. New Brunswick was not as seriously short of coin as were the other colonies. A brisk trade with Nova Scotia kept the colony supplied to a limited extent with copper. The need for copper was not serious before 1830, when a halfpenny was anonymously issued at Saint John.

Miscellaneous Tokens ca. 1830-1845

The first piece was not issued because the name of the city was spelled incorrectly. Saint John is the largest city of New Brunswick, St. John's is the capital city of Newfoundland. Evidently this rarity was made by the manufacturers of the almost equally rare Montreal Ropery halfpenny.

The second piece appeared about 1830. Its reverse die was used also for an anonymous token issued at the same time in Lower Canada (101).

65   66

Breton No.		VG-8	F-12	VF-20	EF-40	BU-60
65	— ST. JOHN'S ... TOKEN					Extremely Rare
66	913 FOR PUBLIC ACCOMMODATION	$13.50	$22.50	$32.50	$55.00	$175.00

SEMI-REGAL TOKENS 1843

In 1841 the provincial government took steps to solve their growing shortage of copper currency by importing £3000 worth of British Imperial pennies and halfpennies. Being sterling, these coins were worth a fraction more in local currency than their face value. The government soon found that they could circulate them only at 1d and ½d local currency, because there was no way to make change for small numbers of pieces.

Only about £150 worth of the Imperial coppers had been put into circulation when the New Brunswick government decided to return the unissued remainder to England and obtain in their place tokens payable in local currency. The government entered into a contract with Mr. William Hammond of Halifax to choose the designs and make the other necessary arrangements for obtaining the new coppers. When the British government was informed of the colony's plans, it was furious. Thus rebuked, the colonial government informed the Colonial Office in London that the contract with Hammond had been cancelled and plans for the new coinage shelved.

The subsequent events are most interesting. The evidence at hand suggests that the New Brunswick government quietly went ahead with their plans and obtained coppers from Boulton & Watt of Soho. The British government knew nothing about them until 1853, when application was made for a fresh coinage of coppers by the unknowing successor of the Lt. Governor under whom the 1843's had been obtained.

67

| 67 | 910 Halfpenny 1843 .... | 4.00 | 6.00 | 12.50 | 35.00 | 135.00 |

68

	Breton No.		VG-8	F-12	VF-20	EF-40	BU-60
68	909	Penny 1843	$5.50	$7.00	$15.00	$40.00	$185.00

PRE-DECIMAL COINAGE 1854

By 1853, when a fresh coinage of pennies and halfpennies was required by the New Brunswick government, the climate in the Colonial Office was more favorable for the issue of local coinages by the British North American colonies. The master tools from the 1843 tokens were forwarded from New Brunswick to the Royal Mint, where they were used as a source of modified designs. These alterations, probably by L.C. Wyon, consisted of the substitution on the obverse of William Wyon's portrait for the British shilling on the halfpenny and that for the British halfpenny on the penny. In addition, the word CURRENCY was used in place of TOKEN on the reverse. The use of CURRENCY indicated the official nature of the issue and also implied Halifax Currency, the standard at the time. Due to a heavy schedule at the Royal Mint, the new dies were sent to the Heaton Mint, where 480,000 pieces of each denomination were struck.

69

| **69** | 912 | Halfpenny 1854 .... | 3.50 | 5.50 | 13.50 | 32.00 | 135.00 |

70

| **70** | 911 | Penny 1854 .... | 4.00 | 7.00 | 15.00 | 40.00 | 185.00 |

LOWER CANADA

New France was conquered by the British in 1760 and ceded to Great Britain in 1763. It was known as the colony of Quebec until 1791. Originally the colony included the St. Lawrence basin and the Great Lakes region, and large areas of territory extending south to the Ohio River. In 1783 the Great Lakes and the upper St. Lawrence were made the boundary with the United States. In 1791 the Great Lakes area was separated from Quebec, which now became the colony of Lower Canada. Lower Canada was predominantly French, and was the largest and most populous of the Canadian colonies.

WELLINGTON TOKENS

No special coinage was struck for Lower Canada until 1837. About 1813 anonymous tokens began to appear. The earliest were the Wellington tokens, brought over by British troops sent to Canada to fight the Americans in 1814. These tokens depicted a bust of the Duke of Wellington, and were very popular. They were often struck over other tokens. Some of them are antedated in order to evade laws passed in 1825 against private tokens.

In 1808 Napoleon sent an army into Spain and Portugal, deposed the king of Spain, and placed his brother Joseph on the Spanish throne. In the same year the British invaded Portugal and won major victories at Vimeira, Talavera, Busaco and Almeida, finally driving the French out in 1811. The action in Spain continued until 1813. Major British victories were scored at Ciudad Rodrigo, Badajoz, Salamanca, Madrid, San Sebastián, Vitoria and Pamplona. Wellington commanded the British forces during most of the period of conflict.

The Wellington pieces dated 1805 and 1811 are of questionable connection to British North America. The reverse of the 1805 token would seem to be the work of Peter Wyon for an Irish piece (also see 237).

In honor of the Peninsular campaigns J.K. Picard of Hull had the battle tokens (73-75) struck by Sir Edward Thomason of Birmingham. Specimens in silver were struck for presentation at Court, Picard having been invited by the Prince Regent to come to London and show his coppers. They are halfpenny size, but there is no expression of denomination, perhaps because they were initially intended to be more in the nature of medalets. In any case they were ultimately used as halfpenny tokens and there was even a brass imitation of one of the varieties which circulated in Canada. Note that only on 74b is the Spanish word *ciudad* (city) spelled correctly.

Numbers 76-79, 81-89 were all designed by Thomas Halliday, the Cossack penny being considered an example of his best work. Of these pieces, most varieties of 76-79, 85-86 were struck over Guppy tokens of Bristol. It is interesting to note that specimens of 86 were overstruck with other designs for use in England, proving that not all the anonymous Wellington tokens of these listed types were sent to Canada.

71   72   73   73b

Breton No.			VG-8	F-12	VF-20	EF-40	BU-60
71	976	WELLINGTON, HIBERNIA, 1805	$7.00	$15.00	$25.00	$50.00	$135.00
72	977	TRADE & COMMERCE, 1811	20.00	30.00	50.00	85.00	200.00
73	987	CUIDAD ... &c·&c·&c, copper	3.75	6.50	9.00	18.50	60.00
73a		Same, silver	65.00	120.00	155.00	240.00	400.00
73b		Imitation of 73, brass	7.00	15.00	25.00	37.50	—

74 obv.   74 rev.   74b rev.

75

74	986	CUIDAD ... MADRID, copper	3.75	6.50	9.00	18.50	60.00
74a		Same, silver	90.00	140.00	190.00	265.00	500.00
74b		CIUDAD (correct spelling), copper	16.00	20.00	30.00	50.00	135.00
75	988	SALAMANCA ... PAMPLUNO	5.50	10.00	20.00	40.00	125.00

Halfpennies

All of the undated halfpennies with HALFPENNY TOKEN on the reverse were produced by Thomas Halliday of Birmingham and most (if not all) were struck over halfpennies of Samuel Guppy.

76

76a

77

76	972	Undated, trident	3.75	5.50	13.50	27.50	100.00
76a		Undated, spear	6.50	11.50	24.00	55.00	135.00
77	971	Undated, large letters	3.75	7.00	15.00	30.00	100.00

The next three pieces, which show Britannia surrounded by a continuous wreath on the reverse, are lightweight and are believed to have been struck by Thomas Halliday on Canadian order. They are linked to the Britannia-eagle series (see pg. 132) through their reverses.

| Field Marshall obv. | Halfpenny obv. | Clockwise wreath | Counterclockwise wreath |

	Breton No.		VG-8	F-12	VF-20	EF-40	BU-60
78	973	FIELD MARSHALL, clockwise wreath				Extremely Rare	
78a		Same, counterclockwise wreath				Extremely Rare	
79	980	HALFPENNY, counterclockwise wreath	$20.00	$32.00	$50.00	$85.00	—

The Marquis Wellington halfpenny was struck by Isaac Parkes of Dublin. It is antedated, since Wellington did not become a marquis until 1814. The tokens of 1814, struck on Canadian order, also were antedated to evade the law against private tokens.

80

| **80** | 978 | MARQUIS WELLINGTON, 1813 .... | 7.00 | 11.50 | 20.00 | 50.00 | 125.00 |

The other halfpennies dated 1813, including the lightweight one dated 1814, were produced by Thomas Halliday. The 1813's were struck over Guppy halfpennies and the 1814 was probably struck on Canadian order.

81-81a

81	969	1813, plain edge	3.75	5.50	10.00	22.50	85.00
81a		1813, engrailed edge	3.75	5.50	10.00	22.50	85.00
82	979	WELLINGTON 1814	3.75	5.50	10.00	22.50	85.00

The halfpenny tokens dated 1816 are lightweight pieces struck by Halliday on Canadian order about 1830.

83   84

	Breton No.		VG-8	F-12	VF-20	EF-40	BU-60
83	981	WATERLOO 1816	$3.75	$5.50	$12.00	$30.00	$100.00
84	531	MONTREAL 1816	3.75	5.50	9.00	20.00	80.00

Pennies

In most cases the pennies produced by Thomas Halliday of Birmingham were struck over penny tokens of Samuel Guppy. It is questionable whether any of the Wellington pennies, particularly the "Cossack" penny (see below), circulated to a large degree in British North America.

Obverse   85   86

			VG-8	F-12	VF-20	EF-40	BU-60
85	970	Undated, no wreath on rev.	25.00	35.00	50.00	75.00	175.00
86		Undated, rev. wreath	20.00	30.00	45.00	60.00	150.00

The next three pennies form a group called the Peninsular Pennies because they were struck for use by Wellington's troops in Portugal and Spain. They were specially designed so that they could not be mistaken for British, Spanish or Portuguese copper coins. The "Cossack" piece is a tribute to the Russian Cossacks, who gave Napoleon's Grande Armée such an uncomfortable time in Russia in 1812 and 1813. All these pieces were struck by Sir Edward Thomason, undoubtedly from dies made by Halliday.

87

87	985	COSSACK PENNY TOKEN	15.00	25.00	37.50	55.00	220.00

Breton No.		VG-8	F-12	VF-20	EF-40	BU-60
88	974 1813 under bust	$15.00	$25.00	$37.50	$55.00	$150.00
89	984 1813 on reverse	12.50	20.00	35.00	60.00	150.00

Anonymous Tokens

Until the mid-1830's, when some of the banks began issuing tokens of their own, the copper currency was provided by merchants and other individuals. It consisted largely of anonymous halfpenny tokens. Some were brought into the colony from the other British North American provinces or from the British Isles in the pockets of immigrants or visitors. Others were surreptitiously imported in quantity and still others were produced locally. The imported tokens were often English or Irish types which had circulated in the British Isles; however, some were new designs struck on Canadian order.

In 1825 the governments of Upper and Lower Canada passed laws forbidding the further importation of private tokens. Due to a loophole in the wording, it was not illegal to import coppers that lacked a date or bore a date prior to 1825. The laws were never corrected and the way was paved for the importation of undated or antedated pieces.

The first anonymous halfpenny attributable to Lower Canada is No. 90, the VICTORIA NOBIS EST token. It was produced by Birmingham coiner Thomas Halliday and the stylistic relationship to the Wellington is unmistakable. Indeed its reverse die is that of the Wellington halfpenny No. 76a. The bust is thought to be that of Lord Nelson and the Latin legend means, "Victory is ours!". Most of this issue was struck over Guppy tokens.

| 90 | 982 VICTORIA NOBIS EST | 3.75 | 5.50 | 15.00 | 32.50 | 150.00 |

Britannia-Eagle Tokens
Original Issue 1813

The original Britannia-eagle tokens of 1813 were struck over Guppy tokens of Bristol, probably for a Boston merchant who settled in Montreal in 1813. Other lightweight pieces dated
1813-1815 are believed to have been struck much later than the dates they bear. Aside from
the difference in weight, the original 1813 issue can be distinguished from the later strikings
having the same date by the larger reverse lettering on the later strikings. Most of the 1815's
were discovered in 1867 still in mint state in a barrel in a warehouse.

91

	Breton No.		VG-8	F-12	VF-20	EF-40	BU-60
91	994	Eagle 1813	$5.00	$10.00	$20.00	$32.50	$110.00

Lightweight Antedated Issues 1813-1815

Counterclockwise wreath obv.   Clockwise wreath obv.   rev.

91a	894	Eagle 1813	10.00	20.00	30.00	40.00	125.00
92		Same 1814	4.00	8.00	15.00	30.00	105.00
93		Same 1815, counterclockwise wreath	6.00	12.00	20.00	40.00	150.00
93a		Same 1815, clockwise wreath	2.50	4.00	7.00	12.00	80.00

The next group of lightweight halfpennies presumably all come from the same coiner, as
they stem from a small number of dies used in various combinations. Some of these combinations were quite inappropriate because the dies were originally designed for coining
various size pieces. For example, the small bust obverse appears to have been made for use
with the COMMERCIAL CHANGE reverse; when it was used with the larger SHIPS COLONIES & COM-
MERCE reverse, a very broad rim resulted on the obverse. Conversly, the large bust obverse,
when used with the smaller COMMERCIAL CHANGE reverse, produced a piece that had little or
no rim design on the obverse.

These pieces were imported about 1830. Their linkage with Lower Canada is unmistakable, since they were later found in hoards in the province of Quebec. It is interesting to note
that among the tokens in one large hoard was a variety of the Ships Colonies & Commerce
token. This piece, No. 13a (see page 120), has always been considered a variety of Breton
997, but it portrays a very different ship. The hull is much shorter than on the varieties of
Breton 997, and the water is very rough.

Obverses

Ship   Large bust   Medium bust

Small bust   Military bust   Military bust
               (open sleeve)   (closed sleeve)

Reverses

WELLINGTON   SHIPS, etc.   COMMERCIAL   TRADE
WATERLOO   CHANGE

	Breton No.		VG-8	F-12	VF-20	EF-40	BU-60
94	1003	Ship, rev. WELLINGTON WATERLOO 1815	$7.50	$12.00	$22.50	$40.00	$110.00
95	1006	Large bust, rev. WELLINGTON WATERLOO 1815	6.00	10.00	20.00	32.50	110.00
96	1002	Large bust, rev. SHIPS, etc.	6.00	10.00	25.00	42.00	130.00
96a		Medium bust, rev. SHIPS, etc.	14.00	22.50	35.00	65.00	165.00
96b		Small bust (broad rim), rev. SHIPS, etc.	20.00	35.00	50.00	80.00	—
97	1007	Large bust, rev. COMMERCIAL CHANGE (no rim)	30.00	50.00	90.00	150.00	—
97a		Small bust, rev. COMMERCIAL CHANGE	5.00	8.00	15.00	25.00	85.00
98	992	Large bust, rev. TRADE 1825	Extremely Rare				
98a		Military bust (open sleeve), rev. TRADE 1825	3.75	5.50	10.00	22.50	60.00
98b		Same, closed sleeve	5.50	10.00	20.00	40.00	125.00

Other Anonymous Issues

99   100

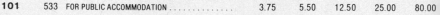

Breton No.			VG-8	F-12	VF-20	EF-40	BU-60
99	1011	Bust 1820, rev. "Commerce"	$5.50	$10.00	$20.00	$40.00	$120.00
100	1001	Ship, rev. "Commerce"		Extremely Rare			

The halfpennies inscribed "For Public Accommodation" were issued about 1830. They were struck with the same reverse die used for 66, the token of Saint John, New Brunswick.

101

101	533	FOR PUBLIC ACCOMMODATION	3.75	5.50	12.50	25.00	80.00

The "Canada" tokens of 1830 and 1841, although seemingly anonymous, are known to have been issued by James Duncan, a hardware merchant of Montreal. He later settled in Charlottetown, Prince Edward Island, where he circulated these pieces until issuing his "cents" in 1855 (Nos. 18-22).

102	532	CANADA 1830	3.75	9.00	15.00	30.00	85.00
103		CANADA 1841	3.75	9.00	15.00	30.00	85.00

Private Tokens
Bearing the Issuer's Name

The private tokens bearing their issuer's names are extremely variable in weight and quality. The only really honest token in this regard is the Molson halfpenny of 1837. The Montreal Ropery halfpenny was issued about 1824, shortly before the firm changed hands. The Mullins token was issued in anticipation that the son would enter into partnership, but this did not happen.

104   105

104	564	R. W. OWEN ROPERY	1,000	1,800	2,800	—	—
105	563	FRANCIS MULLINS & SON ... MONTREAL	10.00	18.00	27.50	50.00	140.00

T.S. Brown, the issuer of 106, was a hardware merchant who took up arms in the Rebellion of 1837, and had to flee to the United States when the rebellion was put down. He remained there until amnesty was granted in 1844.

John Shaw's halfpenny was issued at Quebec in 1837. Shaw withdrew his tokens when the Quebec Bank issued its Habitant tokens the following year.

Breton No.			VG-8	F-12	VF-20	EF-40	BU-60
106	561	T.S. BROWN ... MONTREAL	$4.50	$7.50	$18.00	$32.50	$120.00
107	565	J. SHAW ... QUEBEC	6.00	8.50	22.50	32.50	125.00

The Molson halfpenny was struck in Montreal by Jean Marie Arnault, who also engraved the dies, probably from designs submitted by the Company. The obverse is a copy in reverse of that of a halfpenny token issued in Perth, Scotland, in 1797.

108	562	MOLSON, copper	90.00	120.00	185.00	280.00	500.00
108a		Same, silver (Not struck for circulation)	—	—	—	3,000	4,500

The Roy token was issued in 1837. Specimens on thin flans were mady by a journeyman employed by the manufacturer. This individual would run off a few extra specimens from the dies whenever he needed money for liquor. The appearance of these lightweight sous forced Roy to withdraw his tokens to avoid discredit.

109	671	J. ROY, thick flan	20.00	30.00	50.00	135.00	300.00
109a		Same, thin flan	20.00	30.00	50.00	135.00	300.00

The Bust and Harp Tokens 1820-1825

These halfpennies first appeared in Lower Canada about 1825. Their design was undoubtedly inspired by the Irish regal halfpennies. The originals were struck in Dublin and are dated 1825. They have denticles at the rims. A second pair of dies, with the reverse also dated 1825 but without rim denticles, was prepared. It is assumed that upon instructions from those who ordered the tokens, the date on this second die was altered to 1820 and pieces struck. One may further assume the purpose in overdating was to antedate the tokens so they would not be excluded from importation by the law passed in Lower Canada in 1825. A non-overdated 1820 reverse dies was also used.

1820—0 over 5

Normal date

Originals

	Breton No.		VG-8	F-12	VF-20	EF-40	BU-60
110	1012	Bust and harp 1825	$200.00	$300.00	$600.00	—	—
111		Same, 1820, 0 over 5		Extremely Rare			
111a		Same, 1820, normal date	5.50	10.00	12.50	20.00	—

Vast quantities of imitations (mostly in brass) of the bust and harp halfpennies were locally produced, probably about 1837. The next two tokens were very likely the product of the same "mint." No. 112 is of moderately good quality and is by far the most common today. No. 113 is noticeably cruder, almost of "blacksmith" style (see 259).

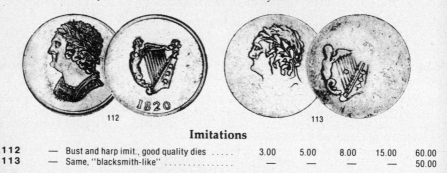

112   113

Imitations

		VG-8	F-12	VF-20	EF-40	BU-60
112	— Bust and harp imit., good quality dies	3.00	5.00	8.00	15.00	60.00
113	— Same, "blacksmith-like"	—	—	—	—	50.00

The next piece is perhaps Lower Canadian, but its attribution to British North America is hardly firm. Considered by some to be part of the "blacksmith" series, its uncertain status dictates that it should be listed here temporarily until conclusive evidence can be found. Note that the bust faces right.

114

114	— Bust and harp, legend	200.00	—	—	—	—

The Tiffin Tokens

About 1832 a Montreal grocer named Joseph Tiffin imported from England copper halfpennies the design of which was a copy of pieces that had circulated twenty years earlier in Great Britain (and perhaps to a much lesser degree in British North America as well). The original pieces were struck by Birmingham coiner Thomas Halliday; they are of good weight, have an engrailed edge and bear Halliday's "H" on the truncation of the bust of George III. Collectors have come to call "Tiffins" any tokens of the bust and commerce 1812 design, whether or not they are the variety issued by him.

The pieces actually circulated by Tiffin appeared later (see below).

115

Halliday Copper Originals

Breton No.			VG-8	F-12	VF-20	EF-40	BU-60
115	960	Halfpenny 1812, with H	$2.50	$6.50	$15.00	$35.00	$125.00

116 obv.   116-117 Rev.

117-118   118-119
Obv.   Rev.

116	959	Penny, 1812 on reverse	6.00	12.50	25.00	40.00	100.00
117	957	Penny, 1812 on both sides	6.00	12.50	20.00	35.00	100.00
118	958	Penny, 1812 on obverse	5.00	8.00	15.00	25.00	75.00
119	958	Penny, 1813 on obverse	6.50	10.50	22.00	35.00	100.00

Halfpennies Probably Circulated by Tiffin

The writings of R.W. MacLachlan suggest that the tokens ordered by Joseph Tiffin in 1832 were halfpennies of the kind shown below. They are of medium weight, are well executed and struck in copper. They are most easily separated from the original strikings by their plain edge and the lack of the letter "H" on the truncation.

Breton No.			VG-8	F-12	VF-20	EF-40	BU-60
120	960	Halfpenny 1812, no H	$3.00	$5.00	$8.00	$15.00	$65.00

Lightweight Imitations in Copper Alloys

Like the bust and harp halfpennies, Tiffin's pieces were soon buried by a vast quantity of lightweight, poorly executed imitations. Various copper alloys were used, so the color of the imitations varies from brassy yellow to the brown of nearly pure copper. These pieces were quite probably produced by the same "mint" that was responsible for the bust and harp imitations. There were two basic obverse designs (wreath running counterclockwise or clockwise) and two reverses (legend and date or date only).

| | Wreath Counterclockwise | Wreath clockwise | Value and date | Date only | |

121	960	Value & date, wreath counterclockwise. . . .	2.50	4.00	8.00	20.00	60.00
121a		Same, wreath clockwise	2.50	4.00	8.00	20.00	60.00
122		Date only, wreath counterclockwise	2.50	3.50	6.00	15.00	60.00
122a		Same, wreath clockwise	2.50	3.50	6.00	15.00	60.00

The Vexator Canadiensis Tokens

These pieces appeared perhaps in the mid-1830's and are close relatives of the "blacksmiths" (see 261 and 262) in that their devices, though very crudely executed, resemble those on the British regal halfpennies. The "classical" Vexators, Breton 558 and 559, have legends which are satirical and at the same time cleverly designed to evade the laws against forgery, sedition and the issue of private tokens.

To ensure that they would be accepted in change, the tokens bore a bust on the obverse and a seated female figure on the reverse, thus superficially resembling English regal copper. To avoid being prosecuted for forgery, the issuers made use of inscriptions quite different from those seen on regal copper.

They are satirical pieces in that the types are caricatures and the legends definitely provocative. The obverse legend as usually read means, "The Tormentor of Canada." The reverse legend means, "Wouldn't you like to catch them." and could allude to those who put the coins into circulation. However, the toils of the law were foreseen here and cleverly avoided. The third letter in the obverse legend is very vague in form, and could easily be an N as an X. The word could then be read as VENATOR and the legend translated as "A Canadian Trapper." The bust is very shaggy and appears to be wearing a fur cap such as trappers wore in those days. The reverse legend could as easily have referred to fur-bearing animals as to the issuers of the tokens. Thus, if caught, the issuers could plead that the pieces were really medalets honoring the fur trade, of which Montreal was in those days an important center.

The date 1811 is clearly an antedate. After going to all the trouble to evade prosecution for forgery and sedition, the issuers were not going to run afoul of the law of 1825 against private tokens. This method of evasion was very easy. The light and variable weight of these tokens also indicates that they are antedated, for nothing as light as these would have been acceptable in 1811.

Who was the "Tormentor of Canada?" Since the tokens are antedated, it certainly was not Sir James Craig, autocratic though he was. It probably was King William IV, whose attitude toward colonies, especially those acquired from other countries in warfare, was very harsh. Almost any of the governors of Lower Canada from 1830 to 1838, or some particularly obnoxious local officials of the period, also could have qualified for this dubious title.

The fur-trade aspect of these tokens is the fruit of brilliant reasoning by Dr. J.P.C. Kent of the British Museum and R.H.M. Dolley of Belfast. The evasion of the laws against forgery was suggested to the author by R.C. Bell of Newcastle-on-Tyne, who pointed out that it was in the technique of the makers of the old English "Bungtown" tokens. It has been known since the time of R.W. McLachlan that these pieces were antedated, but the fact had been almost forgotten in recent years.

There are two very rare Vexators in addition to the "classical" ones. The first is from the reverse die of Breton 558, but has a new obverse, apparently with only the date 1810 in addition to the crude bust. The second is from entirely new dies. There seems to be only a bust on the obverse. The so-called "variety" of Breton 559 with a ML. in the obverse legend is not a variety at all. The ML. simply doesn't show on many of the pieces; they were all struck from the same obverse die.

123 Obverse   124 Obverse   123-124 Rev.

Breton No.			Average Condition
123	558	VEXATOR CANADIN SIS 1811	$125.00
124	—	Obverse dated 1810, but no legend	Extremely Rare

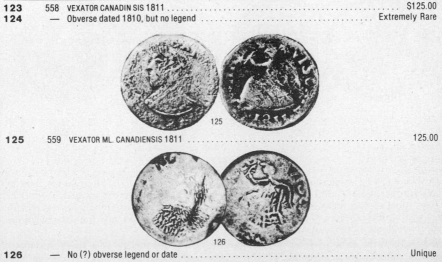

125	559	VEXATOR ML. CANADIENSIS 1811	125.00
126	—	No (?) obverse legend or date	Unique

THE FIRST BANK TOKENS 1835-1837
BANK OF MONTREAL

In 1835 the banks refused to take any more anonymous brass pieces and other metallic trash except by weight. To supply a copper coinage, the Bank of Montreal began issuing halfpenny tokens of good weight. The value was inscribed in French on the reverse, but was incorrectly expressed by the plural form SOUS rather than SOU. This did not hinder their circulation at all. In 1836 the bank received government authority to supply copper, and added its name to the reverse inscriptions, but did not correct the value, for the error was taken by everyone as a guarantee of authenticity. The Bank of Montreal sous were struck in Birmingham. Each year there was an issue of about 72,000.

	Breton No.		VG-8	F-12	VF-20	EF-40	BU-60
127	713	BANK TOKEN MONTREAL	$2.50	$5.00	$12.00	$35.00	$110.00
128	714	BANK OF MONTREAL TOKEN	2.50	5.00	12.00	35.00	110.00

BANQUE DU PEUPLE

The first sou of the Banque du Peuple was the so-called "Rebellion Sou," issued in 1837. It received its name because of the addition of a small star and a liberty cap on the reverse, said to have been done at the instigation of an accountant who favoured the cause of the rebels of 1837. It was soon discovered, and the token was replaced with another type in 1838. The Rebellion Sou was engraved by Jean Marie Arnault of Montreal, who struck about 12,000 pieces. There is considerable variation in size and weight.

The second sou of the Bank du Peuple (130) was issued in 1838 to replace the Rebellion sou. It was struck in Belleville, New Jersey, and about 84,000 were struck.

129	716	"Rebellion" sou	6.00	12.50	30.00	55.00	165.00
130	715	BANQUE DU PEUPLE, "oak" wreath	2.50	5.00	12.00	35.00	110.00

BOUQUET SOUS

The Bouquet Sous are imitations of the Bank of Montreal tokens. The latter pieces were so popular that lightweight imitations soon appeared, bearing a similar obverse bouquet of roses, thistles, shamrocks, and wheat. Inscriptions were entirely in French, however (with the words AGRICULTURE and COMMERCE the same in both languages), and the value was correctly rendered in the singular.

Because of the wide usage of the Bouquet Sous, they became the first series to achieve great popularity with collectors. They have been more thoroughly studied than other colonial issues, and it has been traditional to collect them by die variety.

Bouquet Sous are most easily identified by first counting the number of leaves in the reverse wreath. This number will serve to locate a general area in one of the groups below, after which details may be compared with the notes below the illustrations. Such points as the number and location of shamrocks and relative position of letters, berries, and leaves will serve as guides to identification. To illustrate, an enlarged bouquet token (in this case No. 157) is shown with arrows pointing to the shamrocks, roses, thistles and ears of wheat on obverse. The number of leaves on the wreath can be counted.

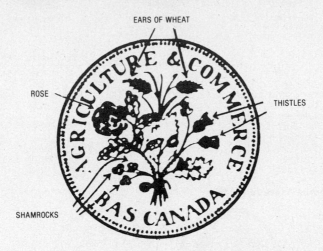

I. Belleville Issues

The Belleville mint was a private company in Belleville, New Jersey, whose production was mainly American tokens.

Sixteen leaves in reverse wreath:

Rev. A—no berry   Rev. B—no berry   Rev. C—berries
left of bow   right of bow   each side of bow

Obv. 1—dots for   Obv. 2—shamrock   Obv. 3—stalk
stops in legend   and large leaf   between thistles
                         lower left   at left

Obv. 4—high bow, shamrock between thistles; thin stops	Obv. 5—2 horizontal thistles; 2 shamrocks lower right	Obv. 6—bent stalk under UL

	Breton No.		VG-8	F-12	VF-20	EF-40	BU-60
131	680	Rev. A, obv. 1	$5.00	$10.00	$22.00	$45.00	$165.00
132	—	Same, obv. 2			Unique		
133	678	Same, obv. 3	3.50	6.50	12.50	30.00	125.00
134	679	Same, obv. 4	3.50	6.50	12.50	30.00	125.00
135	—	Same, obv. 5	—	—	—	—	—
136	681	Rev. B, obv. 5	165.00	250.00	450.00	—	—
137	682	Same, obv. 6	12.50	25.00	40.00	55.00	175.00
138	675	Rev. C, obv. 2	325.00	475.00	850.00	—	—
139	677	Same, obv. 3	165.00	250.00	450.00	600.00	—
140	676	Same, obv. 6	18.00	30.00	45.00	70.00	175.00

Seventeen leaves in reverse wreath:

Rev. D—17 leaves	Obv. 7—rose flanked by 2 pairs of stalks

141	683	Rev. D, obv 1	10.00	15.00	30.00	45.00	160.00
142	—	Same, obv. 5			Extremely Rare		
143	—	Same, obv. 7			Unique		

Eighteen leaves in reverse wreath, no bow:

Rev. E— UN close together	Rev. F— berry left of bottom N	Rev. G— berry over bottom N	Obv. 8— similar to obv. 4; thick stops

144	—	Rev. E, obv. 5			Extremely Rare		
145	688	Same, obv. 7	$6.50	$10.50	$22.00	$40.00	$140.00
146	687	Same, obv. 8	8.50	17.50	28.00	45.00	165.00
147	685	Rev. F, obv. 5	8.50	20.00	55.00	90.00	185.00
148	686	Rev. G, obv. 5	6.50	10.50	22.00	55.00	165.00

Eighteen leaves in reverse wreath, with bow:

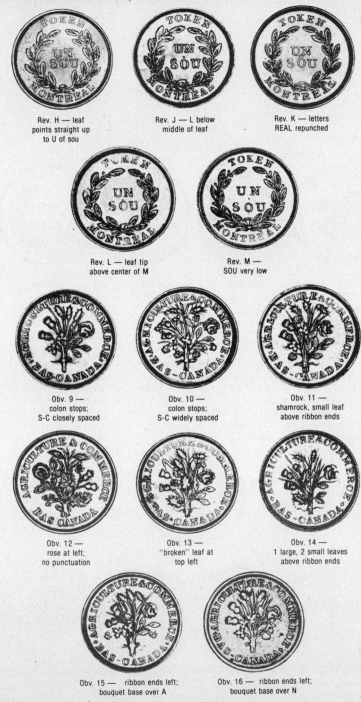

Rev. H — leaf
points straight up
to U of sou

Rev. J — L below
middle of leaf

Rev. K — letters
REAL repunched

Rev. L — leaf tip
above center of M

Rev. M —
SOU very low

Obv. 9 —
colon stops;
S-C closely spaced

Obv. 10 —
colon stops;
S-C widely spaced

Obv. 11 —
shamrock, small leaf
above ribbon ends

Obv. 12 —
rose at left;
no punctuation

Obv. 13 —
"broken" leaf at
top left

Obv. 14 —
1 large, 2 small leaves
above ribbon ends

Obv. 15 — ribbon ends left;
bouquet base over A

Obv. 16 — ribbon ends left;
bouquet base over N

	Breton No.		VG-8	F-12	VF-20	EF-40	BU-60
149	696	Rev. H, obv. 1	$22.50	$38.00	$55.00	$85.00	$220.00
150	691	Rev. J, obv. 9	5.00	10.00	20.00	32.50	150.00
151	695	Rev. K, obv. 1	5.00	10.00	20.00	32.50	150.00
152	692	Same, obv. 4	5.00	10.00	20.00	32.50	150.00
153	693	Same, obv. 7	5.00	10.00	25.00	40.00	200.00
154	694	Same, obv. 10	5.00	10.00	20.00	32.50	150.00
155	697	Rev. L, obv. 11	9.00	15.00	25.00	50.00	250.00
156	698	Same, obv. 12	15.00	25.00	45.00	70.00	235.00
157	699	Rev. M, obv. 12	7.50	13.50	22.50	40.00	160.00
158	703	Same, obv. 13	375.00	550.00	900.00	—	—
159	702	Same, obv. 14	5.50	9.50	20.00	40.00	160.00
160	700	Same, obv. 15	5.50	9.50	20.00	40.00	160.00
161	701	Same, obv. 16	25.00	35.00	50.00	75.00	250.00

Twenty leaves in reverse wreath:

Obv. 17 —	Rev. N —	Obv. 18 —	Rev. P —
2 shamrocks	small bow	no shamrocks	large bow
lower right		lower right	

			VG-8	F-12	VF-20	EF-40	BU-60
162	704	Rev. N, obv. 17	$5.50	$9.50	$20.00	$40.00	$160.00
163	705	Rev. P, obv. 18	7.50	12.50	22.50	40.00	160.00

II. Birmingham Issues

The sous numbered 164 through 169 were struck in Birmingham, England by the same firm that produced the early sous of the Bank of Montreal. These issues can be readily distinguished by the large number of leaves (32-42) in the wreath on the reverse. The bouquet sou assigned number 712 by Breton was exposed as fraud by McLachlan, who described how it was made. All specimens of this variety seen by the authors are fabrications. It is therefore not assigned a number in this catalogue.

Thirty-two leaves in reverse wreath:

Rev. R — 32 leaves

Obv. 19 —	Obv. 20 —	Obv. 21 —	Obv. 22 —
no shamrocks	1 shamrock	2 shamrocks	English legend;
at lower left	at lower left	at lower left	2 roses

Breton No.		VG-8	F-12	VF-20	EF-40	BU-60
164	706 Rev. R, obv. 19	32.50	45.00	65.00	80.00	250.00
165	707 Same, obv. 20	6.50	9.00	25.00	50.00	125.00
166	708 Same, obv. 21	7.00	12.00	25.00	55.00	165.00
167	709 Same, obv. 22	12.00	24.00	37.50	60.00	210.00

Forty-two leaves in reverse wreath:

Rev. S —	Obv. 23 —	Obv. 23a —
42 leaves	1 large, 2 small sham-rocks at lower left	1 shamrock right, 2 left

		VG-8	F-12	VF-20	EF-40	BU-60
168	710 Rev. S, obv. 21	$9.50	$18.00	$32.00	$60.00	$190.00
169	711 Same, obv. 23	7.50	14.00	27.50	50.00	165.00
—	712 Same, obv. 23a		Authenticity Questionable			

III. Montreal Issues

Several varieties of the bouquet sous were produced in Montreal by Jean Marie Arnault. Nos. 171 and 172 are routinely struck over other tokens withdrawn from circulation, quite possibly in 1837. No. 170 was long thought to be No. 171 struck over an Upper Canada sloop token (No. 199); however, closer examination shows that neither of the dies used for the overstriking was that of No. 171 or any other catalogued sou. The lettering is quite small and the bouquet clearly different from that on No. 173-174. It is very possible that the "small letters" sou was a prototype for the sou No. 171 and that the dies were created in both cases for the purpose of overstriking other tokens.

The last two varieties, which share the same obverse, were postulated by Courteau to have been "patterns" for a coinage of sous for one of the Montreal banks, perhaps the City Bank. As this is far from proven, we list these pieces here.

Obv. 24 —	Rev. T —	Obv. 25 —	Rev. U —
small letters in legend	small letters in legend	1 shamrock right, 4 left	16 small leaves

Obv. 26 — 4 shamrocks right; 2 left	Rev. V — 17 leaves with bow

Obv. 27 —
English legend

Rev. W -
½ penny token 1837

Rev. X —
½ penny bank token

	Breton No.		VG-8	F-12	VF-20	EF-40	BU-60
170	—	Rev. T, obv. 24			Unique		
171	674	Rev. U, obv. 25	$5.50	$10.00	$15.00	$32.50	$175.00
172	684	Rev. V, obv. 26	6.50	15.00	30.00	45.00	175.00
173	672	Rev. W, obv. 27			Unique		
174	673	Rev. X, obv. 27			Extremely Rare		

IV. Miscellaneous Issues

The first two varieties probably never circulated; both were unknown until at least the 1860's and do not come in well worn condition. The dies and a few "original" specimens of No. 175 were found in Montreal. A small number of restrikes were struck in various metals after the dies had been fitted with a collar. Most specimens of No. 176 are known as "proofs" and were found in Boston. For that reason this variety has been called the "Boston" sou.

Number 177 is a heavy piece which could well have circulated more in the United States than it did in Canada. Its reverse is thought to have been originally intended for a token for Belleville butcher T.D. Seaman. The U in DUSEAMAN was deliberately made to facilitate passing these pieces off as anonymous cents in the United States.

Obv. 28 —
small bouquet;
no shamrocks

Rev. Y —
small N's

Obv 29 —
shamrocks with
round leaves

Rev. Z —
18 leaves
no bow

Obv. 5 —
(see page 148)

Rev. —
"T. DUSEAMAN
BUTCHER"

175	689	Rev. Y, obv. 28. Original, struck without collar	125.00	200.00	325.00	450.00	—
175a	(689)	Same, restrike, struck with collar	—	—	150.00	225.00	350.00
176	690	Rev. Z, obv. 29; the "Boston" sou	—	—	150.00	225.00	350.00
177	670	Rev. DUSEAMAN, obv. 5	15.00	25.00	40.00	100.00	250.00

LATER BANK TOKENS
Habitant Tokens

The Habitant tokens, so called because they show on the obverse a Canadian habitant in traditional winter costume, were released early in 1838. They were struck by Boulton & Watt. The Bank of Montreal, the Quebec Bank, the City Bank, and the Banque du Peuple participated in the issue, with the bank name appearing on the reverse ribbon. The Bank of Montreal issued 240,000 pennies and 480,000 halfpennies, and each of the others issued 120,-000 pennies and 240,000 halfpennies.

179

	Breton No.		VG-8	F-12	VF-20	EF-40	BU-60
178	522	Halfpenny, CITY BANK	$2.50	$4.00	$6.50	$12.00	$65.00
179		Same, QUEBEC BANK	2.50	4.00	6.50	12.00	65.00
180		Same, BANQUE DU PEUPLE	3.25	6.50	10.00	20.00	75.00
181		Same, BANK OF MONTREAL	3.00	5.00	9.00	20.00	75.00

183

182	521	Penny, CITY BANK	3.00	5.00	9.00	20.00	70.00
183		Same, QUEBEC BANK	4.00	5.50	12.00	22.50	80.00
184		Same, BANQUE DU PEUPLE	6.50	10.00	20.00	30.00	110.00
185		Same, BANK OF MONTREAL	5.00	7.00	12.00	25.00	100.00

Side View Tokens

The "Side View" tokens, so called because they show a corner view of the Bank of Montreal building, were struck by Cotterill, Hill & Co. of Walsall, England. In 1838 the coiners shipped 120,000 pennies and 240,000 halfpennies to Montreal. The bank returned the coins because their workmanship was far inferior to that of the Habitant tokens, and the copper was brassy. The most probable point of objection on the obverse is the trees, which appear "frizzy." The reverse is considerably cruder than that for the Habitant pieces. In 1839 another 120,000 pennies and 240,000 halfpennies arrived, but these were also returned with the complaint that they were even worse than the shipment of 1838.

The reverse of the 1839's is an improvement over the 1838 issue. The fault is in the obverse, which has the bank building rendered in atrocious perspective. Note the portico, for example. These tokens are more expensive than rare today.

187   188

	Breton No.		VG-8	F-12	VF-20	EF-40	BU-60
186	524	Halfpenny 1838	285.00	365.00	475.00	625.00	825.00
187		Halfpenny 1839	285.00	365.00	475.00	625.00	825.00
188	523	Penny 1838	500.00	625.00	800.00	900.00	1,400
189		Penny 1839	500.00	625.00	800.00	900.00	1,400
190		Penny 1839, BANQUE DU PEUPLE			Very Rare		

UPPER CANADA

In 1791 the Great Lakes region was detached from Quebec and organized as the colony of Upper Canada. It is now the Province of Ontario. Very little coined money was in use before 1800. A few of the Wellington tokens trickled in from Lower Canada after 1814, and local tokens appeared about 1812.

The Brock Tokens

The Brock tokens were struck about 1816 to honor one of the heroes of the War of 1812, Major General Sir Isaac Brock. Brock was commander of the British troops in Upper Canada. In July of 1812 he captured Detroit and on 13 October of that year successfully repulsed an American invasion attempt at Queenstown (near Niagara Falls), although Brock himself was killed in the battle. The tokens are light in weight. They soon became too plentiful and fell into discredit. Note the spelling blunder on 191 (BROOK instead of BROCK). No. 193 is a mule struck from very worn dies.

		Ship obv.	Monument obv.		Text rev.			1816 rev.	
191	723	Ship, text			$5.00	$15.00	$28.00	$55.00	$125.00
192	724	Monument, 1816......................			3.75	5.50	11.00	28.00	85.00
193	725	Ship, 1816...........................			24.00	40.00	80.00	—	—

The Sloop Tokens

These tokens feature on their obverses a sloop, which was in those days the chief means of transportation on the Great Lakes. This obverse was the work of John Sheriff of Liverpool. The tokens are heavier, as Upper Canada by this time was using Halifax Currency. Most of them are antedated to evade the law against private tokens enacted in 1825. As this law became a dead letter, later issues bore the actual date of issue. The "hunter" piece (198) is a mule struck from very worn dies. Its reverse die was used previously to strike one of the Nova Scotia tokens (45).

Obverse	Anvil rev.	Upper Canada rev.

Jamaica rev.	Plow rev.	Hunter rev.

Antedated Issues

Breton No.			VG-8	F-12	VF-20	EF-40	BU-60
194	727	Anvil 1820	$5.50	$11.00	$25.00	$40.00	$125.00
195	728	UPPER CANADA on cask, 1821.............	35.00	50.00	70.00	125.00	—
196	729	JAMAICA on cask, 1821	250.00	400.00	550.00	—	—
197	730	Plow 1823	7.50	12.00	22.50	45.00	135.00
198	726	Hunter 1815	22.50	32.50	55.00	—	—

199   200

Contemporaneously Dated Issues

199	730	Plow 1833	3.75	6.50	13.50	22.50	100.00
200	731	Tools 1833, brass	4.50	7.50	17.00	27.50	125.00

The Lesslie Tokens

These tokens were issued by a drug and book firm with shops in Toronto, Dundas, and Kingston. The first halfpennies were issued from 1824 to 1827 and have a plain edge. Note the use of York, which was the old name for Toronto; the change took place in 1834. A second issue of halfpennies (1828-1830) has an engrailed edge and a comma after YORK. The twopence was engraved by Thomas Wells Ingram and was struck at least as early as 1827. A specimen was found in the cornerstone during the demolition of the old Courthouse of Hamilton, Ontario, which was built in that year. Because of its size, the twopence was never popular and many became washers. Both Lesslie denominations are unique in being the only Upper Canada issues containing French in their inscriptions. They have the phrase, LA PRUDENCE ET LA CANDEUR, meaning "wisdom and honesty."

	Breton No.		VG-8	F-12	VF-20	EF-40	BU-60
201	718	LESSLIE & SONS, halfpenny plain edge	$5.50	$9.00	$22.50	$45.00	$110.00
201a		Same, engrailed edge	7.00	12.00	27.50	55.00	135.00

202	717	Twopence 1822	100.00	175.00	300.00	500.00	—

Miscellaneous Tokens

About 1830 tokens inscribed NO LABOUR NO BREAD were imported into Toronto by Perrins Bros., a dry goods firm. Because of the act outlawing private tokens, however, the pieces were seized by the Customs Dept. and ordered to be melted down. A large number of the coppers "fell to the floor", as it has been so quaintly said, and so escaped the melting pot and entered circulation. They were occasionally found in change as late as 1837.

203	1010	NO LABOUR, NO BREAD	$4.50	$9.00	$18.00	$35.00	$125.00

In 1832 a halfpenny token (204) was issued of honest size and weight. It was struck in Birmingham by the firm which struck the thistle tokens of Nova Scotia. Like the Nova Scotia issues of 1832, this piece shows the bust of George IV, even though it was then two years after his death. It is not yet known whether this token is semi-regal or private.

204

Breton No.			VG-8	F-12	VF-20	EF-40	BU-60
204	732	Halfpenny, George IV 1832	$15.00	$25.00	$40.00	$60.00	$125.00

THE NORTHWEST

FUR TRADE TOKENS

What was loosely termed "the Northwest" in colonial times included all of British North America north and west of colonial Canada to the Pacific coast and the Arctic Archipelago. This vast region was the preserve of the Hudson's Bay Company. No settlement took place anywhere in this region before Lord Selkirk opened up the valley of the Red River, later to become the province of Manitoba. Beyond this area the only permanent establishments were the trading posts of the Hudson's Bay Company and its rival, the Northwest Company. After years of bitter strife the two companies merged in 1821.

On the west coast, Vancouver Island was detached from the Company and set up as a Crown Colony. The British Columbia mainland was separated in 1858 as a second Crown Colony. In 1866 these two colonies united, and the united colony entered the Dominion of Canada in 1871. The remainder of the territory of the Hudson's Bay Company was acquired by the Dominion of Canada in 1869.

Northwest Company Token 1820

The Northwest Company token was struck in Birmingham in 1820. It is not known by whom, but its style suggests that it may have been struck by the makers of Nova Scotia coinage of 1823-1843. Many known specimens of this piece were found in the lower valley of the Columbia River in Oregon, which is now in the United States. For this reason it is sometimes considered an American piece. It is also thought of as Canadian because it was issued by a Canadian firm. All but one of the known specimens is holed. It is believed that they were issued holed to facilitate wearing them as medalets or attaching them to garments.

205

205	925	NORTHWEST COMPANY, copper	$650.00	$750.00	$950.00	—	—
205a		Same, brass	600.00	700.00	850.00	—	—

Hudson's Bay Company Tokens

The brass tokens of the Hudson's Bay Company were issued around 1854. At the top of the reverse is the Company's HB monogram, below which are the initials EM for the East Main district, south and east of Hudson Bay. The tokens have been found in northern Quebec and Ontario, and as far west as Manitoba. They are erroneously valued in "new beaver." The unit of the fur trade was the "made beaver," which is an adult beaver skin in prime condition. It was never cut up, so the Company thought that tokens would be the ideal way in which to express fractions of the made beaver. The Indians, however, preferred to trust the Company accounts rather than take the tokens, which were easily lost. For this reason the pieces never circulated in large quantities. When it was decided to redeem them, the tokens were punched on the reverse at the top to show that they had been redeemed and cancelled. The number of unpunched pieces available now suggests that they were not all presented to be redeemed, or that not all company offices punched them as they were redeemed.

	Breton No.		VG-8	F-12	VF-20	EF-40	BU-60
206	929	⅛ made beaver	$32.00	$40.00	$50.00	$70.00	$125.00
207	928	¼ made beaver	32.00	40.00	50.00	70.00	125.00
208	926	½ made beaver	32.00	40.00	50.00	70.00	125.00
209	926	1 made beaver	32.00	40.00	50.00	70.00	125.00

PROVINCE OF CANADA

Bank of Montreal
"Front View" Tokens 1842-1845

In 1841 Upper and Lower Canada were reunited to form the colony or province of Canada. The Bank of Montreal was given the right to coin copper, and it issued 240,000 pennies and 480,000 halfpennies in 1842. A further issue of 1,440,000 halfpennies was released in 1844. The tokens were struck by Boulton & Watt. A halfpenny die was prepared in 1845, and two tokens struck, but the bank did not issue any tokens dated 1845.

In addition to the normal 1842 front view penny, there exists a mule with the Habitant reverse of 1837 (with CITY BANK on the ribbon). It has long been known that dies and other tools connected with the Habitant and front view tokens later fell into the hands of an unscrupulous die sinker named W.J. Taylor and that he used them to produce proofs for sale to collectors. It is also believed that Taylor produced a number of mules that had never been issued for circulation. Many people have generally believed the front view 1837 mule pennies to be just such a concoction. Nevertheless, some pieces recently examined are clearly circulation strikes and are presumably originals produced by Boulton & Watt. Such pieces seem to be inadvertent mules. Because of the relative commonness of the Taylor restrikes compared with the originals, both are listed here.

210   213

	Breton No.		VG-8	F-12	VF-20	EF-40	BU-60
210	527	Halfpenny 1842	$2.00	$4.00	$8.00	$12.00	$75.00
211		Halfpenny 1844	2.25	5.00	10.00	15.00	80.00
212		Halfpenny 1845	—	—	—	—	—
213	526	Penny 1842	3.25	5.00	10.00	15.00	100.00
213a	526a	Mule penny: CITY BANK 1837. rev., original ..	100.00	125.00	175.00	300.00	400.00
213b	—	Same, Taylor restrike	—	—	—	—	400.00

Quebec Bank Tokens 1852

In 1852 the Quebec Bank was allowed to issue pennies and halfpennies because of a serious shortage of copper in Quebec. The Bank of Upper Canada coinage was supposed to be enough for the whole province, but the first two issues of this bank were not delivered until 1853, and the Quebec Bank was desperate. With government sanction the bank issued 240,-000 pennies and 480,000 halfpennies in 1852. A request for permission to issue more was turned down on the grounds that a change to decimal currency was under contemplation, which event took place in 1858. The Quebec Bank pieces were struck by Ralph Heaton & Sons, and are among the most attractive Canadian colonial issues. The obverse features the familiar "habitant" device and the reverse shows the coat of arms of Quebec City.

214   215

			VG-8	F-12	VF-20	EF-40	BU-60
214	529	Quebec Bank halfpenny 1852	$3.50	$5.50	$7.50	$13.50	$100.00
215	528	Quebec Bank penny 1852	4.50	6.50	11.50	18.50	120.00

Bank of Upper Canada Tokens, 1850-1857

The Bank of Upper Canada received the right to issue copper in 1850, after the capital was transferred to Toronto from Montreal. An order was placed at the Royal Mint that same year for halfpennies and pennies. The Province of Canada's agent for coinage was the British firm of Rowe, Kentish and Co. The obverse device is the popular St. George and the Dragon motif and the reverse shows the then obsolete arms of Upper Canada. The master tools were engraved by John Pinches of London, but it is Rowe, Kentish's RK & CO. that appears on the ground line on the obverse.

The pieces dated 1850 were struck at the Royal Mint in 1851 and did not reach Canada until 1852. Some of the pennies have a dot between the cornucopia tips on the reverse. Although this dot seems to have been deliberately added, its significance is not known.

In 1852 a second order was placed. The Royal Mint began the coinage, but was unable to complete it because of more pressing demands. The remaining blanks were transferred to Heaton's Mint in Birmingham and the rest of the order was struck. The Royal Mint strikings probably have the die axes ↑ ↑ ("medal" arrangement), while the Heaton's pieces have the dies ↑ ↓ ("coinage" arrangement).

The 1854 and 1857 issues were also produced by Heaton's. No further orders were placed because of the change to the decimal system of currency in 1858.

In 1863 the Bank complained to the government that because of the introduction of the decimal coins it had not been possible for them to put much of the final order of their tokens into circulation. The government agreed to purchase the tokens and they were stored in Montreal for a number of years. It seems that, through some irregularity (after the Bank had closed in 1867), a portion of the tokens got into circulation. In any case the tokens were moved to Toronto in the early 1870's, sold as copper bullion and melted under government supervision in 1873.

216

	Breton No.		VG-8	F-12	VF-20	EF-40	BU-60
216	720	Halfpenny 1850	$2.00	$3.00	$4.00	$8.00	$45.00
217		Halfpenny 1852, dies ↑ ↑	2.00	3.00	4.00	8.00	45.00
217a		Same, dies ↑ ↓	2.00	3.00	4.00	8.00	45.00
218		Halfpenny 1854, plain 4	2.00	3.00	4.00	8.00	45.00
218a		Same, crosslet 4	25.00	35.00	45.00	60.00	135.00
219		Halfpenny 1857	2.00	3.00	4.00	8.00	45.00

220

220a
Dot between cornucopiae tips

220	719	Penny 1850		2.50	3.25	4.00	10.00	55.00
220a		Same, dot between cornucopiae tips		5.00	8.00	15.00	25.00	80.00

Plain 4   Crosslet 4

	Breton No.		VG-8	F-12	VF-20	EF-40	BU-60
221	719	Penny 1852, dies ↑↓	$3.25	$5.00	$6.50	$12.00	$70.00
221a		Same, dies ↑↑	3.25	5.00	6.50	12.00	70.00
222		Penny 1854, plain 4	2.50	3.25	4.00	10.00	55.00
222a		Same, crosslet 4	10.00	15.00	20.00	35.00	135.00
223		Penny 1857	2.50	3.25	4.00	10.00	80.00

ANONYMOUS AND MISCELLANEOUS TOKENS

This section contains various kinds of tokens which are not included in the sections dealing specifically with tokens of the individual colonies, provinces or geographical regions.

With the exception of the "blacksmith" tokens, most of these pieces are of English or Irish origin, some of which had been used in the British Isles before being sent to Canada. Those of light weight were probably struck on Canadian order. A few, such as the North American token, circulated to a limited extent in the United States near the Canadian border.

The North American Token

The North American token was struck in Dublin long after 1781. It was dated 1781 to evade Canadian laws against the importation of anonymous tokens after 1825. To add to the illusion of age, the token was struck without a collar.

224

224	1013	NORTH AMERICAN TOKEN, copper	$15.00	$25.00	$60.00	$80.00	$175.00

The Success to Trade Token

Number 225 is an anonymous English piece with altered legends. The phrase "Success to Trade" was punched over "George III Rules," and "Commerce" was punched over "Britannia."

225

	Breton No.		VG-8	F-12	VF-20	EF-40	BU-60
225	983	SUCCESS TO TRADE	25.00	40.00	75.00	115.00	250.00

Other Issues

The pieces numbered 226 through 231 were engraved by Thomas Halliday and struck in Birmingham. The "Irish" piece, number 226, evidently was used in Ireland before being sent to Canada, for specimens have been found there.

226   227

	Breton No.		VG-8	F-12	VF-20	EF-40	BU-60
226	1009	Irishman in wreath	$8.00	$12.00	$20.00	$40.00	$130.00
227	966	FOR GENERAL ACCOMMODATION	3.25	5.00	10.00	27.50	100.00

The RH tokens have sometimes been attributed to Richard Hurd of Montreal. In light of available evidence, however, it is more reasonable to consider them English. Even if Hurd also ordered pieces of this design, it is likely that only the halfpenny on the thin flan was involved.

228   229   230

	Breton No.						
228	991	RH Farthing	40.00	60.00	95.00	140.00	335.00
229	990	RH Halfpenny, thick flan	6.50	11.00	22.50	35.00	100.00
229a		RH Halfpenny, thin flan	8.50	14.00	27.50	40.00	125.00
230	989	RH Penny	15.00	22.50	37.50	60.00	250.00

The ship tokens, 231 through 233, are lightweight tokens struck probably on Canadian order. The reverse of 232 is that of a halfpenny token of Shaw, Jobson & Co. of Roscoe Mills, Sheffield, England, whose initials S.J & Co. can be seen on the bale. The ship on this piece flies a pennant from the mainmast.

A second variety dated 1812 appears to be a direct copy by another coiner and can be distinguished by the presence of a pennant flying from the foremast (the Halliday variety has none). The 1815 issue was by Halliday, using the same obverse die as in 1812 and a new reverse die.

231

Breton No.		VG-8	F-12	VF-20	EF-40	BU-60
231	1005 HALFPENNY TOKEN, no date; rev. ship	$9.00	$14.00	$18.00	$36.00	$125.00

232   No pennant   Pennant on foremast

232	1004 HALFPENNY TOKEN 1812, rev. ship, no pennant	11.00	22.50	36.00	50.00	125.00
232a	Same, with pennant	5.50	11.00	22.50	36.00	100.00
233	HALFPENNY TOKEN 1815, rev. ship	5.50	11.00	22.50	36.00	100.00

The Anchor and H halfpennies are rather crudely made. It has been said that they were issued in Halifax, Nova Scotia, but this has not yet been proved. An 1814 date has been reported but cannot be confirmed.

234

234	— Anchor and H, 1816	—	—	—	—	—

Doubtful Pieces

The five tokens listed here have been traditionally included in Canadian collections but which are more properly placed in the English or Irish category. While they may have circulated in British North America in extremely small quantities, none was specifically imported. The BRITISH COLONIES tokens were originally sent to Jamaica for circulation as pennies. No. 236 was issued for use in British Guiana.

	Breton No.		VG-8	F-12	VF-20	EF-40	BU-60
235	993	TO FACILITATE TRADE 1825	7.50	14.00	27.50	42.50	130.00
236	967	TRADE & NAVIGATION 1838	7.50	14.00	27.50	55.00	150.00

237	975	HIBERNIA 1805, penny	$22.50	$36.00	$55.00	$85.00	$235.00

The Hibernia penny (237) is an anonymous Irish token designed by Peter Wyon.

The two pennies with the "Tiffin" obverse and the inscription COMMERCE on the reverse are English tokens, produced by Thomas Halliday.

238	—	COMMERCE	27.50	38.00	45.00	70.00	200.00
239	—	COMMERCE 1814	27.50	38.00	45.00	70.00	200.00

The "Blacksmith" Tokens

This fascinating group of tokens derives its name from a quaint legend that attributes their origin to a Montreal blacksmith, who made them to pay for liquor. Whatever their origin, it is clear that the blacksmith tokens were not produced by a single source and arose over a period of some years. They could have appeared as early as about 1820, when the tokens then in circulation had been largely decried and the only acceptable coppers were the battered, worn-out old British and Irish regal halfpennies of George III. In any case they were still being introduced as late as 1837. The blacksmiths were initially copper, but the late issues tended to be brass.

In a traditional sense the blacksmiths have been defined as specially produced imitations of worn British and Irish regal halfpence. Indeed, the first blacksmiths were just that, but the series grew more complex with the passage of time. Later issues imitated popular tokens in circulation at the time and yet other pieces were of "original" designs resulting from the muling of various dies or the use of dies that were not copying anything.

The blacksmith technique was to leave the designs unfinished and to engrave in very low relief. The devices were often reversed compared to those being copied and usually there was no legend or date. To further heighten the appearance of age and wear, the copper pieces were darkened by heating before being passed into circulation.

The series was almost completely ignored by the earlier writers, Breton including only two in his work. They were described in detail by Howland Wood, whose 1910 monograph is still the standard reference.

The nature of blacksmiths makes them difficult to grade and, in any case, most pieces fall within a rather narrow range of condition. Therefore, the prices for pieces in this series are given for "Average Condition" only. Some of the extremely rare varieties are not priced.

Imitations of British Regal Halfpennies

Obverses:

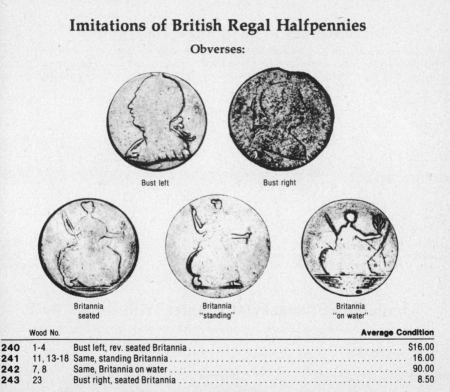

Bust left   Bust right

Britannia seated   Britannia "standing"   Britannia "on water"

	Wood No.		Average Condition
240	1-4	Bust left, rev. seated Britannia	$16.00
241	11, 13-18	Same, standing Britannia	16.00
242	7, 8	Same, Britannia on water	90.00
243	23	Bust right, seated Britannia	8.50

The next two pieces are of a rather complex nature. There is a group of tokens generally considered U.S., called "bungtowns." These are imitations of British and Irish halfpence, where the legend has deliberately been garbled to circumvent the laws against counterfeiting. The first piece (244) could well be a U.S. "bungtown" shipped to Lower Canada. (So many of them have been found in Canada that there can be no doubt of their right to be called Canadian.) The legends are GLORIOUS III ● VIS (instead of GEORGIUS III REX) on the obverse and BITIT ● (instead of BRITANNIA) on the reverse. It was thought by Wood to be an *imitation* of a bungtown; however, the relatively high quality of the lettering leads us to believe it to be a U.S. product.

The legend on the second piece (245) is much cruder and more difficult to read. The letters which show suggest that this token is a copy of the "bungtown" issue.

244   245

	Wood No.		Average Condition
244	33	Bust right, GLORIOUS III ● VIS	12.50
245	34	Bust left, GLO ● III VIS (?)	Extremely Rare

Imitations of Irish Regal Halfpennies

In addition to a plain harp on the reverse there are some curious pieces with a harp surrounded on the sides and bottom by a nondescript design. This design has generally been believed to have resulted from deterioration of the die, but this is only partially correct. Much of it was *engraved*.

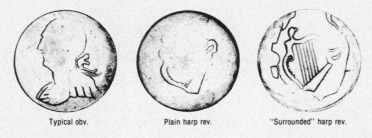

Typical obv.   Plain harp rev.   "Surrounded" harp rev.

246	6	Bust left, plain harp	$16.00
247	5, 12	Same, "surrounded" harp	16.00
248	35	Obverse of 245, rev. smaller harp (not shown)	Extremely Rare

Imitations of Regal Halfpennies With Only a Bust

This is a group consisting of uniface strikings from the obverse dies for some of the preceding pieces, but mostly from dies apparently intended to be used alone. Most were unknown to Wood and all are extremely rare and therefore not priced.

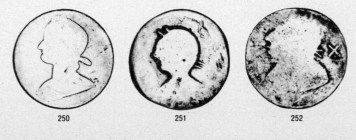

250   251   252

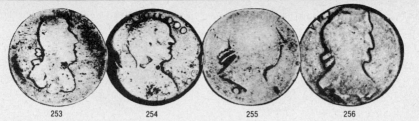

253   254   255   256

	Wood No.		Average Condition
249	(34)	Obverse of 245	—
250	42	Bust left, single ribbon end	—
251	—	"Horned" bust left	—
252	39	Bust left, × behind	—
253	—	Narrow bust right	—
254	43	Bust right, dots at rim	—
255	—	Bust right, dot below	—
256	—	Thick bust, legend behind head	—

Imitations of Ships, Colonies and Commerce Tokens

The next two pieces, not found in Wood, are rare and have both been included in Lees under 5. Recently, however, their obverses have been shown to be from different dies. The first (No. 257) has faint rim beads on the obverse, a distinct ball at the top of each mast and a thin line extending back from between the two waves just below the ship's stern. The classical Lees 5 (258) lacks rim beads, has indistinct mast tops and no line between the waves at the rear. In addition all known examples are from a badly cracked die.

257   258

	Lees No.		Average Condition
257	5	Drooping flag, incomplete ship	Extremely Rare
258	5	Same, no beads either side	Extremely Rare

Other Imitating Designs

259   260

	Wood No.		G-4	VG-8	F-12
259	21, 22	"Bust & Harp-like" 1820	$175.00	$225.00	$325.00
260	19	"Tiffin-like" 1820, copper	140.00	175.00	275.00
260a	20	Same, brass	140.00	175.00	275.00

261　　　　　262

Wood No.			Average Condition
261	—	"Vexator-like" 1811 (?), uniface	Extremely Rare
262	—	Same, no date (?), uniface	Extremely Rare

263

263	31	"Sloop-like," wreath	Unique

Miscellaneous "Original" Designs

Some of the tokens in the blacksmith series fall into a category which can be called original designs. The dies, individually or in combination, did not copy an existing design. The first two pieces are from one die for an imitation of a regal halfpenny, and the other for an imitation of the SHIPS COLONIES & COMMERCE tokens. The reverse die of 264 is the same as the obverse die for 258.

264　　　　　　　　　　　　265

	Wood No.		G-4	VG-8	F-12
264	9	Bust, rev. ship		Extremely Rare	
265	10	SHIPS COLONIES etc., rev. "surrounded" harp	$125.00	$185.00	$240.00

The reverses of 266 and 267 are said to be from very worn reverse dies for standard type tokens. In the first case it is the Upper Canadian sloop 197 or 199 and in the second it is a U.S. "hard times" token (Low 19). The obverse of 267 also strongly resembles that of 98a. Whether the dies which struck these blacksmith issues are really those that struck the tokens they resemble is not yet established.

266   267

	Wood No.		Average Condition
266	45	Bust, rev. TO FACILITATE TRADE	Extremely Rare
267	46	Bust, rev. U.S. "hard times" token	Extremely Rare

The "Mexican" bouquet sou has what appears to be a copy of a State of Chihuahua copper coin (1883-1856) depicting a standing Indian for its reverse design. The obverse die is probably a copy of a bouquet sou die, rather than a deteriorated original die.

268

268	—	"Mexican" bouquet sou	$500.00

The next group of "original" designs stems from five kinds of dies used in various combinations. The RISEING SUN TAVERN piece has been tentatively linked to a Tavern in Toronto; however, this is not certain. It is interesting that two of the dies are apparently discarded reverse dies from metallic store cards of N.S. Starbuck & Son and J. & C. Peck, both of Troy, New York.

Bust obv.

Eagle obv./rev.

RISEING SUN   Starbuck rev.   Peck rev.
TAVERN rev.

Wood No.			G-4	VG-8	F-12
269	24	Bust, RISEING SUN TAVERN	$125.00		
270	26	Bust, eagle	Extremely Rare		
271	25	Bust, STARBUCK	Extremely Rare		
272	27	Eagle, STARBUCK	Extremely Rare		
273	28	Eagle, PECK	Extremely Rare		
274	30	Eagle, eagle	Extremely Rare		
275	29	STARBUCK, PECK	Extremely Rare		

The next three tokens are of completely new designs, but are nevertheless generally considered to be part of the blacksmith series.

276

Wood No.			Average Condition
276	—	Windmill, rev. NO CREDIT	$800.00

277

| **277** | 32 | Anchor, rev. shield .... | 135.00 |

278

| **278** | — | Balance, rev. tools and star .... | Extremely Rare |

A GUIDE FOR ATTRIBUTING TOKENS

The listings of tokens in the main body are arranged according to the colony for which they were struck or where they were most used. Many of the pieces bear some indication of the colony of issue, in the form of either a city in the colony or the colony name itself. However, others do not, and as an aid to finding such pieces in the catalogue listings, the table below was constructed. To find a given token the following rules should be noted:

1. Pieces with the name of a city or the colony are NOT included in this list if they are listed under the expected colony.
2. If one or both sides of the token has a legend, consult the lists of legends.
3. Where a token has two legends on the same side — one around the outside and the second (usually the value) in a circle in the centre — the legends are listed separately.
4. When there is no legend or the legend is indistinct, the lists of designs should be consulted.

PIECES WITH LEGENDS

Legend	Haxby-Willey Token Nos.
AGRICULTURE & COMMERCE · BAS CANADA	177
BRITISH COLONIES	235
BRITIT	244
CANADA 1830	102
1841	103
CANADA HALF PENNY TOKEN	101
COMMERCE (undated)	80,224
1814	239
COMMERCE RULES THE MAIN	225
COMMERCIAL CHANGE	97-97a
COSSACK PENNY TOKEN	87
EXECUTIVE EXPERIMENT	267
FARTHING TOKEN 1812	228
FIELD MARSHALL WELLINGTON	
(undated)	71, 76-78a, 81-81a, 85-86
1813	88
FISHERIES AND AGRICULTURE	18-19
FOR GENERAL ACCOMMODATION	227
FOR PUBLIC ACCOMMODATION	101, 237
FOR PUBLICK ACCOMMODATION	9
FOR THE CONVENIENCE OF TRADE	31
GENUINE BRITISH COPPER (undated)	36
1815	39
GLO III · VIS (?)	244
GLORIOUS III · VIS	245, 248-249
H	234
HALFPENNY or HALF PENNY	40-42, 102-103
HALFPENNY or HALF PENNY TOKEN —	
(undated)	19,24-25, 28, 39, 76-77, 90, 227, 231
1812	24, 115, 120-121a, 232
1813	25, 28, 82-81a, 91-93a
1814	31, 229-229a
1815	36, 38, 40, 233
1816	84,234
HB EM ⅛ (¼, ½ or 1) NB	206-209
HIBERNIA 1805	71, 237
HISPANIUM ET LUSITANIUM RESTITUIT WELLINGTON	73-75
JB (script)	42
MACHINE SHOP, etc.	271-272, 275
MAGDALEN ISLAND TOKEN	1
MARQUIS WELLINGTON 1813	80
NEMO ME IMPUNE LACESSIT	43
NO CREDIT	276
NO LABOUR NO BREAD	203

Legend	Haxby-Willey Token Nos.
NORTH AMERICAN TOKEN 1781	224
NORTH WEST COMPANY	205-205a
ONE CENT 1855	18
ONE HALFPENNY TOKEN (undated)	8
1820	50
ONE PENNY	237
ONE PENNY TOKEN (undated) 26-27a, 85-86, 88, 118-119	
1812	116-117
1813	26, 89
1814	27-27a, 230
PAYABLE AT THE STORE OF J. BROWN	43
PECK'S PATENT, etc.	273-275
PURE COPPER PREFERABLE TO PAPER	23-28, 226-227, 236
RENUNILLOS VISCAPE 1811	123-126
RH (script)	228-230
RISEING SUN TAVERN	269
SHIPS COLONIES & COMMERCE	10-15b, 96-96b, 257-258, 265
SHIPS COLONIES & COMMERCE 1815	8-9
SPEED THE PLOUGH	17-17c
SPEED THE PLOUGH HALFPENNY TOKEN	203
SUCCESS TO THE FISHERIES	17-17c
SUCCESS TO TRADE 1812	225
SUCCESS TO NAVIGATION & TRADE	38
T. DUSEAMAN BUTCHER · BELLEVILLE	177
THE ILLUSTRIOUS WELLINGTON	83
TO FACILITATE TRADE (undated)	266
1825	98-98b, 235
TOKEN 1820	205-205a
TRADE & COMMERCE 1811	72
TRADE & NAVIGATION (undated)	50
1812	24
1813	23, 25-26, 28
1814	27-27a
1838	236
VE?ATOR CANADIN SIS	123-124
VE?ATOR CANADIENSIS	125
VICTORIA NOBIS EST	90
VIMIERA·TALAVERA·BADAJOZ·SALAMANCA·VITTORIA	89
VIMIERA·TALAVERA·BUSACO·BADAJOZ·SALAMANCA	87
WATERLOO HALFPENNY 1816	83
WELLINGTON HALFPENNY TOKEN	79, 82
WELLINGTON WATERLOO 1815	94-95

PIECES WITHOUT LEGENDS

Designs	Haxby-Willey Token Nos.	Designs	Haxby-Willey Token Nos.
Anchor/shield	277	Bust/eagle	270
Balance scale/tools and star	278	Bust/harp	113-114, 246-248
Bouquet/dancing Indian	268	Bust/harp 1820	111-112, 259
Bust left (uniface)	249-52, 262	Bust, harp 1825	110
Bust right (uniface)	253-256	Bust/ship	264
Bust 1811? (uniface)	261	Eagle/eagle	274
Bust/seated female	240, 242-243	Ship/1858	6
Bust/standing female	241	Ship/seated female	100
Bust 1820/seated female	99	Sloop in wreath/anvil, shovels in wreath	263
Bust/seated female 1820	260-260a		
Bust in wreath/seated female 1812	122-122a		

TRADE, ADVERTISING, AND TRANSPORTATION TOKENS

Trade and advertising tokens appeared in the developing portions of the Dominion after 1880. They were issued by rural storekeepers and city firms in the West and in the north of Ontario as a means of enticing customers to return to their place of business. Given out in change, they could only be redeemed in the locality or at the shop of the issuer. In many cases they augmented the local supply of cash. Saskatchewan saw an enormous quantity and variety of these pieces in use, in denominations ranging from one cent to ten dollars. Large numbers were issued in Manitoba, Alberta, and British Columbia.

There was also a great variety of tokens issued which were redeemable in goods or services. Cordwood tokens, pool checks, hotel and restaurant tokens, barber shop tokens, cigar store tokens, dairy tokens, and bread tokens abound in all provinces. A special class of tokens good for some service are transportation tokens. These were issued to pay the fare by bus, street car or ferry in various localities, or to pay tolls for the use of bridges and tunnels. The famous Bout de l'Isle tokens are an example of tokens issued to pay tolls, in this case over a series of bridges near Montreal. One of the earliest fare tokens is the Montreal & Lachine Railroad token.

TRADE TOKENS

Pool check   Cigar store token   Hotel token

Another item now becoming very popular is the trade or souvenir coin. This is a sort of cross between a trade token and a commercial medal, for it is issued by a local organization or municipality for temporary use as money within the limits of a municipality, and commemorates or honours some important local event or historical personage. Usually these pieces are issued with a value of one dollar, and collectors have called them trade dollars, but their appearance in other denominations necessitates their being called by some other name, for by no conceivable stretch of the imagination ought a fifty-cent trade coin be called a trade dollar.

One of the earliest of these pieces was the dollar struck in 1960 for the golden jubilee of the founding of Prince Rupert, British Columbia. They have been most widely used in Western Canada, but have recently spread into the East.

Dairy token   Bread token

Barber shop token   Ferry token

Montreal and Lachine
Railroad Token

It was found that ordinary railway tickets were not convenient for use among the Indians and workmen on the Lachine Canal, who formed the bulk of third class travel on the Montreal & Lachine Railroad Company.

These tokens were therefore imported from Birmingham, England. They were strung on a wire as they were collected by the conductor.

Article reprinted from ''An Introduction to Coin Collecting'' with the kind permission of the Canadian Numismatic Association.

7
DOMINION OF CANADA NOTES 1867-1935

TRANSITIONAL ISSUES

The newly formed government of the Dominion of Canada decided to utilize the large stockpiles of Province of Canada notes which had only been in circulation for a short time. These notes were not withdrawn from circulation and became the first issue of Dominion notes. In addition to the Province of Canada type notes payable at Toronto or Montreal the newly formed Dominion government had to prepare notes payable in the Maritimes. Notes prepared for New Brunswick were overprinted with a horizontal blue ST. JOHN in addition to the regular vertical green markings PAYABLE AT TORONTO (on $1 to $50 notes). Nova Scotia notes were specially prepared ($5 note only) with a green PAYABLE AT HALIFAX ONLY appearing vertically at each end of the face.

As the types payable only at Toronto or Montreal were previously issued by the Province of Canada, they will not be listed here. All notes have the engraved signature of T.D. Harington at the right and the manuscript signature or various individuals at the left. After 1871 all Provincial issue notes were withdrawn and replaced by Dominion of Canada notes.

Toronto / St. John Issue

	VG	Fine	VF
Province of Canada Type — Payable at:			
$5 payable at Halifax	$950.00	$1,900	$2,900
$1 overprinted ST. JOHN	900.00	1,800	2,800
$2 overprinted ST. JOHN	750.00	1,500	2,200
$5 overprinted ST. JOHN	1,000	2,000	3,000
$10, $20, or **$50** overprinted ST. JOHN	No notes known to exist		

25 CENT NOTES ("SHINPLASTERS")

The first issue of 25 cent notes was an emergency issue to halt the large amount of United States silver coinage circulating at par in Canada. At that time the U.S. dollar was worth only 80¢ Canadian and was discounted 20% at banks in Canada, with the result that individuals had to bear the loss. The Canadian government hoped to replace the need for U.S. silver with an issue of Canadian coins. In order to fill the time delay required to produce the large quantity of Canadian coins needed, it was decided to meet the shortage by issuing 25¢ notes. These were never intended to be more than a temporary issue but they proved so popular with the public that the government was forced to produce further issues in 1900 and 1923.

The expression "shinplaster" has been attributed to the use of such low denomination notes by soldiers of the Revolutionary war period as a lining to protect their ankles and shins from chafing by their boots.

1870 Issue

Vignette: Britannia; signatures: right (engraved): T.D. Harington, left (engraved): W. Dickinson. There were three series: the A series (issued 1870), the B series (issued 1871-ca. 1885) and the no letter or "plain" series (issued ca. 1885-1900). The series letter, when present, is located at the lower left just below the 0 of 1870.

Series letter location

Variety/Signatures	Good	VG	Fine	VF	EF	Unc
25¢ A series	$35.00	$100.00	$200.00	$350.00	$700.00	$1,500
B series	10.00	20.00	35.00	95.00	325.00	850.00
"Plain" series	7.00	15.00	30.00	55.00	130.00	500.00

1900 Issue

Vignette: Britannia; signature (engraved): various (see below).

25¢ J.M. Courtney	4.00	6.50	13.50	25.00	50.00	125.00
T.C. Boville	3.00	6.00	9.00	16.50	30.00	100.00
J.C. Saunders	5.00	10.00	15.00	35.00	65.00	140.00

1923 Issue

Vignette: Britannia; signatures (engraved); various (see below). The first printing has AUTHORIZED BY R.S.C. CAP. 31. above the signature at the left and a red check letter A, B, C, D, E, H, J, K, L or M to the left of the number. Later printings lack this statement, and a black check letter (to the left of the left 25) replaces the red one. All notes bear the seal of the Department of Finance at the right.

AUTHORIZED, etc.   No AUTHORIZED, etc.

Major Variety/Signature at Left	Good	VG	Fine	VF	EF	Unc
25¢ AUTHORIZED, etc.						
G.W. Hyndman	$8.50	$15.00	$32.50	$55.00	$120.00	$300.00
No AUTHORIZED, etc.						
G.W. Hyndman	8.50	15.00	32.50	55.00	120.00	300.00
S.P. McCavour	3.00	5.50	9.50	17.50	30.00	110.00
C.E. Campbell	3.50	6.50	10.50	20.00	35.00	125.00

ONE DOLLAR
1870 Issue

Vignettes: Jacques Cartier (left) and "Canada" (right); signatures: T.D. Harington (engraved at right), W. Dickinson (engraved at left) and that of various persons (written vertically positioned at one end, usually the left). The city payable is indicated on the back of each note. In addition the extremely rare notes issued in Manitoba have a black MANITOBA stamped vertically on the face at the right end of PAYABLE AT MONTREAL or TORONTO varieties.

The Toronto issue was heavily counterfeited. The counterfeits can be most easily recognized by the presence of D4 (check letter D, plate number 4) twice on their face and a crude black dot for Cartier's eye.

Major Variety	Good	VG	Fine	VF	EF	Unc
$1 1870 Back reads Payable at:						
Montreal	$95.00	$250.00	$500.00	$900.00	$1,800	$3,000
Toronto	95.00	250.00	500.00	900.00	1,800	3,000
MANITOBA stamped on either of above	No notes known to exist					
Halifax	275.00	500.00	1,100	—	—	—
St. John	425.00	900.00	1,750	—	—	—
Victoria	—	5,000	9,000	—	—	—

1878 Issue (Dufferin)

Vignette: the Countess of Dufferin, wife of the Governor General, and on the back the Great Seal of Canada; signatures: T.D. Harington (engraved at right) and that of various persons (written at left). The city payable is indicated on both the face (lower left) and the back. The initial issue had a frame (border) consisting of a scallop-like design with a large "scallop" in each corner. It was replaced in 1881 with a modified design due to some notes of the original issue being altered to $4's. The frame of the new design contains 1 ONE DOLLAR repeated with a 1 in each corner, plus other differences.

Scalloped Frame   Lettered Frame

Major Variety/Signatures	Good	VG	Fine	VF	EF	Unc
$1 1878 Scalloped Frame on Face — Back reads Payable at:						
Montreal	$100.00	$250.00	$500.00	$1,000	$2,000	$4,250
Toronto	100.00	250.00	500.00	1,000	2,000	4,250
Halifax	375.00	750.00	1,500	—	—	—
St. John	400.00	1,000	1,750	3,000	—	—
$1 1878 Lettered Frame on Face — Back reads Payable at:						
Montreal	17.50	40.00	80.00	175.00	375.00	800.00
Toronto	17.50	40.00	80.00	175.00	375.00	800.00
Halifax	300.00	600.00	1,000	1,600	4,000	—
St. John	350.00	700.00	1,200	1,750	—	—

1897 and 1898 Issues (Aberdeen)

Vignettes: the Countess of Aberdeen, the Earl of Aberdeen (Governor General 1893-1898), a logging scene and on the back the center block of the Parliament buildings in Ottawa; signatures: J.M. Courtney (later T.C. Boville) engraved at the right and that of various persons written at the left.

1897 Face   1897 Back   ONE's curve inward   ONE's curve outward

The face tint (background colour) on the 1897 issue is green and the design on the back contains a large 1 at each end. Probably to better distinguish it from the 1897 $2, the colour of the face tint on the $1 was changed to brown and the notes redated 1898. It had also been found that the large 1's on the back of the original design tended to disfigure the portraits on the face (by showing through the paper), so the 1898 issue has a modified back where three small counters replace each of the large 1's. The initial 1898 back has the small ONE at each end curving inward; this was later changed to have the ONE'S curving outward.

These issues mark the termination of domiciling for this denomination.

	Good	VG	Fine	VF	EF	Unc
$1 1897 (green tint)	$90.00	$235.00	$500.00	$1,000	$1,650	$3,400
$1 1898 (brown tint)						
ONE's on back curve inward						
Signed J.M. Courtney	22.00	40.00	85.00	175.00	350.00	900.00
ONE's on back curve outward						
Signed J.M. Courtney	15.00	27.50	50.00	100.00	250.00	750.00
T.C. Boville	15.00	27.50	50.00	100.00	250.00	750.00

1911 Issue (Grey)

Vignettes: the Earl of Grey (Governor General 1904-1911) and the Countess of Grey; back design: the same as the second design for the 1898 issue; signatures: T.C. Boville (engraved at the right) and that of various persons (written at the left).

The first notes of this issue had a green signature pane across the bottom. On later printings a black line was added along the top edge of the panel.

All green panel

Black line at
top of panel

Major Variety/Signatures	Good	VG	Fine	VF	EF	Unc
$1 1911 all green signature panel	$12.00	$20.00	$40.00	$90.00	$150.00	$600.00
black line at top of signature panel	12.00	20.00	35.00	80.00	135.00	475.00

1917 Issue (Princess Pat)

Vignettes: Princess Patricia of Connaught and on the back the centre block of the the original Parliament buildings. The first printings have a plain green ONE on each side of the portrait on the face side, have the written signatures of various persons at the left and the engraved signature or T.C. Boville (later J.C. Saunders) at the right. In 1922 the government switched over to countersigning the notes by printing; as a security device the seal of the Department of Finance was added with the second signature. The initial printings involving machine countersigning were with the notes of the original design (ONE at right), so a transitional variety with the seal over the ONE was created. The final issue lacks the ONE at the right, allowing the Finance Department seal to be more easily seen.

ONE alone
at right

Seal over ONE
at right

Seal alone
at right

	Good	VG	Fine	VF	EF	Unc
$1 1917 Plain ONE at right:						
Signed Boville at right	$10.00	$20.00	$35.00	$70.00	$135.00	$375.00
Signed Saunders at right	10.00	25.00	40.00	80.00	150.00	450.00
Black Seal over ONE at right:						
Signed Hyndman-Saunders	12.00	30.00	50.00	90.00	160.00	500.00
Seal alone (no ONE) at right						
Signed Hyndman-Saunders	12.00	30.00	50.00	90.00	160.00	500.00

1923 Issue (George V)

Vignette: King George V and on the back the Library of Parliament; signatures: various (see below), all engraved. On this issue the seal of the Department of Finance comes in various colours, the purpose of which was to aid in sorting the notes when they came back in for destruction.

Seal Colour/Signatures	Good	VG	Fine	VF	EF	Unc
$1 Black Seal at right						
Hyndman-Saunders	$10.00	$20.00	$35.00	$70.00	$175.00	$450.00
McCavour-Saunders	8.00	20.00	35.00	70.00	165.00	400.00
Campbell-Sellar	7.00	14.00	18.50	32.00	75.00	200.00
Campbell-Clark	7.00	14.00	18.50	32.00	75.00	200.00
Red Seal at right						
McCavour-Saunders	9.00	20.00	32.00	70.00	165.00	450.00
Blue Seal at right						
McCavour-Saunders	7.00	15.00	25.00	45.00	110.00	350.00
Green Seal at right						
McCavour-Saunders	7.00	15.00	22.50	40.00	100.00	325.00
Purple-Brown Seal at right						
McCavour-Saunders	7.00	15.00	22.50	40.00	100.00	325.00
Lilac Seal at right*						
McCavour-Saunders	65.00	135.00	250.00	525.00	1,000	2,500
Campbell-Sellar	85.00	240.00	525.00	1,000	1,750	3,400

*All of the scarce lilac seal notes have a C prefix in the note number and have a small C-1 to the right of the seal. Purple-brown seal notes do not come with this letter.

TWO DOLLARS
1870 Issue

Vignettes: Generals Wolfe and Montcalm, the ill-fated commanders of the British and French forces in the Battle of the Plains of Abraham at Quebec City in 1759, and "civilization" (center); signatures: T.D. Harington (engraved at right), W. Dickinson (engraved at left) and that of various persons (written, vertically positioned at one end, usually the left). The city payable is indicated on the back of each note. In addition, the extremely rare notes issued in Manitoba have a black MANITOBA stamped vertically on the face at the right end of PAYABLE AT MONTREAL or TORONTO varieties.

Major Variety	Good	VG	Fine
$2 1870 Back reads Payable at:			
Montreal	$600.00	$1,200	$2,200
Toronto	600.00	1,200	2,200
MANITOBA stamped on either of the above	1,250	2,600	—
Halifax	800.00	1,600	3,000
St. John	1,000	1,900	3,250
Victoria	No notes known to exist		

1878 Issue (Dufferin)

Vignette: the Earl of Dufferin, Governor General 1872-1878 and on the back the Great Seal of Canada; signatures: T.D. Harington (engraved at right) and that of various persons (written at left). The city payable is indicated on both the face (lower left) and the back. Both the Montreal and Toronto issues were heavily counterfeited; it is likely that this is the reason for the early retirement of the whole issue compared to the corresponding $1 issue. The counterfeits have a rather inferior portrait and all known examples have at least a single 1 in the serial number. The counterfeits have curved topped 1's, whereas the genuine notes have flat topped 1's. Unfortunately, most of the surviving notes of the Toronto and Montreal varieties are the counterfeits.

Flat topped 1
(Genuine)

Curved top 1
(Counterfeit)

	Good	VG	Fine
$2 1878 Back reads Payable at:			
Montreal	$475.00	$1,000	$1,750
Toronto	475.00	1,000	1,750
Halifax	750.00	1,500	2,400
St. John	850.00	1,600	2,550

1887 Issue (Lansdowne)

Vignettes: the Marchioness of Lansdowne, the Marquis of Lansdowne (Governor General 1883-1888) and on the back "Quebec!", showing Jacques Cartier and his men aboard ship. The back is bi-coloured for security reasons and is the only Dominion note to have such a back.

	Good	VG	Fine	VF	EF	Unc
$2 1887 (Lansdowne)	$175.00	$300.00	$550.00	$1,150	$1,750	—

1897 Issue (Wales)

Vignettes: Edward, Prince of Wales (later King Edward VII), men cod fishing from a boat and on the back field workers harvesting grain; signatures: J.M. Courtney (later T.C. Boville) engraved at the right and that of various persons written at the left. The first printings have a red-brown back; this was soon changed to dark brown.

Major Varieties/Signature	Good	VG	Fine	VF	EF	Unc
$2 Red-Brown Coloured Back						
Signed J.M. Courtney	$100.00	$200.00	$375.00	$750.00	—	
Dark Brown Coloured Back						
Signed J.M. Courtney	35.00	60.00	125.00	200.00	600.00	2,000
Signed T.C. Boville	35.00	60.00	125.00	200.00	600.00	2,000

1914 Issue (Connaught)

Vignettes: the Duke of Connaught (Governor General 1911-1916), the Duchess of Connaught and on the back the Canadian coat-of-arms, along with those of the provinces; signatures: the initial design has the statement WILL PAY TO THE BEARER ON DEMAND in a curved line over the large 2 counter in the center of the face. On later printings this statement is in a straight line. Initially the notes also have an olive TWO on each side of the portrait on the face side, have the written signature of various persons at the left and the engraved signature of T.C. Boville (later J.C. Saunders) at the right. In 1922 the government switched over to countersigning the notes by printing; as a security device the seal of the Department of Finance was added with the second signature. The first printings involving machine countersigning were with notes of the second design (straight WILL PAY, etc. and TWO at the right), so a transitional variety was created. The final issue lacks the TWO at the right, allowing the Finance Department seal to be more easily seen.

Curved WILL PAY, etc.   Straight WILL PAY, etc.

$2 Plain TWO at right						
Curved WILL PAY, etc.						
Signed Boville	$12.00	$35.00	$75.00	$125.00	$285.00	$800.00
Straight WILL PAY, etc.						
Signed Boville	14.00	40.00	85.00	135.00	300.00	850.00
Signed Saunders	18.00	50.00	100.00	175.00	325.00	950.00
Black Seal over TWO at right						
Straight WILL PAY, etc.						
Signed Saunders	70.00	110.00	220.00	350.00	700.00	1,300
Seal alone (no TWO) at right						
Straight WILL PAY, etc.						
Signed Saunders	40.00	75.00	160.00	250.00	475.00	1,100

1923 Issue (Prince of Wales)

Vignettes: Edward, Prince of Wales (later King Edward VIII) and on the back the coat-of-arms of Canada; signatures: various, all machine signed, (see below). On this issue the seal of the Department of Finance comes in various colours, the purpose of which was to aid in sorting the notes when they came back in for destruction.

Major Varieties/Signatures	Good	VG	Fine	VF	EF	Unc
$2 Black Seal at right						
Hyndman-Saunders	$22.00	$45.00	$90.00	$200.00	$400.00	$1,000
McCavour-Saunders	14.00	32.00	75.00	165.00	350.00	875.00
Campbell-Sellar	10.00	22.00	42.00	95.00	200.00	550.00
Campbell-Clark	10.00	22.00	40.00	80.00	175.00	500.00
Red Seal at right						
McCavour-Saunders	13.50	30.00	65.00	150.00	300.00	825.00
Blue Seal at right						
McCavour-Saunders	12.50	30.00	65.00	150.00	300.00	850.00
Campbell-Sellar	12.50	30.00	65.00	150.00	300.00	850.00
Green Seal at right						
McCavour-Saunders	25.00	45.00	100.00	300.00	600.00	1,650
Purple-Brown Seal at right						
McCavour-Saunders	22.50	42.00	95.00	275.00	550.00	1,500

FOUR DOLLARS
1881 Issue (Lorne)

Vignette: the Marquis of Lorne (Governor General 1878-1883); signatures: J.M. Courtney engraved at the right and that of various persons written at the left. As a security device the notes were printed on watermarked paper (they were the only Dominion notes that were) and bear an orange Great Seal of Canada at the right on the face side. The colour of the seal is sometimes brown due to oxidation of the ink.

$4 1882	200.00	400.00	750.00	1,500	—	—

1900 and 1902 Issues (Minto)

Vignettes: the Countess of Minto, the Earl of Minto (Governor General 1898-1904), the locks at Sault Ste. Marie, connecting Lakes Superior and Huron and on the back Parliament Hill as seen from the Ottawa River to the east; signatures: J.M. Courtney (1900 and the 1902 issue with the 4's at the top) or T.C. Boville (1902 issue with the FOUR'S at the top) engraved at the right and that of various persons written at the left. On the initial printings (dated 1900) the U.S. side of the locks was portrayed. This error was corrected in 1902 and the design redated. In 1911, on the eve of the introduction of the $5 notes and the withdrawal of the $4's, a third variety (with FOUR'S at the top for easier recognition of the denomination) was issued because of a pressing need for paper money.

1900 Issue   1902 Issue (4's at top)

1902 Issue (FOUR's at top)   Back (all issues)

Major Variety/Signatures	Good	VG	Fine	VF	EF	Unc
$4 1900	$135.00	$250.00	$500.00	$1,000	$2,000	$3,000
$4 1902 Large 4's at top						
Signed J.M. Courtney	150.00	300.00	600.00	1,250	2,100	3,500
Large FOUR's at top						
Signed T.C. Boville	100.00	200.00	425.00	900.00	1,750	2,800

FIVE DOLLARS
1912 Issue (Train)

Vignette: the "Maritime Express" travelling through the Wentworth Valley in Nova Scotia and on the back a large Roman numeral V in the centre. The first printings have a FIVE counter on each side of the vignette on the face, the written signature of various persons at the left and the engraved signature of T.C. Boville at the right. In 1922 the government switched over to countersigning the notes by printing; as a security device the seal of the Department of Finance was added with the second signature. The initial printings involving machine countersigning were with notes of the original design (FIVE at the right), so transitional notes with the seal over the FIVE were created. A signature change also occurred at this time. The final issue lacks the FIVE at the right, allowing the Finance Department seal to be more easily seen.

FIVE alone   Seal over FIVE   Seal alone
at right   at right   at right

Major Variety/Signatures	Good	VG	Fine	VF	EF	Unc
$5 Plain FIVE at right						
Signed T.C. Boville at right	$40.00	$85.00	$140.00	$275.00	$450.00	$750.00
Blue Seal over FIVE at right						
Signed T.C. Boville at right	110.00	200.00	325.00	500.00	700.00	1,100
Signed J.C. Saunders at right	100.00	160.00	325.00	500.00	700.00	1,100
Seal alone (no FIVE) at right						
Signed Hyndman-Saunders	35.00	70.00	110.00	200.00	325.00	575.00
McCavour-Saunders	300.00	650.00	900.00	1,150	1,500	2,200

1924 Issue (Queen Mary)

Vignettes: Queen Mary, wife of King George V and on the back the east block of the Parliment buildings; signatures: W. Sellar at the right and C.E. Campbell at the left, both printed on with the Department of Finance seal after the rest of the note had been printed. Although they were dated 1924, these notes were not issued until 1934, just before the withdrawal of the Dominion notes and the introduction of the Bank of Canada notes. Because of this, the notes of this issue are often encountered in high grade.

$5 1924	250.00	500.00	750.00	1,250	2,000	3,000

HIGHER DENOMINATIONS

The Dominion government also issued $50, $100, $500 and $1000 notes for circulation, although the two higher denominations were used almost exclusively in transactions between banks. The earliest issues were domiciled: The $50 and $100 notes came payable at Montreal or Toronto and the $500 and $1000 of 1871 came payable at Montreal, Toronto, Halifax, St. John, Victoria, Winnipeg, or Charlottetown.

$50	**1872**		Extremely Rare				
$100	**1872**		Extremely Rare				
$500	**1871**		No notes known to exist				
$500	**1911**	—	$1,500	$2,000	—	—	—
$500	**1925**	—	1,500	2,000	—	—	—
$1000	**1871**		No notes known to exist				
$1000	**1911**	—	1,750	2,000	—	—	—
$1000	**1925**	—	1,500	2,000	—	—	—

8

BANK OF CANADA NOTES
1935 TO DATE

INTRODUCTION

The Bank of Canada was created by the Central Bank Act of 1934. Under this Act, the Bank was given sole responsibility for the issuance and management of Canadian paper money as well as being responsible for the national debt and giving advice to the government on monetary policy. The Bank of Canada while dealing directly in ordinary banking, would loan money to the chartered banks as well as accept deposits from them.

Commencing business on March 11th, 1935, the Bank of Canada assumed responsibility for all Dominion of Canada notes still in circulation which it would replace with the new Bank of Canada 1935 issue notes. Although chartered banks were allowed to continue issuing their own notes into the mid 1940's, they had to drastically reduce their note circulation and in fact the last date on a chartered bank issue was 1943 (Royal Bank of Canada $5). During the latter part of the 1940's, the chartered banks actively withdrew their notes and in 1950 transferred to the Bank of Canada a sum of money equal to the face value of their notes outstanding as of December 31, 1949 ($13,302,046.60). As of January 1st, 1950 the Bank of Canada assumed responsibility for the redemption of these notes.

All Bank of Canada notes have been printed on blank note paper containing randomly scattered green planchettes (tiny discs of paper embedded in the white paper during its manufacture as an anti-counterfeiting device). Two security printers in Ottawa produce the notes: the British American Bank Note Company, Ltd., and the Canadian Bank Note Company, Limited.

1935 ISSUE

The Bank of Canada's first issue of notes was put into circulation early in 1935. The official changeover date from Dominion notes to Bank of Canada notes was March 11, 1935 and thereafter the Dominion notes were rapidly retired. The new Bank of Canada notes were small size (about 152 x 72 mm) to decrease printing costs. They consisted of two separate emissions, one English and one French, for each denomination making 18 different notes in all. The portrait on the face is positioned at the left end.

Face side with portrait at left   Back with allegorical vignette

Design Details

Denom.	Basic Colour	Portrait	Back Design
$1	Green	King George V	Allegorical figure of Agriculture
$2	Blue	Queen Mary	Mercury with implements of transportation
$5	Orange	Prince of Wales, later Edward VIII, then Duke of Windsor	Allegorical figure of Power
$10	Purple	Princess Royal	Allegorical figure of Harvest
$20	Rose pink	Princess Elizabeth, now Elizabeth II	Worker showing produce to Agriculture
$50	Brown	Duke of York, later George VI	Allegorical figure of Invention with radio

Design Details

Denom.	Basic Colour	Portrait	Back Design
$100	Dark Brown	Duke of Gloucester	Allegorical scene of Shipping with industry
$500	Tan	Sir John A. Macdonald, first Prime Minister of the Dominion in 1867	Allegorical scene showing Produce
$1000	Olive Green	Sir Wilfrid Laurier, Prime Minister 1896-1911	Allegorical figure of Security

Dates, Signatures and Numbering

All notes of this issue bear "ISSUE OF 1935" (or its French equivalent), the facsimile signatures of Deputy Governor (of the Bank) J.A.C. Osborne and Governor G.F. Towers, and at the right the seal of the Bank. The numbering system was the same as that used for the final issues of Dominion notes. That is, the notes were numbered in groups of four; each note within a given group received the same series letter and number (in red at top). The individual notes within a group were differentiated from each other by a black check letter, A, B, C or D. All notes of the French issue were series F, while those of the English issue were series A (except that B was also used for the $1 because the A series was completed). Within each series the numbers could go from 1 (preceded by various amounts of 0's) to 1000000.

Denomination	Good	VG	Fine	VF	EF	Unc
English Issues:						
$1	$5.00	$10.00	$15.00	$22.50	$40.00	$135.00
$2	10.00	20.00	32.00	55.00	140.00	275.00
$5	12.00	25.00	40.00	75.00	150.00	550.00
$10	14.00	27.50	40.00	60.00	110.00	500.00
$20 Large seal	40.00	90.00	140.00	235.00	500.00	1,750
$20 Small seal	32.00	70.00	110.00	200.00	450.00	1,600
$50	75.00	135.00	250.00	475.00	850.00	2,000
$100	—	150.00	250.00	425.00	750.00	1,400
$500	—	1,000	2,000	3,000	4,500	6,500
$1000	—	—	1,150	1,400	1,650	2,500
French Issues:						
$1	9.00	15.00	25.00	45.00	85.00	200.00
$2	20.00	50.00	90.00	225.00	400.00	1,100
$5	20.00	50.00	70.00	150.00	250.00	850.00
$10	18.00	35.00	60.00	110.00	235.00	800.00
$20	50.00	125.00	250.00	500.00	850.00	2,500
$50	85.00	250.00	425.00	900.00	1,400	3,000
$100	—	220.00	400.00	800.00	1,200	2,100
$500	—	1,350	2,500	4,800	6,000	9,000
$1000	—	—	1,450	1,750	2,000	4,000

GEORGE V
Silver Jubilee Commemorative 1935

In addition to the regular denominations, the Bank of Canada issued $25 notes to mark the 25th anniversary of the accession of George V. There were separate English and French issues like the notes of the Bank's first issue; however, the $25 notes were strictly a special commemorative issue and were not part of the first issue. This is emphasized by the different issue date on the notes (May 6, 1935) and the date span 1910-1935 at the top. The portraits of King George V and Queen Mary are shown in the center on the face and a view of Windsor Castle appears on the back. The face tint and back colour is royal purple. The signatures and numbering are as for the regular 1935 issue.

Denomination		Good	VG	Fine	VF	EF	Unc
$25	English issue	$200.00	$385.00	$525.00	$850.00	$1,250	$2,300
	French issue	325.00	750.00	1,000	1,500	2,250	3,500

1937 ISSUE

Under King Edward VIII the preparation of new issue of Bank of Canada notes was begun. Upon Edward's abdication in December 1936, the portrait of his brother, the Duke of York, was substituted and work continued on the new issue. The portrait of the new monarch, King George VI, had already been used on the $50 1935 notes when he was the Duke of York. A number of major changes took place from the previous issue. The King's portrait is in the centre of the face side and was used on all denominations from $1 to $50. The $100 note has Sir John A. MacDonald (same portrait as on the 1935 $500 note) and the $1000 denomination once again had Sir Wilfrid Laurier. The $500 denomination was discontinued. The use of one bilingual note rather than two separate monolingual notes for each denomination was instituted, as the cost of preparing separate English and French issues had simply been too high. The text and denominations are in French on the right side and English on the left.

Back Design Details

All the allegorical back designs of the 1937 notes were the same as those used in 1935, although they did not necessarily appear on the same denominations as previously. The backs were also made bilingual and small changes in the design were made. Several denominations also changed colour from the 1935 issue.

Face with portrait in centre   Back with allegorical vignette

Denom.	Basic Colour	Back Design	Denom.	Basic Colour	Back Design
$1	Green	Same as 1935	**$20**	Olive Green	As $500, 1935
$2	Dull Red	As $10, 1935	**$50**	Orange	Same as 1935
$5	Blue	Same as 1935	**$100**	Brown	Same as 1935
$10	Purple	As $2, 1935	**$1000**	Pink	Same as 1935

Dates, Signatures and Numbering

All notes bear the date January 2, 1937 but only the denominations $1 to $100 were released at that time. The $1000 note was not released by the Bank of Canada until the early fifties although the Osborne-Towers signatures indicate that they were printed much earlier. All notes bear the facsimile signature of Governor G.F. Towers at the right. Three different

Deputy Governors served during the period of these notes: J.A.C. Osborne, D. Gordon and J.E. Coyne. The numbering system was changed beginning with the 1937 issue. The serial number of each note consists of a two-letter prefix, expressed as a fraction, followed by a number. The lower letter in the fraction is the denominational letter (a given letter was used on only one denomination) and the upper letter is the series letter (which could be used on any denomination). Within each series the numbers could go from 0000001 to 10000000 with the number printed twice on the face of each note.

Denom.	Good	VG	Fine	VF	EF	UNC
Notes signed J.A.C. Osborne at Left:						
$1	$3.50	$6.00	$10.00	$20.00	$40.00	$100.00
$2	7.00	15.00	22.50	45.00	100.00	225.00
$5	35.00	110.00	165.00	250.00	500.00	1,200
$10	12.00	25.00	40.00	75.00	120.00	425.00
$20	30.00	60.00	100.00	140.00	250.00	500.00
$50	75.00	140.00	265.00	550.00	1,250	2,500
$100	—	110.00	165.00	250.00	450.00	850.00
$1000	—	—	1,100	1,250	1,500	2,000
Notes signed D. Gordon at Left:						
$1	—	$ 3.50	$ 4.50	$ 6.50	$ 8.50	$ 15.00
$2	—	7.00	10.00	17.50	25.00	40.00
$5	—	7.00	10.00	17.50	25.00	40.00
$10	—	12.50	17.50	20.00	30.00	50.00
$20	—	22.00	27.50	30.00	35.00	60.00
$50	—	55.00	60.00	75.00	90.00	135.00
$100	—	105.00	110.00	135.00	175.00	300.00
Notes signed J.E. Coyne at Left:						
$1	—	$ 3.50	$ 4.50	$ 6.50	$ 8.50	$ 15.00
$2	—	7.00	10.00	17.50	25.00	40.00
$5	—	7.00	10.00	17.50	25.00	40.00
$10	—	12.50	17.50	20.00	30.00	50.00
$20	—	22.00	27.50	30.00	35.00	60.00
$50	—	55.00	65.00	75.00	100.00	145.00
$100	—	105.00	110.00	135.00	175.00	300.00

1954 ISSUE

Upon the death of George VI in 1952, a new issue of Canadian paper currency was prepared for the incoming monarch, Elizabeth II. A number of marked departures from previous issues were incorporated. All denominations bear the portrait of the Queen and it is positioned at the right end of the face where it would get less wear by folding than the centre portraits of the 1937 issue. The face tint (background colour) is more complex than the previous notes, the allegorical vignettes on the backs of the 1937 issue were replaced by real-life Canadian scenes.

The issue was withdrawn beginning in 1970 because the prefix letters were almost entirely used up. There was also a large number of counterfeits appearing on this issue, particularly on the higher $50 and $100 denominations. The later signature varieties of these denominations were replaced quickly and are relatively scarce.

Face with Queen's portrait at right

Back with Canadian scene

Back Design Details

Basic colours for all denominations were carried over from the previous issue.

Denom.	Back Design	Denom.	Back Design
$1	Western prairie and sky	$20	Laurentian Hills in winter
$2	Country valley in Central Canada	$50	Atlantic seashore
$5	Northern stream and forest	$100	Mountain, valley and lake
$10	Rocky Mountain peak	$1000	Village, lake and hills

Date, Signatures and Numbering

All notes of the first issue of Elizabeth carry the designation OTTAWA, 1954. There are five signature combinations in this issue:

J.E. Coyne and G.F. Towers (all with "Devil's Face")
J.R. Beattie and J.E. Coyne (with and without "Devil's Face")
J.R. Beattie and L. Rasminsky
G. Bouey and L. Rasminsky
R.W. Lawson and G. Bouey

For denominations of $5 and up, some of the later signature combinations were not printed.

The numbering on the notes is as previously described on the 1937 issue except that after 1968 the number range in any given series was changed to run from 0000000 to 9999999, the zero note being removed and destroyed prior to issue. Each denomination letter was used for up to 250,000,000 notes and eventually every possible denomination letter except Q was used.

VARIETIES

Asterisk Note
(replacement)

Prior to the 1954 issue, replacement notes (to replace ones that were spoiled during printing) were individually made up with exactly the same serial numbers as those that were spoiled. In order to eliminate the nuisance of preparing new notes, a new system was devised for use with the 1954 issue. The Bank of Canada began printing series of independently numbered notes with an asterisk (*) preceding the serial number to replace defective notes. No asterisk notes were printed for the $50, $100 or $1000 denominations.

"Devil's face"
in Queen's hair

Modified hair

Shortly after the 1954 issue notes appeared in circulation, it was noticed that certain highlighted portions of the Queen's hair created the illusion of a Devil.s face peering out from behind her ear. This was not an "error", nor was it the result of a prank but was simply a faithful copying of the original photograph used as the model. The "Devil's Face" portrait created enough controversy that it was decided to modify her hair thereby creating two varieties of the Queen's portrait on this issue.

Devil's Face Portrait		Regular Issue					Asterisk Issue				
Denom.	Signatures	VG	Fine	VF	EF	Unc.	VG	Fine	VF	EF	Unc.
$1	Coyne-Towers	1.75	2.50	3.75	10.00	17.50	110.00	185.00	350.00	550.00	1,000
$1	Beattie-Coyne	1.50	2.00	2.75	7.50	12.50	100.00	150.00	300.00	500.00	800.00
$2	Coyne-Towers	3.00	4.50	6.50	13.50	22.50	120.00	200.00	325.00	650.00	1,200
$2	Beattie-Coyne	2.75	3.75	6.00	12.00	20.00	100.00	165.00	300.00	625.00	950.00
$5	Coyne-Towers	-	10.00	16.50	25.00	55.00	400.00	700.00	1,250	2,100	3,500
$5	Beattie-Coyne	-	8.00	12.00	16.50	25.00	175.00	300.00	675.00	1,100	2,000
$10	Coyne-Towers	-	17.50	22.00	30.00	55.00	210.00	350.00	550.00	850.00	1,500
$10	Beattie-Coyne	-	12.00	16.50	25.00	50.00	165.00	265.00	450.00	750.00	1,200
$20	Coyne-Towers	-	25.00	50.00	100.00	150.00	375.00	525.00	900.00	1,300	2,000
$20	Beattie-Coyne	-	22.00	40.00	55.00	120.00	225.00	350.00	550.00	900.00	1,500
$50	Coyne-Towers	-	-	55.00	80.00	175.00	Not Printed				
$50	Beattie-Coyne	-	55.00	75.00	125.00	250.00	Not Printed				
$100	Coyne-Towers	-	-	110.00	125.00	175.00	Not Printed				
$100	Beattie-Coyne	-	-	120.00	150.00	250.00	Not Printed				
$1000	Coyne-Towers	-	-	-	1,100	1,200	Not Printed				

Modified Portrait		Regular Issue					Asterisk Issue				
Denom.	Signatures	VG	Fine	VF	EF	Unc.	VG	Fine	VF	EF	Unc.
$1	Beattie-Coyne	-	1.25	1.75	3.00	8.00	3.00	4.50	6.50	15.00	25.00
$1	Beattie-Rasminsky	-	-	1.75	2.50	4.00	-	-	3.00	4.00	5.00
$1	Bouey-Rasminsky	-	-	-	1.75	2.50	-	-	4.00	5.00	6.00
$1	Lawson-Bouey	-	-	-	2.00	3.00	-	-	5.00	6.00	10.00
$2	Beattie-Coyne	-	2.50	3.25	7.00	13.50	4.00	6.00	10.00	25.00	50.00
$2	Beattie-Rasminsky	-	-	2.25	3.50	4.50	-	-	3.00	4.00	5.50
$2	Bouey-Rasminsky	-	-	2.25	3.50	4.50	-	-	4.00	5.00	6.50
$2	Lawson-Bouey	-	-	2.50	4.00	5.00	-	-	4.00	6.00	8.00
$5	Beattie-Coyne	-	7.00	10.00	15.00	30.00	10.00	15.00	20.00	35.00	60.00
$5	Beattie-Rasminsky	-	-	7.00	8.00	12.00	-	7.00	9.00	12.00	22.00
$5	Bouey-Rasminsky	-	-	7.00	8.00	12.00	-	7.00	9.00	12.00	22.00
$10	Beattie-Coyne	-	12.00	13.50	17.50	30.00	-	18.00	22.50	40.00	65.00
$10	Beattie-Rasminsky	-	-	12.00	15.00	25.00	-	12.00	15.00	25.00	35.00
$20	Beattie-Coyne	-	-	25.00	36.00	85.00	-	30.00	50.00	100.00	175.00
$20	Beattie-Rasminsky	-	-	25.00	36.00	55.00	-	30.00	45.00	75.00	135.00
$50	Beattie-Coyne	-	-	60.00	70.00	90.00	Not Printed				
$50	Beattie-Rasminsky	-	-	-	65.00	85.00	Not Printed				
$50	Lawson-Bouey	-	80.00	100.00	150.00	250.00	Not Printed				
$100	Beattie-Coyne	-	-	-	125.00	150.00	Not Printed				
$100	Beattie-Rasminsky	-	-	-	125.00	150.00	Not Printed				
$100	Lawson-Bouey	-	-	-	125.00	150.00	Not Printed				
$1000	Beattie-Coyne	-	-	-	-	1,050	Not Printed				
$1000	Beattie-Rasminsky	-	-	-	-	1,050	Not Printed				
$1000	Bouey-Rasminsky	-	-	-	-	1,050	Not Printed				
$1000	Lawson-Bouey	-	-	-	-	1,050	Not Printed				

CENTENNIAL OF CONFEDERATION COMMEMORATIVE ISSUE 1967

As part of the 1967 Centennial celebration, special $1 notes were issued. The face is the same as that of the 1954 issue, except for the addition of the maple leaf symbol for Confederation and some wording changes. However, the prairie scene on the 1954 $1 back was replaced with a view of the first Parliament buildings. This vignette was originally engraved in 1872 and saw use on the face of the $100 Dominion notes. For the 1967 Bank of Canada notes certain portions (e.g. the sky) were re-engraved.

In addition to the regular serial number and asterisk issues released for circulation, a special collectors issue was prepared with the dates 1867   1967 replacing the serial numbers and were available only from the Bank of Canada at face value (although many later entered circulation). The collectors issue has remained very common, as they were hoarded by the public. The regular serial number issue are not nearly as common. All notes are signed J.R. Beattie/L. Rasminsky and bear the date OTTAWA 1967.

$1 — 1967 Commemorative (1867 1967 collectors' issue)

			EF	Unc
$1	**1967**	Confederation, regular serial number	$2.00	$4.00
		Confederation, Asterisk Issue	4.00	8.00
		Confederation, Collector's Issue 1867 1967	1.50	2.50

MULTICOLOURED ISSUE 1969-1975

In 1969 the release of a completely new and more modern series of Canadian notes began. In producing this series, the Bank of Canada was concerned with producing notes that would be virtually impossible to counterfeit. Counterfeiting of notes of the 1954 was increasing and so the most advanced security features were incorporated into the new designs to eliminate problems with counterfeits. At the same time the Bank of Canada wished to update the style of the notes, maintaining a high artistic standard. For the first time since the 1937 issue, portraits of former Canadian Prime Ministers replace that of the ruling British Monarch on some denominations.

The common feature of the notes of this new series are a portrait at the right and Canadian coat-of-arms at the left end of the face side, multicoloured back and a more extensive use of colour generally, as well as deeper engraving giving the notes more of a "feel". The serial numbers are in red at the left and in blue at the right. To date all denominations to $100 have been released and there are no plans to date to issue a $1000 note in the new issue and where needed, $1000 notes of the 1954 issue are still in circulation.

Face side with portrait at right

Back with Canadian scene

Design Details

Denom.	Basic Colour	Portrait	Back Design
$1	Black	Queen Elizabeth	Ottawa River and Parliament Buildings
$2	Terra cotta	Queen Elizabeth	Eskimos preparing for a hunt
$5	Blue	Sir Wilfrid Laurier	Fishing boat on the west coast
$10	Purple	Sir John A. Macdonald	Oil refinery
$20	Olive Green	Queen Elizabeth	Rocky Mountains and lake
$50	Bright red	W.L. McKenzie King	Dome formation from R.C.M.P. "Musical Ride"
$100	Dark brown	Sir Robert L. Borden	Maritimes dock scene

Dates, Signatures and Numbering

For the first time the various notes of a Bank of Canada issue do not all bear the same date. This is because the multicoloured notes required several years to design and produce and so each denomination was released separately. The year shown on the notes and the actual months and years of their first release are as follows:

$1 — 1973 (June, 1974)	$10 — 1971 (Nov., 1971)	$100 — 1975 (May, 1976)
$2 — 1974 (Aug., 1975)	$20 — 1969 (June, 1970)	
$5 — 1972 (Dec., 1972)	$50 — 1975 (Mar., 1975)	

The check letter system for numbering is as on the previous issue, except that the two letters are beside each other instead of in the form of a fraction. The left letter signifies denomination and the right letter indicates the series. Within each series the numbers go from 0000000 to 9999999, the zero note being removed and destroyed prior to issue. Since the series letters may include all letters from A to Z (except I,O or Q), each denomination can use 23 different series, or 230,000,000 notes. In 1981 a triple letter prefix was introduced to provide a wider range of series to be used to meet future demand.

There are three signature combinations on this issue:

J.R. Beattie and L. Rasminsky

G.K. Bouey and L. Rasminsky

R.W. Lawson and G.K. Bouey

Replacement of defective notes by asterisk notes was continued with the multicoloured issue on all denominations but was discontinued when the new triple letter prefix notes were introduced. Replacement notes are now indicated by using the letter "X" for the third letter of the prefix.

Denom.	Signature / Variety	Regular Issue Unc.	Replacement Note Issue* Unc.
$1	Lawson-Bouey / 2 letter prefix	$1.50	$2.00
$1	Lawson-Bouey / 3 letter prefix	1.25	1.75
$2	Lawson-Bouey / 2 letter prefix	3.25	4.00
$2	Lawson-Bouey / 3 letter prefix	2.75	4.00
$5	Bouey-Resminsky / 2 letter prefix	8.50	12.00
$5	Lawson-Bouey / 2 letter prefix	7.50	10.00
$10	Beattie-Rasminsky / 2 letter prefix	15.00	20.00
$10	Bouey-Rasminsky / 2 letter prefix	20.00	35.00
$10	Lawson-Bouey / 2 letter prefix	14.00	17.50
$10	Lawson-Bouey / 3 letter prefix	12.00	15.00
$20	Beattie-Rasminsky / 2 letter prefix	25.00	35.00
$20	Lawson-Bouey / 2 letter prefix	22.50	30.00
$50	Lawson-Bouey / 2 letter prefix	60.00	70.00
$50	Lawson-Bouey / 3 letter prefix	55.00	65.00
$100	Lawson-Bouey / 2 letter prefix	115.00	135.00
$100	Lawson-Bouey / 3 letter prefix	110.00	125.00

* Replacement notes using 2 letter prefixes have an asterisk preceeding the serial number. Replacement notes with 3 letter prefixes are designated by the use of an "X" for the 3rd letter of the prefix.

BLACK SERIAL NUMBER ISSUE 1979

In 1979 the Bank of Canada released $5 and $20 notes in a new format. The basic style of the multicoloured issue was retained but there were several changes. In order to make it easier to distinguish the $20 from the $1 note, the orange and pink colours on the $20 note were strengthened while the green tones were diminished, creating a greater colour contrast between the two denominations.

The major change in the design was the removal of the words BANK OF CANADA-BANQUE DU CANADA from below the vignette on the back. New black serial numbers were put in this position replacing the red and blue serial numbers on the note faces.

These notes were introduced as an experiment to produce notes that would be machine readable but the experiment was unsuccessful and no further denominations were made in this series.

Dates, Signatures and Numbering

Both denominations occur with the Lawson-Bouey signatures only. The black serial numbers differ from the previous issues in not using letters in the prefix, having eleven digits. The first number indicates denomination and the next 3 digits indicate series. The last seven digits are the note numbers going from 0000000 to 9999999 as in the past. Replacement notes are not indicated by an asterisk with this issue. The $5 note was issued in October 1979 and the $20 note in December 1978.

Denom.	Date	Variety/Signature	Uno.
$5	**1979**	Lawson-Bouey	$6.00
$20	**1979**	Lawson-Bouey	22.00

9
BULLION VALUES

Silver and gold coins are often purchased by dealers strictly for their "bullion" or "melt" value — a term which refers to the value of the precious metal content in the coins.

The majority of Canadian coins have been struck from precious metals and the bullion grade and weight of these coins is a matter of public record. These facts have been stated throughout this book. By following the examples illustrated under the bullion charts, anyone can easily determine a fair bullion value without concern of getting fair value for precious metal content.

Determining the Value
of Gold and Silver Coins

There is usually a difference of 15 to 25% between the calculated price of gold and silver bullion coins and the actual amount paid by a buyer. There are several reasons for this. Remember, the gold or silver buyer is a middleman and must make a profit for the use of his time, knowledge and investment. The buyer will have to pay refining costs as well as pay shipping to and from the refinery. He will also have to accommodate a large amount of bullion coins before it is profitable to ship to a refiner since the larger amount sent results in a lower refining cost for each ounce refined. Sometimes this delay means a risk since the price of gold or silver may drop drastically before the buyer can have the coins refined.

Silver Coins

The daily spot price of silver is always stated in troy ounces and all dealers buy and sell silver by the troy ounce. You need only know the weight and fineness of a silver coin and using the example calculation below, you can arrive at the melt value for any given daily silver price. The weight and fineness (composition) of all silver Canadian coins are listed thoughout this catalogue. To convert grams to troy ounces, multiply grams by .0321 (1 Troy Ounce = 31.103 Grams).

Now remember, when you sell to a dealer, he will be buying at a discount from this price, usually 15-25% less to cover costs and still make a reasonable profit.

Gold Coins

The daily spot price of gold is usually stated in troy ounces (although sometimes in pennyweights). Once again however you need only to know the weight and fineness of a gold coin to calculate the melt value at any daily gold price. The weight (in grams) and fineness (composition) of all Canadian gold coins are listed throughout this catalogue. To convert grams to troy ounces, multiply grams by .0321 (1 Troy Ounce = 31.103 Grams). To convert Pennyweights to Troy ounces, divide Pennyweights by 20. Gold fineness is also often expressed in karats:

Karats	Fineness	Purity
24k	.999	99.9%
22k	.916	91.6%
18k	.750	75.0%
14k	.585	58.5%
10k	.417	41.7%

Now remember, when you sell to a dealer, he will be buying at a discount from this price, usually 15-25% less to cover costs and still make a reasonable profit.

Silver Bullion Value of Canadian Silver Coins

Coin Denomination	Years of Issue	Coin Weight Grams	% of Silver Content	Silver Troy Ounce	Silver Value - Canadian Dollars									
					S1	S2	S4	S6	S8	S10	S20	S30	S40	S50
5-cents	1858-1919	1.166	.925	.0346	.035	.07	.14	.21	.28	.35	.69	1.04	1.38	1.73
5-cents	1920-1921	1.166	.800	.0299	.03	.06	.12	.18	.24	.30	.60	.90	1.20	1.50
10-cents	1858-1919	2.333	.925	.0693	.07	.14	.28	.42	.55	.69	1.39	2.08	2.77	3.46
10-cents	1920-1967	2.333	.800	.0599	.06	.12	.24	.36	.48	.60	1.20	1.80	2.40	3.00
10-cents	1967-1968	2.333	.500	.0374	.04	.08	.15	.23	.30	.37	.75	1.12	1.50	1.87
25-cents	1870-1919	5.810	.925	.173	.17	.35	.69	1.04	1.38	1.73	3.46	5.19	6.92	8.65
25-cents	1920-1967	5.832	.800	.1498	.15	.30	.60	.90	1.20	1.50	3.00	4.50	6.00	7.50
25-cents	1967-1968	5.832	.500	.0936	.09	.19	.37	.56	.75	.94	1.87	2.81	3.74	4.68
50-cents	1870-1919	11.620	.925	.3450	.35	.69	1.38	2.07	2.76	3.45	6.90	10.35	13.80	17.25
50-cents	1920-1967	11.664	.800	.2995	.30	.60	1.20	1.80	2.40	3.00	6.00	9.00	12.00	15.00
1 Dollar	1935-1967	23.327	.800	.5990	.60	1.20	2.40	3.60	4.80	6.00	12.00	18.00	24.00	30.00
1 Dollar*	1971-date	23.327	.500	.3744	.37	.75	1.50	2.25	3.00	3.74	7.49	11.23	14.98	18.72
NEWFOUNDLAND														
5-cents	1865-1944	1.166	.925	.0346	.035	.07	.14	.21	.28	.35	.70	1.04	1.40	1.75
5-cents	1945-1947	1.166	.800	.0299	.03	.06	.12	.18	.24	.30	.60	.90	1.20	1.50
10-cents	1865-1944	2.333	.925	.0693	.07	.14	.28	.42	.55	.69	1.39	2.08	2.77	3.47
10-cents	1945-1947	2.333	.800	.0599	.06	.12	.24	.36	.48	.60	1.20	1.80	2.40	3.00
20-cents	1865-1912	4.712	.925	.1399	.14	.28	.56	.84	1.12	1.40	2.80	4.20	5.60	7.00
25-cents	1917-1919	5.832	.925	.1732	.17	.35	.69	1.04	1.39	1.73	3.46	5.20	6.93	8.66
50-cents	1870-1919	11.664	.925	.3463	.35	.69	1.39	2.08	2.77	3.46	6.93	10.39	13.85	17.32

* Collectors Issues

Example:

To calculate the price of a silver coin:

A Canadian coin made of .800 silver weighs 23.327 grams
Multiply weight 23.327 grams × .0321 = .7488 Troy oz.
Multiply .7488 Troy ounce × .800 fineness = .599 Troy oz. of silver

If silver is worth $20.00 an ounce, then this coin is worth:
$20.00 × .599 = $12.00 Bullion value. (Collector value may be greater.)

Gold Bullion of Canadian Coins

Coin Denomination	Years of Issue	Coin Weight Grams	% of Gold Content	Gold Troy Ounce	Gold Value - Canadian Dollars									
					$25	$50	$100	$200	$300	$400	$500	$600	$700	$800
CANADA														
£1 Sovereign	1908c-1919c	7.99	.917	.236	5.90	11.80	23.60	47.20	70.80	94.40	118.00	141.60	165.20	188.80
5 Dollars	1912-1914	8.3591	.900	.2419	6.05	12.10	24.19	48.38	72.57	96.76	120.95	145.14	169.33	193.52
10 Dollars	1912-1914	16.7181	.900	.4838	12.10	24.19	48.38	96.76	145.14	193.52	241.90	290.28	338.66	387.04
20 Dollars	1967	18.2733	.900	.5287	13.22	26.44	52.87	105.74	158.61	211.48	264.35	317.22	370.09	422.96
100 Dollars	1976	13.3375	.583	.2501	6.25	12.51	25.01	50.02	75.03	100.04	125.05	150.06	175.07	200.08
100 Dollars	1976-1980	16.9655	.9166	.500	12.50	25.00	50.00	100.00	150.00	200.00	250.00	300.00	350.00	400.00
S50 Maple Leaf	1979-date	31.1	.999	1.000	25.00	50.00	100.00	200.00	300.00	400.00	500.00	600.00	700.00	800.00
S10 Maple Leaf	1981-date	7.77	.999	.250	6.25	12.50	25.00	50.00	75.00	100.00	125.00	150.00	175.00	200.00
S5 Maple Leaf	1981-date	3.11	.999	.100	2.50	5.00	10.00	20.00	30.00	40.00	50.00	60.00	70.00	80.00
NEWFOUNDLAND														
2 Dollars	1865-1888	3.3283	.9166	.0981	2.45	4.91	9.81	19.62	29.43	39.24	49.05	59.86	68.67	78.48

Example

To calculate the price of a gold coin:

A Canadian Gold Coin made of .900 gold weighs 16.718 grams
Multiply weight 16.718 grams × .0321 = .5366 Troy oz.
Multiply .5366 Troy ounce × .900 fineness = .4829 Troy oz. of gold

If gold is worth $400.00 an ounce, then this coin is worth:
$400.00 × .4829 = $193.00 Bullion value (collector value may be greater)

10
GLOSSARY

ALLOY: Mixture of more than one metal, usually preceded by the name of the most predominant or most important metal in the mix, such as nickel alloy.

ASSAY: The analytical test to determine the purity and weight of metal.

BAGMARKS: Slight scratches and nicks acquired by coins in contact with others in a mint bag. Most common on large and heavy silver and gold coins.

BILLON: A low-grade alloy used for some minor coin issues consisting usually of a mixture of silver and copper, and sometimes coated with a silver wash.

BLANKS: Flat round metal discs or planchets from which the coins are made.

BROCKAGE: Formerly any misstruck coin, now specifically refers to a coin having one side normal and the opposite side having the same design only as an incuse "mirror image."

BULLION: Uncoined gold or silver in the form of bars, ingots and plates. Bullion value is a term used in reference to the value of the metal content in gold and silver coins.

BUSINESS STRIKE: Any coin struck with the intention of circulating.

CAMEO-EFFECT: A description of the appearance of certain gold and silver proof coins which have frosted devices on highly polished fields.

CLASHED DIES: Damaged dies caused by the absence of a planchet at the time of striking. Each die retains a portion of its opposite's design, in addition to its own. The resulting coins show a partial impression of the reverse design on the obverse and/or vice versa.

CLIPPED PLANCHET (CLOSE PLANCHET): A planchet less than fully round due to the adjacent planchet having been punched too closely, or having been punched too closely to the edge of the metal sheet.

DEBASEMENT: Debasement of a coin takes place when the issuing authority reduces the purity of the metal, lowering the intrinsic value of the coin but circulating it at par with the previous coins of the original purity.

DENTICLES: Tooth-like projections running inside the rim of a coin.

DEVICE: Any design feature appearing on the obverse, reverse or edge of a coin.

DIADEMED: A coin where the portrait head has a headband or fillet as a sign of royalty.

DIE: Engraved metal pieces used to impress the design of a coin on a blank planchet.

DIE AXIS: The vertical axes of the two dies when striking a coin or medal are indicated by arrows; with the obverse die assumed to be upright and the relative position of the reverse die indicated by a second arrow. Medal struck pieces have both dies upright (↑ ↑); coin struck, the reverse appears upside down (↑ ↓).

DIE CRACK: A stress crack on a die producing a raised line on the pieces struck.

DIE POLISHING LINES: Minute scratches on the die from polishing which produce very fine raised lines on some well struck coins.

ESSAI: A trial piece from dies already accepted for regular coinage. It may bear a date or mint mark other than on the coins issued for circulation or it may be a different metal.

EXERGUE: The lower part of a coin or medal which is usually divided from the "field" by a line under which is contained the date, place of minting or engraver's initials.

FIELD: Areas on either side of a coin not occupied by portrait, design or description.

FLAN: See BLANKS.

GEM: A relatively flawless piece of superlative quality.

HAIRLINES: Minute lines or scratches on a coin caused by cleaning or polishing.

HIGH POINTS: The highest points on the design of a coin. The first points to show wear.

INCUSE: Coins with either obverse or reverse design sunk below the coin's surface.

IRIDESCENT: Multi-coloured blending or toning usually found in older uncirculated coins.

KARAT: The degree of fineness of gold. Pure gold is 24 karats and most gold coins have a fineness of 22 karats.

LAMINATED PLANCHET: A "peeling off" of a top layer of the metal of a planchet.

LEGEND: The principal inscription on a coin.

LUSTRE: The sheen on the surface of an uncirculated coin caused by the centrifugal flow of metal on striking. Mint lustre (bloom) is somewhat frosty in appearance as opposed to the mirror-like fields of a proof. An important indicator of a coin's condition, lustre is worn through with the slightest circulation. Chemical cleaners can destroy it. Once gone lustre cannot be restored.

MAJOR VARIETY: A coin of the same date, mint mark and denomination as another, but struck from another pair of dies and having at least the major device added, removed or redesigned.

MATTE PROOF: A proof coin for which the planchet is treated in a manner other than polishing. A dull and grainy finish is achieved.

MEDAL: A commemorative metal piece in honour of a person or event. Not money.

MEDALET: A small medal, usually smaller in diameter than a fifty-cent piece.

MILLED EDGE: [1] Prior to use of collar dies the edge design was milled onto the blank before minting; [2] using collar dies, flan edges are milled so that the border or design will be adequately raised when struck.

MINOR VARIETY: A minor variety is one with all major devices the same as another, but with some easily recognizable variation.

MINT ERROR: An incorrectly struck or defective coin produced by a mint.

MINT MARK: Letter designation for a branch mint product.

MULE: A coin struck from dies not designed to be used together.

OBVERSE: The "face-up" side of the coin, regarded as more important than the reverse side and usually bearing the portrait of the monarch.

OVERDATE: The date made by an engraver at the mint punching one or more numbers on a previously dated die.

OVERSTRIKE: A coin where part of the design, particularly the date, appears over another design or date.

PATINA: Originally: a green or brown surface film (from oxidation) found on ancient copper and bronze coins; now refers to toning on any coin.

PATTERN: A design suggested for a new coinage, struck in a few examples but not adopted. If adopted for regular coinage with the same date, the piece ceases to be a pattern.

PIEDFORT: A type of pattern struck on a thick flan. Probably, piedforts were struck for use by coiners as models when making actual coins.

PLANCHET: See BLANKS.

PROOF: [1] A special striking of a coin, produced to show to those who have the right to choose the design for the coinage, a design at its best. Proofs are carefully struck by gentle pressure, usually at least twice, from carefully polished dies, on polished flans. The minutest details of the design are thus made clear. The term does NOT refer to the condition of the coin. [2] A bank note or other form of paper money specially printed as a sample or specimen but not intended for circulation.

REEDED EDGE: Minted vertical serrations on the edge of a coin.

RELIEF: Where the lettering and design are raised above the surface of the coin.

RESTRIKE: Any coin struck later than the date appearing on the coin.

REVERSE: Opposite from obverse. The back or "tails" side of a coin.

ROTATED DIE: Dies are positioned and locked on a coining press by means of a key. When these keys come loose, rotation can occur resulting in the next coin being struck with the obverse and reverse dies rotated. Coins struck from rotated dies are errors.

SPECIMEN: [1] A coin or bank note prepared, often with special care, as an example of a given issue. Sometimes, particularly with bank notes, surcharged with "SPECIMEN" or a similar word. [2] A synonym for a numismatic item, e.g., a very rare specimen.

SPURIOUS: A false piece made to deceive, often an original creation rather than a copy of a known item. Not genuine, counterfeit, false.

TOKEN: Usually a piece of durable material appropriately marked and unofficially issued for monetary, advertising, services or other purposes.

TRADE DOLLAR: A token used by a municipality primarily as a tourism promotion, and redeemable in most stores in the issuing municipality.

VIGNETTE: A pictorial element of a bank note design that shades off gradually into the surrounding unprinted paper or background rather than having sharp outlines or a frame.

WIRE EDGE: Slight flange on coins or medals caused by heavy striking pressure, often characteristic on Proof coins (also KNIFE EDGE). The metal is squeezed up the side of the die faces by the collar die.

WORKING DIE: Used to strike coins. Not a master die, etc.

UNISAFE COIN FOLDERS

The Most Popular Coin Folder on the Market Today!

UNISAFE Folders offer the following features:

- Sturdy vinyl covered dura-board gives the folders a solid feel
- Finished in Royal Blue, with silver embossing on the front cover
- Striking silver coin ont he front cover of each folder to match the coins it holds
- Pages open flat for convenient viewing
- Every folder complete with four crystal clear vinyl pages permitting two-sided viewing
- New shape for pocket opening permits easy access to coin while preventing it from falling out
- Data sheet on inside cover of dated folders shows collector the proper layout for his coins — Blank folders show mintage information
- All folders are indexed for reordering purposes

ALL CANADIAN COIN FOLDERS
$1.95 EACH

No.	Title/Titre
DATED FOLDERS	
141	Canada Cents 1858-1920
142	Canada Cents 1920-date
143	Canada 5 Cents 1922-date
144	Canada 10 Cents 1920-date
145	Canada 25 Cents 1937-date
146	Canada 50 Cents 1937-date
147	Canada Dollars 1935-date
BLANK FOLDERS	
142B	Canada Cents
143B	Canada 5 Cents
144B	Canada 10 Cents
145B	Canada 25 Cents
146B	Canada 50 Cents
147B	Canada Dollars

NEW
No. 130 WORLD COIN FOLDER:
6 pages fitting all sizes of World Coins $2.95

Folders are available coast-to-coast at your favorite dealer,
stationery or bookstore, or through:
UNITRADE ASSOCIATES
P.O. Box 172, Station A, Toronto, Ontario M5W 1B2

UNIMASTER COIN ALBUMS

The most attractive coin albums money can buy!

Attractive gold-stamped, brown-grained vinyl binders will make a handsome addition to any library. Inside, the loose-leaf crystal-clear pages and slides display your coins perfectly without any chance of a coin ever falling out. Each slide has a description and date strip which means your album can never become outdated. Additional pages with blank date strips and binders are available.

Ref.	Album	Pages	Retail
151	Large Cents 1858-1920	2	$7.95
152	Small Cents 1920-date	3	9.50
153	Cents Blank	5	11.95
154	5¢ Silver 1858-1921	2	7.95
155	5¢ Nickel 1922-date	3	9.50
156	5¢ Blank	5	11.95
157	Dimes 1870-date	4	10.95
158	Dimes Blank	5	11.95
159	Quarters 1870-date	4	10.95
160	Quarters Blank	5	11.95

Ref.	Album	Pages	Retail
161	Halves 1870-1945	3	$9.50
162	Halves 1946-date	3	9.50
163	Halves Blank	5	11.95
164	Dollars 1935-date	4	10.95
165	Dollars Blank	5	11.95
166	Mint Sets	5	11.95
Also available - Blank pages & binders			
150	Blank Binders - No Titles		$4.95
"A"	30-pocket pages for 1¢ to 25¢	ea.	1.50
"B"	16-pocket pages for 50¢ to $1	ea.	1.50
"C"	2-pocket pages for Mint Sets	ea.	1.50

Unimaster Coin Albums are available through your local coin dealer or directly from the distributor. Orders to the distributor should include $1.50 per order for postage and handling.

UNITRADE ASSOCIATES
127 Cartwright Avenue, Toronto, Ontario M6A 1V4

Tel: (416) 787-5658

Telex: 06-969719

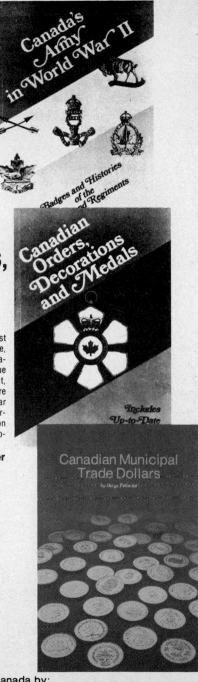

The fascinating story of the Royal Canadian Mint and the coins it proudly produces

The Royal Canadian Mint celebrates its 75th anniversary with a book for every numismatist.

First, this is a book of history. It begins centuries ago, before the idea of the Mint was even conceived, when trading was done with furs, and coins were in short supply. It takes us to the turn of the twentieth century, when nationalism created the demand for a Canadian mint, and brings us to the present day, and the stories behind our modern circulating coins and special issues.

Yet also, this is a book of people. John Cabot walks its pages. So does Winston Churchill, Earl Grey, Barbara Ann Scott, Edward VIII, Elizabeth II and Lord Simcoe.

But most of all, this is a book filled with an unprecedented wealth of information, certain to fascinate any reader who has ever felt the lure of coins and their story.

Its title is "Striking Impressions"– and the words are apt in every way. The book, written by Dr. James A. Haxby to fill a notable gap in numismatic literature, is striking in its detail, striking in its scholarship, and most of all, striking in its readability.

A few of the remarkable stories hidden in the pages of "Striking Impressions":

☐ The rush for gold in B.C. and the Klondike.

☐ The debates which led to the establishment of the Royal Canadian Mint.

☐ The Mint's production of gun parts during World War I.

☐ The public hoarding of tombac alloy during World War II.

☐ The expansion of the Mint's realm, to include minting for other nations.

Be sure to order your copy now.

"Striking Impressions" is available, in both English and French editions, for just $25.00 Cdn. ($22.00 U.S.). Order your copy (copies) now by returning the order form below.

OFFICIAL ORDER FORM

Please send me:

Qty _____ "Striking Impressions" in English at $25.00 each. (Cdn) $ _____
Qty _____ «Pièces à l'appui» in French at $25.00 each. (Cdn) $ _____
Total value of the order. (Cdn) $ _____

OR

Qty _____ "Striking Impressions" in English at $22.00 each. (U.S.) $ _____
Qty _____ «Pièces à l'appui» in French at $22.00 each. (U.S.) $ _____
Total value of the order. (U.S.) $ _____

Name _____

Address _____

City _____ Prov/State _____ Postal/Zip _____

Correspondence/Correspondance: English/Anglais _____ French/Français _____

Method of Payment ☐ Certified cheque or money order payable to the Royal Canadian Mint
☐ Visa ☐ MasterCard ☐ Am. Ex. Expiry date _____

Credit Card No. | | | | | | | | | | | | | | | |

Cardholder's Address _____

Cardholder's Signature _____

Return to: Royal Canadian Mint, P.O. Box 445, Station A, Ottawa, Ontario, Canada K1N 9H3

06

Important Notice: The Mint reserves the right to refuse or limit orders, and is not responsible for any duty charged upon entry to a foreign country. Please allow 6 to 8 weeks for delivery. Valid in Canada and U.S.A. only.

Royal Canadian Mint   Monnaie royale canadienne

Canada